PLATE I

PLATE 2

PLATE 3

PLATE 4

PLATE 5

PLATE 6

PLATE 7

PLATE 8

PLATE 9

PLATE 10

PLATE II

PLATE 12

PLATE 13

PLATE 14

PLATE 15

PLATE 16

SAGA LAND

Praise for *Saga Land*

'A fascinating insight into Iceland's little-known history
and literature, and a compelling story of one
man's quest to reclaim his identity.'
Financial Review

'Digressive and compendious, it is a book that resists narrow
classification … Fidler and Gislason immerse themselves in every
experience and encounter, and the reader along with them.'
Sydney Morning Herald

'Usually I read non-fiction in small bites, squeezed in between
my reading of novels. I read *Saga Land* in one big gulp.
It was utterly mesmerising.'
Kate Forsyth

RICHARD FIDLER
& KÁRI GÍSLASON

SAGA LAND

ABC
Books

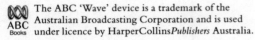 The ABC 'Wave' device is a trademark of the Australian Broadcasting Corporation and is used under licence by HarperCollins*Publishers* Australia.

First published in 2017
This edition published in 2018
by HarperCollins*Publisher*s Australia Pty Limited
ABN 36 009 913 517
harpercollins.com.au

Copyright © Richard Fidler and Kári Gíslason, 2017

HarperCollins*Publishers*
Level 13, 201 Elizabeth Street, Sydney, NSW 2000, Australia
Unit D1, 63 Apollo Drive, Rosedale, Auckland 0632, New Zealand
A 53, Sector 57, Noida, UP, India
1 London Bridge Street, London SE1 9GF, United Kingdom
Bay Adelaide Centre, East Tower, 22 Adelaide Street West, 41st floor, Toronto, Ontario, M5H 4E3
195 Broadway, New York NY 10007, USA

National Library of Australia Cataloguing-in-Publication data:
Fidler, Richard, author.
Saga land / Richard Fidler and Kári Gíslason.
978 0 7333 3970 7 (paperback)
978 1 4607 0820 0 (ebook)
Notes: Includes index.
Subjects: Old Norse literature.
Family mysteries—Iceland—Biography.
Iceland—Description and travel.

Cover and internal design by Evi Oetomo and Daniel New, OetomoNew Studio
Maps by Clare O'Flynn/Little Moon Studio
Typeset in Minion Pro Regular by Kirby Jones
Printed and bound in Australia by McPherson's Printing Group
The papers used by HarperCollins in the manufacture of this book are a natural, recyclable product made from wood grown in sustainable plantation forests. The fibre source and manufacturing processes meet recognised international environmental standards, and carry certification.

To my saga teachers Martin Duwell,
Vésteinn Ólason and Stefanie Gropper.
– *KG*

To the unknown saga authors, for leaving us
everything except your names.
– *RF*

A snapping bow, a burning flame,
A grinning wolf, a grunting boar,
A raucous crow, a rootless tree,
A breaking wave, a boiling kettle,
A flying arrow, an ebbing tide,
A coiled adder, the ice of a night,
A bride's bed talk, a broad sword,
A bear's play, a prince's children,
A witch' s welcome, the wit of a slave,
A sick calf, a corpse still fresh,
A brother's killer encountered upon
The highway a house half-burned,
A racing stallion who has wrenched a leg,
Are never safe: let no man trust them.

—'Hávamál' ('Advice from Odin')

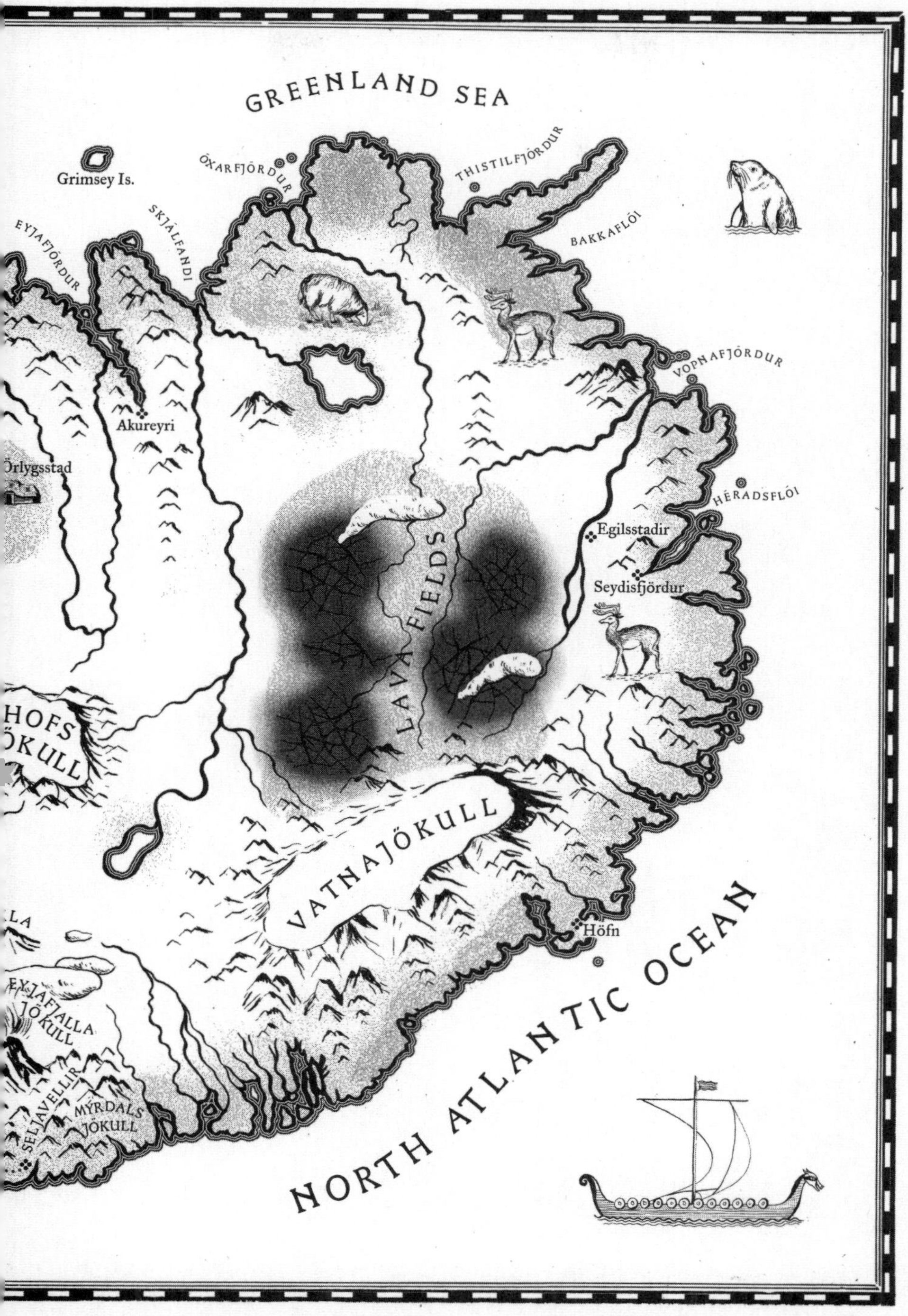

GREENLAND SEA

Grimsey Is.

ÖXARFJÖRDUR

THISTILFJÖRDUR

BAKKAFLÓI

EYJAFJÖRDUR

SKJÁLFANDI

VOPNAFJÖRDUR

Akureyri

HÉRADSFLÓI

Örlygsstad

Egilsstadir

Seydisfjördur

LAVA FIELDS

HOFS JÖKULL

VATNAJÖKULL

Höfn

EYJAFJALLA JÖKULL

SELJAVELLUR

MÝRDALS JÖKULL

NORTH ATLANTIC OCEAN

Contents

Timeline

20 million years B.C.E.	Iceland formed by string of volcanic eruptions in the North Atlantic.
8th–9th century AD	Irish-Scots monks, the Papar, sail to Iceland and form scattered hermit settlements.
793	Norse raiders attack monastery at Lindisfarne off the northeast coast of England, marking the start of the Viking age.
870	Harald the Finehair becomes the first king of a unified Norway.
874	Viking settlement of Iceland begins.
930	The first Althing is proclaimed under the Law Rock at Thingvellir.
947	Norway adopts Christianity.
961	Warrior-poet Egil Skallagrímsson composes the poem 'Lament for My Sons'.
977	Gísli the Outlaw dies in the northwest fjords of Iceland.
986	The first Norse colonies in Greenland founded by Erik the Red.
988	The Varangian Guard is founded in Constantinople by Emperor Basil II, drawing Vikings from across Northern Europe into its service.
990	Death of warrior-poet Egil Skallagrímsson.
992	Death of Gunnar of Hlídarendi.
999	Leif Eriksson explores the coast of America.
1000	Iceland officially converts to Christianity.

1003	Kjartan Ólafsson is killed in mid-west Iceland.
1010	Lawyer Njál Thorgeirsson is killed by burning at his farm in southern Iceland.
c. 1010	Colonising expedition of Karlsefni and Gudríd to North America.
1060	Gudrún Ósvífsdóttir dies at Helgafell.
1104	Massive eruption at Mount Hekla. Ash and poison gas create widespread devastation across Iceland.
1110	King Sigurd Jerusalem-Farer of Norway arrives in Constantinople.
c. 1120	Saga-writing begins to flourish in Iceland. Ari the Wise starts work on *Íslendingabók, The Book of Icelanders*.
1179	Snorri Sturluson is born in Hvamm.
1199	Snorri marries Herdís.
1201	Snorri's daughter Hallbera is born.
1202	Snorri and Herdís move to Borg.
1203	Jón Little Trout is born.
1206	Snorri settles at Reykholt.
1207	Snorri's daughter Thórdís is born to his mistress Oddný.
1208	Snorri's daughter Ingibjörg is born to another mistress, Gudrún.
1215	Snorri becomes lawspeaker.
1217	Haakon IV is proclaimed King of Norway.
1218	Snorri travels to Norway by royal invitation.
1220	Snorri returns to Iceland and is accused of conniving to bring Iceland under Haakon's rule.
c. 1220	Snorri writes the *Prose Edda*.
1221	Snorri resumes his role as lawspeaker of the Althing.
1224	Snorri enters into a common-law marriage with Hallveig Ormsdóttir.

1229	Snorri's son-in-law Thorvald is burnt to death in his farmhouse.
	Thorvald's sons attack Sturla's farm. Snorri's son Jón Little Trout goes to Norway.
1230	Truce between Snorri and Sturla.
	Sturlunga Saga records Snorri as writing sagas at Reykholt.
c. 1230	Composition of *Egil's Saga* and *Heimskringla*, Snorri's history of the Norwegian kings.
1231	Volcanic eruption off the coast of Iceland.
	Snorri's daughter Hallbera dies.
	Jón Little Trout dies in Norway.
1232	Sturla's men kill Thorvald's sons.
	Snorri's son Oraekja begins a rampage across Iceland.
	Sturla goes to Norway and meets Haakon IV.
1233	Oraekja moves to attack Reykholt. Snorri consents to give Oraekja his farm at Stafholt.
1235	Sturla returns to Iceland from Norway, charged with bringing Iceland under his rule.
1236	Sturla marches on Reykholt; Snorri and Hallveig flee.
	Oraekja is gelded by Sturla at Surt's Cave.
1237	Snorri flees to Norway and conspires with Earl Skuli.
1238	The Battle of Orlygsstad: fifty-six are killed, including Sturla.
1239	Snorri defies Haakon by returning to Iceland.
	Earl Skuli revolts, launches a coup d'état against Haakon and proclaims himself king.
c. 1240	Composition of *The Saga of Gísli*.
1240	Earl Skuli is killed, ending the rebellion against Haakon.
	Haakon authorises Snorri's son-in-law Gizur Thorvaldsson to kill Snorri.

1241	Hallveig dies.
	Snorri is murdered at Reykholt by Gizur's men.
c. 1245	*Laxdaela Saga* written by an unknown author.
1258	Gizur named Earl of Iceland by King Haakon.
1262	Iceland is incorporated into Norway. End of the Icelandic commonwealth.
c. 1270	Composition of *Njál's Saga*.

Cast of Characters

THE ICELANDERS

Ari the Wise, Iceland's first historian, author of the Book of Icelanders.

Árni Magnússon, the nation's greatest manuscript collector and antiquarian.

Árni the Quarrelsome, Snorri's son-in-law and Hallbera's husband, briefly.

Ásgerd, wife of Thorkel (Gísli's Saga).

Aud the Deep Minded, first settler and leader in the midwest of Iceland.

Aud, wife of Gísli the Outlaw.

Bödvar, son of Egil Skallagrímsson (Egil's Saga).

Bolli Thorleiksson, best friend and foster-brother of Kjartan Ólafsson (Laxdaela Saga).

Egil Skallagrímsson, a warrior-poet from Borg in the midwest (Egil's Saga).

Gest Oddleifsson, a prescient man, interpreter of dreams.

Gísli the Outlaw, poet, Norse settler in the Westfjords.

Gizur Thorvaldsson of Haukadalur, the first earl of Iceland.

Gudríd the Far Travelled, explorer of the New World, alongside her husband Thorfinn Karlsefni.

Gudrún Ósvífsdóttir, a woman from Laugar (Laxdaela Saga).

Gunnar of Hlídarendi, a warrior and farmer in the south (Njál's Saga).

Hallbera Snorradóttir, daughter of Snorri Sturluson.

Hallgerd, Gunnar's wife (Njál's Saga).

Hallveig Ormsdóttir, the richest woman in Iceland, Snorri Sturluson's wife.

Höskuld, foster-son of Njál.

Hrefna, Kjartan's wife (Laxdaela Saga).

Ingibjörg Snorradóttir, Snorri Sturluson's daughter and wife of Gizur.

Ingólf Arnarson, first Norse settler of Iceland.

Jón Arason, last Catholic bishop of Iceland.

Jón Little Trout, Snorri's eldest son.

Jón Loptsson, Snorri's foster-father.

Jón Magnússon, Pastor at Eyri.

Kjartan Ólafsson, a man from Laxárdalur (Laxdaela saga).

Kolbein the Younger, chieftain and ally of Gizur Thorvaldsson.

Leif Eriksson, explorer and first European to discover America.

Melkorka, an Irish slave brought to Iceland (Laxdaela saga).

Njál, lawyer and farmer in the south.

Oraekja Snorrason, second, illegitimate son of Snorri Sturluson.

Otkel, Gunnar and Hallgerd's neighbour (Njál's Saga).

Sighvat Sturluson, Snorri's older brother.

Skarphédin, Njál's oldest son.

Snorri Sturluson, Lawspeaker, saga author.

Snorri Thorvaldsson, younger son of Thorvald, who seeks revenge
against Sturla for his killing.

Sólveig Saemundsdóttir, wife of Sturla.

Sturla Sighvatsson, rival and nephew of Snorri Sturluson.

Sturla Thórdarson, author of Sturlunga Saga, another of Snorri's
nephews.

Thórd Sturluson, Snorri's eldest brother.

Thórdís Snorradóttir, second daughter of Snorri, wife of Thorvald.

Thórdís, sister of Gísli the Outlaw.

Thorfinn Karlsefni, explorer and leader of the expedition to America.

Thorgerd, Egil's daughter (Egil's Saga).

Thorgrím, Gísli's brother-in-law, husband of Thórdís (Gísli's Saga)

Thorkel, Brother of Gísli (Gísli's Saga).

Thorvald of Vatnsfjördur, Snorri's son-in-law, husband of Thórdís,
briefly.

Véstein, Gísli's best friend (Gísli's Saga).

THE NORWEGIANS

King Haakon IV, (r. 1217–1263), king of Norway and eventual ruler of Iceland.

King Harald the Finehair (r. 872–930), first king of Norway.

King Harald The Hard Ruler (r. 1046–1066), Viking warrior, commander of the Varangian Guard in the Eastern Roman Empire, and unsuccessful claimant to the English throne.

King Sigurd Jerusalem-Farer (r. 1103–1130), leader of the Norwegian crusade in Palestine.

Skuli Bardarson, nobleman and claimant to the throne against Haakon IV.

THE GREENLANDERS

Erik the Red, founder of the settlements at Greenland.

Freydís Eriksdóttir, daughter of Erik the Red, expeditioner to America.

GODS AND MONSTERS

Brokk, a dwarf master smith.

Fenris, the wolf monster.

Frey, god of the summer and the fruit of the earth.

Heimdall, watcher on the Bifrost.

Hel, daughter of Loki, guardian of the realm of the unworthy dead.

Kvasir, the wisest man who ever lived. His blood is the chief ingredient of the Mead of Poetry.

Loki, trickster, shape-shifter, bane of the Aesir, destined to play a key role in their doom at Ragnarok, the twilight of the gods.

The Norns, three female beings who dwell at the foot of Yggdrasil and rule the destiny of gods and men.

Odin, chief of the Aesir, the god of war, death and poetry. Also known as Allfather, Spear-Shaker, Glad-of-War, High, Just-as-High and Third.

Sif, goddess of the earth, wife of Thor, famous for her golden hair.

Surt, fire giant who wields a flaming sword of destruction, whose flames
will one day engulf the Earth.

Thor, god of thunder, the most revered of the Norse gods among the early
Icelanders.

Tyr, god of heroic glory, who loses his hand to the Fenriswolf.

Ymir, the ancestor of the frost giants, whose body is butchered by Odin
and his brothers to create the heavens the waters and the earth.

THE AUSTRALIANS

Kári Gíslason, an academic drudge.

Richard Fidler, a peripheral media personality.

About this book

I've begun studying Icelandic, and I believe that the literature
produced during the Middle Ages in that remote island close to
the Arctic Circle is one of the most important in the world.

—Jorge Luis Borges

A THOUSAND YEARS AGO, in the northwest of Iceland, there lived a poor farmhand named Audun. One summer, a ship put in at the nearby harbour, and Audun was able to give its captain some good advice and help him sell his wares. In return for these kindnesses, the captain offered Audun free passage to Greenland.

Audun sold his sheep and gave the local farmer enough money to pay for three years' food and lodgings for his mother. Then he boarded the ship, which carried him away to the Western Settlement of Greenland.

Among the Greenlanders there was a hunter named Erik, who had captured a polar bear. Audun decided to buy the bear, even though it cost him nearly all his remaining money. He planned to give the magnificent creature to King Svein of Denmark, who he heard was a good man.

Along the way, Audun and the bear travelled through Norway, where they were brought before the Norwegian king, known as Harald the Hard Ruler. Harald offered to purchase the bear from Audun at a high price, but Audun politely declined, and told Harald it was his intention to make a gift of it to King Svein of Denmark. Harald pointed out irritably that he was at war with Svein; nonetheless he did consent to let Audun proceed through his lands, so long as he promised to return with an account of his journey.

Audun and the polar bear travelled south to Denmark, where the last of Audun's money ran out. He was forced to beg for food for himself and the bear on the streets.

Audun went to see a man named Aki, who was a steward of the Danish king. He told Aki of his plan to give the creature to King Svein and asked him for food for the bear, which was now close to starvation.

'I will not give you food,' said Aki. 'But I am prepared to purchase a half-share in the bear. Then you will have money to feed it.'

Audun was very unhappy with this arrangement, but he could see no alternative, so he accepted Aki's offer. The two men and the polar bear went to see the king, and a large crowd followed them to the royal table.

The king asked Audun which country he was from.

'I am an Icelander,' he said. 'I purchased this bear in Greenland with all that I had, and I meant to make a gift of it to you. I saw King Harald and he gave me leave to pass through his lands, even though he wanted the bear for himself. Then I met this man, Aki, who would not help me unless I sold him a half-share in the bear. And now the gift has been spoilt.'

'Is this man speaking the truth, Aki?' asked the king.

Aki said, 'Yes he is, my lord, which is why I insisted he should keep the other half.'

King Svein said, 'You were a little man and I made you an important one. Was it right for you to impede someone who had spent everything he had on this priceless gift? Even our enemy King Harald saw fit to let this man travel in peace. Get out of my sight, Aki, and leave this land forever. As for you, Audun, I feel as much in your debt as if you had given me the whole bear.'

The king invited Audun to stay with him a while. Then he agreed to sponsor Audun on a pilgrimage to Rome.

On his way back from Rome, Audun became ill and ran out of money. He returned to Denmark a thin and filthy vagabond. He was too ashamed to show himself to King Svein in church, but during evening prayers the king noticed him lurking in the corner.

'You have changed,' he said, taking Audun by the hand.

The king ordered a bath to be prepared for Audun, and gave him the clothes he himself had worn during Lent. He invited Audun to stay with him and become his cup-bearer. But Audun insisted he had to return to Iceland, because his time was up, and the money he had provided for his mother had run out, and he could not bear to think of her living in poverty.

'You must truly be a man of good fortune,' said the king. 'It is the only reason you could give for leaving that does not offend me.'

King Svein furnished Audun with a ship and many gifts, including a magnificent arm-ring that he took from his own arm. Then he bade the Icelander farewell.

Audun sailed up the coast of Norway, and stopped at the court of King Harald to tell the king of his journey, just as he had promised.

Harald asked Audun if he had given King Svein the bear.

'Yes I did, my lord,' he replied.

'How did he repay you?'

'Well, first of all, by accepting it.'

'I would have repaid you in that way as well,' said the king. 'Did he give you anything else?'

'He gave me food and a pouch of silver so I could go to Rome on a pilgrimage,' said Audun.

'I would have done that for you too. What else did he give you?'

'He invited me to stay with him when I returned from Rome, even though I looked like a beggar,' said Audun. 'He also gave me the fine clothes he had worn during Lent.'

'It is no great thing to treat a beggar this way, and I too would have done this,' said the king. 'What else did he give you?'

'He gave me a handsome ship to return home in, laden with fine wares.'

'That was generous of him, but I too would have done this. Was there anything else?'

Audun said, 'He gave me another purse of silver so I would not be penniless if my ship got wrecked off the coast of Iceland.'

'Now, that was *truly* generous,' said the king, 'and more than I would have done. Was there anything else?'

'He gave me a gold arm-ring,' said Audun, 'and told me not to part with it, unless I found myself under a heavy obligation to some great man, such that I would wish to give it to him. And now I give it to you, my lord, for it was in your power to have me killed and to take my precious bear, yet you let me travel in peace. I owe all my good fortune to you.'

Harald admitted that King Svein had very few equals, even though they were not friends, and he accepted the arm-ring. He ordered Audun's ship to be handsomely fitted out, and gave him a sword and cloak. They were both treasures, even though Harald said they were merely small gifts.

Audun sailed back that summer to Iceland, where he was acknowledged as a man of the greatest good fortune. Many good people are descended from him.

'AUDUN AND THE POLAR BEAR' is a small, finely wrought fable, but it holds many of the qualities of the great Icelandic sagas: the tale is told tersely, and contains real historical figures. The main character's honour is central to the story, and Audun quietly holds to it, at the risk of great suffering to himself. Also typical of the sagas is the beautiful strangeness of the tale. When the intricacies of the plot fade from the memory, that odd image of the starving Icelander wandering the streets of the Danish town with a polar bear lingers in the mind. The one element that distinguishes this tale from the great sagas, apart from its brevity, is its happy ending. Nearly always, the men and women of the sagas of Iceland are not rewarded for honourable behaviour, but destroyed by it.

The Icelandic sagas are the stories of the Viking families who settled on that impossible island a thousand years ago. These are not mere heroic fantasies – they're stories of flesh-and-blood people whose existence is also recorded in the family genealogies of the time. These records extend right up to the present day, allowing Icelanders to trace their ancestors all the way back to the saga characters.

The word *saga* simply means 'a telling'. Over time, the stories of these people were continually refined and retold, transfixing one generation after another. These 'tellings' relied on careful memorisation, but they might simply have faded away into the cold air were it not for an astonishing outburst of literary activity in the thirteenth century, when the sagas were at last transmitted from the voice to the page in lean, elegant prose. The greatest resource of this sparsely populated, volcanic island turned out to be the stories of its inhabitants.

The Icelandic sagas were written at a time when the fashion in medieval Europe was for chivalric tales like *Le Morte D'Arthur* and *Sir Gawain and the Green Knight*. Those courtly works from a more temperate climate resemble exquisitely embroidered silk, whereas the sagas might be made from rough hessian cloth, impregnated with ash and the scent of cold seawater. And yet this coarse fabric can hold the finest and subtlest emotions, revealed in strange and shocking moments. Like any great work of literature, the sagas reward second, third and fourth readings, and they surrender new meanings each time.

To a large extent, these classic tales from a distant north have somehow slipped past the notice of the rest of the world, but their influence on modern literature has been profound. Jorge Luis Borges discovered the sagas as a boy in his father's library in Buenos Aires. As an adult he paid tribute to their originality: 'In the twelfth century,' he wrote, 'the Icelanders discovered the novel … a discovery, not unlike their discovery of America, that remains so well concealed and barren from the rest of the world.' Borges felt compelled to make several trips to Iceland, and it was in Reykjavík that he finally summoned the courage to kiss Maria Kodama, his Japanese–Argentine assistant. He was blind, and seventy-one years old, and it was the first time in fifty years that a woman had not spurned him. Later he would write:

I want to recall that kiss, the kiss
You bestowed on me in Iceland.

THE ENGLISH POET W.H. Auden, whose name so closely resembles that of our man with the polar bear, was also introduced to the sagas by his father. Like Borges, he made pilgrimages to Iceland, which he sometimes called 'Saga Land'. Auden was shocked by the uncompromising and violent world the sagas describe, but, as he discovered, there's a great deal more to the lives of these Vikings than extortion and revenge. Those of us who grew up with the caricature of the mindless Viking brute, hacking and slashing his way through medieval Europe, are likely to be as shocked by the emotional complexity and tenderness of Viking family life and friendship portrayed in the sagas as they are by the extremities of violence.

The people of the sagas can seem both familiar to us and profoundly strange. This, for the two of us, is one of the deepest pleasures of the sagas, and we've endeavoured to honour that paradox. The stories, as we tell them here, are very much our versions, and are by no means definitive. We've shorn away much of their long and complex genealogies and some of the local detail. In so doing, we hope we've been able to distill their emotional intensity, as well as their weird and often confronting beauty.

THERE ARE FOUR different kinds of saga within the pages of this book.

Firstly, there are the classic family sagas that we have read and loved, which take place in tenth-century Iceland – the Iceland of the Viking era. Then there's the saga of one man, Snorri Sturluson, the greatest of the saga authors, who, in the thirteenth century, wrote down some of these tales onto vellum manuscripts. There are some scattered tales that we picked up along the way. And finally, there is a present-day family story that is Kári's *own* family saga. In the course of our journey, these four kinds of saga became interconnected and we had no desire to pull them apart.

The division of the stories came quite naturally to us. Kári has told the family sagas, and the story of his own history with Iceland. Richard has written the story of Snorri Sturluson's turbulent life, and an assortment of other tales, which concern a witchcraft trial, the chess match of the century, and Iceland's most haunted house and its role in ending the Cold War.

A BRIEF WORD on names. The Icelandic alphabet contains characters unfamiliar to English speakers, which we've altered here and there for the sake of simplicity. Audun, for example, is properly spelt 'Auðunn' in Icelandic. 'Au' is pronounced a bit like the 'i' in 'girl', and the 'ð' makes a 'th' sound like in 'weather', so his name is pronounced as 'I-thun' – with the stress, as in all Icelandic names, on the first syllable. Likewise, the name of the saga character Hallgerdur, the most dangerous woman in Iceland, should be spelt 'Hallgerður'. The 'a' is the same as in the English 'father', 'll' comes out as 'tl', and so in Icelandic the name is 'Hatl-gerth-ur'. Gudrún, the main character of another saga we tell later in the book, is Guðrún, in Icelandic a lovely-sounding name that translates as 'God's Rune'.

THIS ASSEMBLY OF stories and experiences is very much a reflection of the nature of our journey – or rather the two journeys that we made, one in high summer, the other in December, the darkest month of winter. On the first trip, we enjoyed long days of crystalline brightness; on the second, relentless wind, sleet that stung the skin, and such brief hours of daylight that we sometimes didn't notice them. But, of course, we wanted to experience both extremes, for they are both very present in the stories we've told. Sun on the fields, in the fjords, and also

Iceland of the silent snow and of the fervent water.
Iceland of the night that vaults
over wakefulness and dreams.

Kári Gíslason & Richard Fidler, 2017

Part

I

To Iceland

Iceland, the largest of the northern islands, lies at
the distance of three natural days' sail from Ireland,
toward the north. It is inhabited by a race of people
who use very few words, and speak the truth.

—Gerald of Wales, *The Topography of Ireland*, 1185

MY FRIEND KÁRI is a Viking. When he said he was going to
Iceland, I told him I was coming with him.

Iceland had been flickering in the back of my imagination since
I was a boy. On the desk in my bedroom I had a tin globe of the
world, the size of a soccer ball, and I often stared at its northernmost
islands, where all the lines of longitude converged on the spindle at
the top. There were places with exotic names – Iceland, Greenland,
Baffin Island – but only Iceland was marked with a mysterious city,
abbreviated to 'Reyk.' on my globe. I wondered how people could
build a city so close to the North Pole. What did they do there? How
did they live in all that ice and snow?

Kári Gíslason was born in that faraway city of Reykjavík. English
is his primary language, but he speaks Icelandic fluently. Kári
looks the part of a Viking: he's six foot four and he struggles to get

comfortable while flying in an economy seat. Although he's lived in Australia most of his life, Kári loves his birthplace with all the tragic passion of an exile living thousands of miles from his rightful home. He likes to quote W.H. Auden, who knew the island well, and who said he was 'never not thinking about Iceland'.

I came to know most of Kári's life story before I met him. Some years ago he wrote a memoir called *The Promise of Iceland*. I read the book and then interviewed him about it on my radio show. Afterwards, we found ourselves talking outside the studio for another hour or so. The lift kept arriving to take him to the carpark, but we kept deferring his departure.

He and I discovered we had much in common: we had similar taste in books and music, we both had young families, and we happened to live just a few blocks from each other. We began to meet regularly for lunch.

Kári was an author and established academic, but he'd retained something of the passionate aesthete he undoubtedly was in his twenties. I liked the way he lugged his favourite novels around with him in his briefcase, and admired his ability to pull an apposite quote from thin air. In 2013, he and I both participated in a literary event, in which we were invited to compose and recite a letter to 'The Woman Who Changed My Life'. I did the obvious thing and wrote about Khym, my wife. Kári, who loves D.H. Lawrence, dedicated his to Lady Chatterley.

ONE AFTERNOON, KÁRI made a passing reference to the sagas of Iceland. I had a vague and incorrect idea that the sagas were like *Beowulf*, tales of warriors fighting trolls and giant monsters.

'Oh no, not at all,' he said. 'The sagas are not fantasy. They're the family stories of the Vikings who settled in Iceland in the Middle

Ages. They're about real men and women. I think they're the greatest stories ever written.'

'So tell me a saga story,' I said.

He thought for a moment, placed his large hands on the table, and then the tale of Gunnar, the warrior who hated killing, and his wife Hallgerd, the most dangerous woman in Iceland, came tumbling out of him.

GUNNAR HAD RETURNED to Iceland after winning wealth and honour in Norway. He was a powerful athlete: instead of mounting his horse as most men did, he would use his halberd to vault himself onto the horse's back. It was said that he could jump as far backward as he could forward.

In the summer, Gunnar came to the assembly at Thingvellir wearing a fine cloak given to him by the King of Norway. He was walking through the gorge when he saw Hallgerd, who was known as the most dangerous woman in Iceland …

Kári told the tale with a quiet intensity, re-enacting Gunnar's pole vault with an imaginary spear. Suddenly, the saga of Gunnar and Hallgerd blazed across the distance of a thousand years from that impossible island at the top of the world.

The Book of Settlements

ICELAND SITS UP HIGH in the North Atlantic, just below the Arctic Circle. Its landmass spreads across a crack in the Earth's surface, along the fault line between the North American and the Eurasian tectonic plates.

The island emerged from the sea around 20 million years ago, created by a series of volcanic eruptions along the Mid-Atlantic

Ridge. As the land cooled and quietened, the tectonic forces below the surface formed fjords, crevasses and bony ridges under a blanket of snow and ice. The volcanic pressure and the crushingly heavy glaciers keep the landscape in a state of constant, slow-moving disruption.

Iceland lay quiet and uninhabited for countless millennia. Its existence seems to have been imagined or suspected centuries before any human actually set foot on the island. The ancient geographer Strabo, living in faraway Asia Minor, recorded a Greek sailor's tale of a mythical island called Thule,* which was said to lie 'six days' sail north of Britain, near the frozen sea'. In the Middle Ages, a fantastical account was written of the voyage of St. Brendan, the sixth-century Irish monk, who was said to have sailed into the North Atlantic, where he saw a 'crystal pillar' and a volcanic island that 'seemed like a giant globe of fire', where 'the sea on every side boiled up and foamed.'

THE STORY OF THE FOUNDING of Iceland is recorded in a medieval manuscript called *Landnámabók – The Book of Settlements*. According to its authors, the first people to settle in Iceland were not the seafaring Vikings, but Irish monks. These men of God, whom the Norse people called the Papar, committed themselves to an astonishingly perilous sea voyage, making their heroic crossings from Ireland in narrow sailboats, made of wicker and oak-tanned oxhide. The Irishmen brought bells, books and croziers to this new, empty land, where they shivered in huts and caves, carving crosses into the rock walls. These scattered hermits were entirely unprepared for the arrival of the pagan Vikings, as was most of northern Europe.

---

*   'Thule' was the name commonly used by medieval Europeans for Iceland. 'Ultima Thule' denoted the lands beyond the northern border of the known world, a name later given to Greenland.

Continental Europe was, in the ninth century, a broadly Christian domain, but the borders of Christendom were under siege from every direction: from Muslims in the south of Spain, from the Mongol invasions in the east, and by the sudden, shocking arrival of hordes of Viking heathens from the north. Driven by overpopulation in their Scandinavian homelands, the rapid spread of the Vikings at this time might be likened to spilling a bucket of water across a stone floor: a people who had been almost entirely unknown to Europeans were suddenly right there, charging across their northern frontiers.

The Viking Age began on the afternoon of 8 June 793, when a party of Norse raiders pulled their longboats ashore on the tidal island of Lindisfarne, in northeast England, where a Christian monastery had been founded more than a century earlier. The island's small community of monks could only look on in horror as the band of tattooed, axe-wielding pagans strode into their courtyard and church. The Vikings, meeting with very little resistance, hacked down several of the clerics and drowned a few more in the sea, before seizing the monastery's treasures and hauling them onto their boats.

Soon, more longships packed with heavily armed Vikings were making landfall on the beaches and in the waterways of England, Ireland, France and Russia. Christians living close to the front line of these attacks feared the invaders were the instrument of God's will, a punishment for their sins. In their terror, they sent up an urgent prayer: 'A furore Normannorum libera nos, Domine' – 'Deliver us from the Northmen's fury, O Lord'.

First the Norsemen came to plunder, then to establish trading posts and farms in these milder climates. While the Danish Vikings spread down into continental Europe, those from Norway sailed west to occupy the outer British islands – first the Orkneys and Shetlands, then the Faroes and Hebrides.

Inevitably, one of their seaworthy ships would press further into the achingly cold waters of the North Atlantic, in search of an island whose existence was still just a rumour.

THE BOOK OF SETTLEMENTS records that the first Norse voyager to set foot in Iceland was a man named Naddodd, who stayed only briefly and named it Snaeland – Land of Snow.

The next Viking to 'discover' Iceland was a Swede named Gardar, who circumnavigated the island in 870 and spent a winter in the north. He renamed it 'Gardar's Island' before sailing back to the mainland, never to return.

Years later another Norseman named Flóki went looking for Gardar's Island with a group of followers and slaves. Flóki brought three ravens on his ship and set them free.

The first flew over the stern and never came back.

The second flew up into the air and returned to the deck.

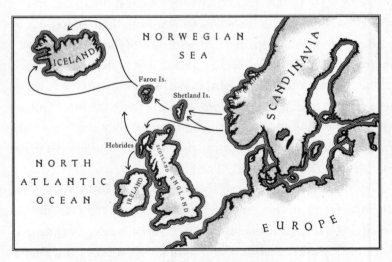

The Norse Settlement of Iceland

The third raven flew straight ahead, and led them to the Westfjords of Iceland.

Flóki and his men brought their cattle ashore and established a small settlement, but the winter that followed was harsh and the animals died. Flóki cursed the cruel, cold land. One day he climbed up onto a headland and saw drifts of ice in the fjord, and so he renamed the island 'Iceland' and this time the name stuck.

Flóki returned to Norway with nothing good to say about the place. But one of his men, Thórólf, took a different view: he spoke of Iceland as a paradise, where 'butter dropped from every blade of grass'. Thórólf was widely ridiculed for this and was thereafter known as 'Thórólf Butter'.

THE MASS SETTLEMENT of Iceland finally got underway in 874 AD, when a Viking named Ingólf sailed out of Norway looking for the land 'Flóki of the Ravens' had spoken of. Ingólf was accompanied by his wife Hallveig and some slaves.

After four days at sea, they caught sight of the Icelandic coast. As the boat approached the shoreline, Ingólf pulled apart the timbers of his high seat and tossed them overboard. He told his slaves that wherever the timbers washed ashore was where they would settle.

The timbers were eventually found in an inlet that Ingólf named Reykjavík – Smoky Bay – for the steam they saw blasting out of the hot springs.

Ingólf and his band of settlers set up a farm on the bay. The land was poor, but there were plenty of fish, and they soon found deposits of bog iron in the marshy springs for making swords and axes.

Reports of the success of the new settlement in Iceland arrived in Norway, where people were said to be chafing under the oppressive rule of King Harald the Finehair.* Thousands of Norwegian farmers sold their goods and sailed to this new land to the west, where they heard there was plentiful farmland for the taking. They were a hybrid group of pioneers: while the men were primarily of Nordic ancestry, almost two-thirds of the women had their ancestral roots in the British Isles, having been brought over as wives or as slaves from Viking settlements in Ireland.

The settlers set up farms on the coastal plains and in the fjords and valleys, which were often lush and grassy in the summer months. They built longhouses made of timber and stone, insulated with thick blankets of turf.

Soon enough, the Viking settlers began to encounter those Irish monks who had come to Iceland decades earlier. One account, written centuries later, blandly records that the monks did not want to share the island with heathens and left Iceland of their own accord. But it seems more likely the Vikings dealt with these monks as they'd always dealt with Christians unfortunate enough to be dwelling in lands they wanted for themselves.

Either way, the presence of the Irish monks on the island abruptly ceased, and within just sixty years of Ingólf's arrival, all of Iceland's farmlands were occupied by the Vikings. The coastal lands had been well forested when the Vikings came, but in a short time, most of the birch trees were cut down to create pastures and provide timber. The newly exposed topsoil was worn away by rain and wind, and it became harder to extract food from the land. From now on,

---

* Harald had not always been known by this name. Years earlier, as an ambitious warlord, Harald had sworn he would not cut or comb his hair or beard until he had brought all of Norway under his rule. This had taken a decade to accomplish, and so he came to be known in this time as 'Harald the Shaggy'. When at last he unified Norway in 872, the thickets of his ten-year-old growth were shorn away, and he took on a much more pleasing appearance, which earned him his new moniker.

Icelanders would have to gather driftwood, or import timber from Norway.

LAND WAS PARCELLED OUT by the chieftains of Iceland, who met in local assemblies to make laws, just as they had done in Norway. They were more or less of equal standing. They were not warlords or petty kings.

It seems never to have occurred to the Icelanders that they should have a monarch or titled aristocrats. Iceland was too distant from the continent to be at serious risk of a full-scale armed invasion, so its chieftains had no need to forcibly extract taxes to fund an Icelandic army or a navy. Perhaps their bitter memories of Harald the Finehair had made them allergic to overbearing rulers. So Iceland came into nationhood quite naturally as a kind of republic, or commonwealth. Arguably, it's Iceland, not America, that should be seen as Europe's first New World society, founded by migrants looking to get out from under an oppressive king.

A MAP OF THE NORSE WORLD in the Middle Ages might appear to the modern eye as a scattering of isolated outposts, separated by stretches of icy water, but the sea-going Vikings saw their realm quite differently: as a network of settlements connected by maritime highways, which they traversed with comparative ease, trading goods, information and ideas. No single settlement, even those as far-flung as Iceland or Greenland, existed in total isolation from the others. Even so, there must have been times when the Icelanders felt very far away from the rest of the world, and that their existence had been forgotten, if it was ever remembered in the first place.

In the summer, they tended to their crops and their sheep, and fed the animals on the fine long grass. Some pushed their boats out into the fjords to catch haddock and cod, which was dried and salted for those times when food was scarce.

The winter months were long and the very idea of 'daytime' lost much of its meaning. Families kept inside their cramped stone-and-turf longhouses while the snowstorms roared outside in the darkness. This was a time for men and women to sit around the fire in the centre of the house. They would spin and weave, or make tools, spears and axes. Children would play on the dirt floor and climb into the rafters.

While they worked with their hands, the men and women passed the time by telling stories of themselves and their families. These tales would be repeated and memorised word-for-word, and perhaps they grew a little with each telling.

This was how the Icelanders remembered Gísli the fugitive; and Egil, the ruthless warrior-poet who was undone by the drowning of his young son; and Gudrún, who engineered the death of the man she loved the most.

Ambitious Icelanders knew they'd have to leave for years at a time to make their name and their fortune. Some travelled east to Byzantium and to the Holy Land, while others sailed west all the way to America, where they traded and fought with native Americans, centuries before Columbus's voyage to the New World. When they returned to Iceland, new sagas were composed to tell of their exploits.

THE SAGA STORY that Kári had told me of Gunnar and Hallgerd had stuck in my mind, and so a week later, I picked up a compendium of the Icelandic sagas from the classics shelf of my local bookshop. As I read them, I was surprised by their speed and precision. The streamlined narratives shift and move unpredictably. The inner lives of the men and women of the sagas are profoundly enigmatic: there are no soliloquies, they never reveal what they're thinking. We have to understand them through what they say and do.

That such a cold and remote island with only a thin scattering of people could generate such a rich body of work seemed to me something of a miracle. Why had I known so little of the sagas until now?

The Vikings of the sagas share our contemporary pre-occupations with love and family and status. They experience all the great emotions and the petty ones too. But there is one element of their lives that can seem strange to us: the Viking concept of honour. Honour drives people in the sagas to do shocking things. It's the reason why they will hold fast to a terrifying course of action, knowing it will result in their destruction, or that of the person dearest to them.

'The thing to understand about Viking honour,' Kári told me, 'is that it's finite. Honour isn't like love, it's not like something that grows from a seed. It's more like currency – there are only so many coins to go around. You can't earn honour; you have to take it from someone else.'

'What if you rescue someone from drowning? Do you earn honour from that?'

'No. The sagas don't tend to record good deeds. In the Viking world, you don't gain honour from doing the right thing. But you can lose it if you don't.'

I asked if this concept applied to women as much as men.

'Oh yes,' he said, 'absolutely. In the sagas, women defend their honour as fiercely as men. And the revenge they extract to defend that honour can be shocking to modern readers.'

THE WHOLE PROJECT of Iceland as a nation was, for many centuries, a marginal thing. Icelanders have always struggled to keep their grip on a violent, inhospitable landscape and to sustain their thin lines of contact with a distant Europe. At times they feared their civilisation might just peter out altogether.

Iceland has never been a rich country. The Norse people left no castles or great ruins on the island. The only real proof they existed at all in those distant centuries comes from the sagas they wrote to sing themselves into the landscape of their new home.

'The sagas are the true castles of Iceland,' Kári told me one afternoon at his house. 'They're the stories that created the island's sense of itself. I think that without the sagas, Icelanders would forget how to be themselves.'

I could see how important they were to Kári's sense of himself as well.

KÁRI WAS PLANNING to spend a month in Iceland in the northern summer of 2015. I suggested I go with him, and that we make a radio series together on the sagas. We decided I would record Kári as he told the stories from the sagas of the Viking men and women who lived in Iceland a thousand years ago. And we would do this in the very places where the events in the sagas unfolded. We would travel across the country, hiking into the fields and rocky fjords and isolated farms to speak the words of Kári's Viking ancestors into the stones and streams of Iceland.

BUT THERE WAS ANOTHER, much more personal reason for Kári to go to Iceland: a deeper mission tangled up inside a family mystery.

CHAPTER TWO
(Kári)

A Gift

WHEN I WAS A BOY IN ICELAND, a family friend called Gunnar used to take me out fishing on his small boat *Svanur*, 'The Swan'. For most of the year, he kept the boat stored in a garage cramped by a Lada station wagon and a long wooden table that he used for cleaning and filleting the fish. But at the beginning of summer he'd tow *Svanur* down to the ashen beach near his house and then wait for a calm day to take her onto the water.

Gunnar was nearing retirement when Mum and I first met him and his wife Lilja, during a holiday in Porta Rosa, Slovenia. In one of our first conversations, he asked me if I liked fishing, and I told him that I hadn't tried it. I ate my share of fish, but I hadn't ever caught one.

When we returned from our holidays, Gunnar rang Mum to ask if I'd like to join him on his next fishing trip. He said we'd catch enough *ýsa*, haddock, to freeze and last the winter. Mum said I could go if I wanted to go, but only if I brought back some fish for us, as well.

On the day of the trip, Lilja gave me one of the jumpers she knitted for a local cooperative that sold woollen clothes. Gunnar and I set out, and as we got past the headlands of the bay, Gunnar switched on his sonar and passed the rudder over to me. I felt utterly released, and part of the life of the sea.

We sailed towards the white light of the horizon, until a shoal of haddock appeared on the sonar and Gunnar turned off the engine. We dropped long lines to the bottom with five hooks each. A light smell of fuel hung over the boat as it swayed; there was cracked paint under my fingers as I held on to the wooden sides.

We pulled in the first fish, cut the gills. A line of shining blood was smeared along the floor of the boat.

I could have stayed on the water forever. Soaking up the sea, the steady work of fishing, and the company of a gentle man who would gradually adopt Mum and me into his own family. I had only the barest understanding of why he wanted us.

On the way back to shore, he let me steer again, and sat just in front of me and lit a cigar. The smoke circled and drifted in lovely patterns over the cabin, trailing around me before it blew out to the sea. I wished the day weren't almost over, and sailed the tug as slowly as I could, drifting off course until Gunnar pointed out that we were going the wrong way.

It was time to go back in.

The author on board *The Swan*

ONE OF GUNNAR'S hands was deformed; it was much smaller than his good hand, and curled into itself. Whenever I was with him in town, joining him on errands, I noticed that he kept it hidden by his side or in the fold of his good arm. But on the boat he was relaxed about it. He knew I didn't care. The look of his hand had never bothered me in the slightest. I didn't ask him about it.

Nor did Gunnar ever ask me about *our* missing parts, Mum's and mine, although I expect he'd heard about them here and there. He never tried to unwrap or define the problems I had to do with my father. During our trips together, he chose instead to leave them, like fish that are too small to keep and have to be thrown back into the water. He chose to let me be with him as a kind of extra grandson.

It was a relief that he didn't. There were times when I needed to think about it, but when I was with him on the water I was happy merely to drift.

A Gap in the Records

MY FATHER AND I first met when I was seven. He came to visit Mum at our apartment in Reykjavík. I can still see him at the door: a handsome man with light brown hair and a hesitant smile, who must have been in his early forties. He said hello, and then, without telling me who he was, asked if Mum was home.

'Yes,' I said. He waited, standing there a little uneasily, but he didn't seem to mind that I was staring at him and not moving off to fetch Mum. I couldn't quite leave, but I didn't know what to say to stretch out the moment.

All I knew for certain was that it was him.

Eventually, he reached into his pocket and gave me some change, and I called out to Mum. While they talked, I ran across the road

and bought myself a bottle of 7Up. When I came back, he was gone.
I went back across the road and bought another one.

Such is my first memory of him, although in fact *he*'d seen *me*
many times before. During the early years, he sometimes visited us
in the evenings, after I'd gone to sleep. He was worried that if I saw
him, I might recognise him and call out in the street one day. He was
nervous, and I was a gregarious child; I'm sure he was right, and that
I would have approached him – on one of those days when I wasn't
satisfied just to drift, but wanted something more from him instead.

A few years before, my mother Susan had found herself in Iceland, as
surprised as her family all the way back in Australia. When her marriage
had ended in 1967, she'd decided to travel. The man she'd loved, Ed,
had left her for another woman. Together, they'd been explorers of a
kind: they'd met in the Australian Navy, and then together had worked
on the ski fields and at Outward Bound, at a camp on the Hawkesbury
River. They had been travellers, and now she travelled on without him.

In any case, it was something of a family ailment to sort out one's
troubles in this way. Her father Harold had been restless, especially
after his service in the Royal Navy in World War II, and already the
family had moved backwards and forwards several times between
England and Australia.

But Mum was much more than merely restless. She was seeking
out her own adventures, to quench a thirst for the world that had
begun when she was just a girl, and the family had made their first
sea voyage to Australia. She loved the sea and ports in particular. And
that strangely intoxicating, addictive feeling of being somewhere
unfamiliar.

First, she took a ship to Japan, and from there one to Russia,
where she boarded the Trans-Siberian Railway. Then another ship,
a ferry to her birthplace in England. And then, of all things, she

saw an advertisement for a job as an English-speaking secretary in Reykjavík, at a small firm of importers. It sounded like the end of the world, and so she took the job. How could you not?

At the end of that year of escaping her failed marriage, my mother began to work at the firm. The office was in the centre of town, halfway up a cobbled street called Grjótagata. It was only steps away from the harbour, the docks. And also from the country's oldest ruin: a rock outline of a Viking longhouse that dated back to the 870s, and marked the first attempts by Ingólf and his fellow settlers to live on this distant island.

Mum fell in love with it all – especially Esja, the mountain that stood across the bay to the north, and the people, who were also always a little distant, but kind as well. They accepted her as a stray from the wider world beyond, and I think they liked that about her. She fitted in, because she was self-contained and perhaps a little lost. Like Iceland could seem.

But Iceland could also be a lonely place, and so unlike England and Australia – no pubs or places to meet new friends, and very little in the way of casual social life. At night, the streets downtown were empty and dark. And the night was such a long one: it started at three in the afternoon, and went on for hours after she got to work each morning. Back home, people had called Iceland the end of the world. Mid-winter in 1970, it very nearly was.

But in workplaces in those days, it was customary to have morning and afternoon coffee together. Now and again, one of the younger men, Gísli, would smile at Mum from across the room. Not such a big deal, but noticeable, at least in Iceland, where people were so much slower to open up, reserved and quiet in a way that she liked. Who, then, was this charmer who smiled at her and sometimes lingered outside her office?

One day, he began to follow her home. I'm not sure how she felt about this. Probably a little uneasy. But in those days, at least in faraway Iceland, I suppose it was still considered romantic. The following day, he started throwing snowballs at her from the other side of the street. Little wonder that she fell for him.

Or is it? Mum's always been a bit coy about that. When I ask her what she saw in him, her eyes seem to dart across the possibilities. It doesn't feel like evasiveness; more, I think, a sign that over forty years later she's still working it out. He was handsome, yes, and nicely mannered. But most of all perhaps, he was an answer to the mystery of why she'd come to Iceland in the first place. A thirst for adventure, a willingness to go with it.

They began a relationship. But she wondered about him. Why was this handsome man in his thirties still unattached? Most of the good ones were gone. So, one day she asked. 'Why aren't you married?'

My father Gísli looked at her as though she were joking. Of course he was married. He had five children. Surely she knew that. This was Iceland; everybody knew everyone else's business.

WHEN I WAS BORN a year or so later, my father asked Mum to keep his identity as my father a secret. He told her that it would ruin his family life if the truth of their affair came out.

She didn't want to do that to him or his family. Instead, she chose silence: she left the 'Name of Father' line of my birth certificate blank, and from then on she held true to her promise to him.

When their relationship ended, I think Mum more or less gave up on men. Instead, she began to live an even quieter and more solitary life that would mainly be about me, and how we might get through our strange situation together. She would be raising a boy who would never know his father. But she did tell me his name, and about the promise she'd made.

I accepted that promise as my own, but I was less accepting of Mum's choice of solitude. I liked nothing more than making new friends of strangers, especially male strangers who I thought would make good husbands for her. She was a shy person, and I expect she found my youthful interference almost unbearably embarrassing. But even as I looked around for others, and then other things to do, I didn't stop wanting my father, not yet, or wanting to please him. Even though my situation was unusual, my love for him was boundless. This may seem strange, but wanting to know him was not conditional on his wanting to know me. And that feeling, of wanting him, would last almost until he died.

When I was ten, Mum and I left for England, and four years later we settled back in Australia, close to where Mum's family lived. I went to high school in an outer suburb of Brisbane called Brighton, which, like its English counterpart, was stretched across the foreshore.

Then, during a gap year between school and university, I accepted one of the invitations that the ocean seemed to offer to retrace my steps. I made my way back to Europe, and eventually also to Reykjavík.

It was the eve of my eighteenth birthday, and I called my father.

On a windy September afternoon, we went for a drive together. I expected to be impressed by him, for in my mind's eye I still held a rather lovely image of him from when I was younger and he stood at our door. But something had changed: for the first time in my life I wondered what Mum had seen in him. Maybe this was because he took all the back roads, so that we wouldn't be seen together. Somehow, his appearance was folded into that nervousness.

As we drove, he talked about my mother. Gísli recalled her loyalty to him, and the promise she'd made him all those years before. He explained that his situation hadn't changed since then. He was still married and still had his other children to think of.

He then asked me to make the same promise as my mother had made: to keep the truth to myself. His life would be ruined if the secret came out; that is, if *I* came out.

Would I do as my mother had done, and protect him?

'Yes, I will,' I said. 'I won't tell anyone. I haven't come all this way to make things hard for you.'

I meant it. I desperately didn't want him to suffer. How could anyone want their parent to suffer? But what *had* I come all this way for, then? What was I doing in his car? I suppose I was knocking on his door, as he had once knocked on ours, trying to offer him something he already had with his family at home – a faithful son, a fish from the sea that was worth keeping. But, just as suddenly as it had appeared, my offer seemed ridiculous, too exposing. And so, instead, I asked if he could help me with money.

'What for?' he asked.

I hadn't been prepared for questions. 'I'm starting university next year.'

'How much would you like?' he asked. 'Things are a bit tight at the moment. We're about to go to Spain.'

'I don't know.'

'A hundred dollars?'

'Okay.'

We drove to a bank, where he took out 100 dollars in Icelandic kronur and gave the notes to me. I wished that I hadn't asked. The whole thing felt like a failed bribe attempt. But I took the money and thanked him. And with that we said goodbye.

Letters

FOR A LONG WHILE, I thought that this was how things were going to end between my father and me. He didn't want a relationship, and, like Mum, I had no wish to destroy his family life. He loved his wife and children, and I didn't think I had the right to alter their view of him. Looking back at it today, I see that over the years I'd come to accept and naturalise my place as the secret child of the family.

And yet when I got back to Brisbane and enrolled in university, something else began to harden in me. At first it was a bitter feeling, and one that didn't offer me much sense of what to do. But gradually a different kind of anger grew alongside it. I wanted another go at that conversation that I'd had with him, so that I could answer his question in a different way. I wanted to say *no*, I wouldn't be silent.

In 1999, almost ten years after he and I had met and gone for our drive together, I won a small grant through my university, and was given the chance to return to Iceland. I'd begun a PhD in medieval Icelandic literature; my topic involved the concepts of authorship revealed by the family sagas, how they were written anonymously and yet also seemed to reflect the creative design of individuals. The sagas seemed to be both communal and individual, a combination that intrigued me.

By then, my attitude to my own family saga had changed: I didn't believe in the secret any more. But now that I was presented with the chance to act, I suddenly felt unsure again.

One afternoon, I caught the bus up to the summit of Mount Coot-tha, a hill in Brisbane's western suburbs. There's a café there, and a lookout. Mostly, it's where tourists go to take pictures of the city. But I found it a good place to think, to sit for a while and make notes in my journal. On this occasion, I sat there for most of the day, sipping coffee and wondering whether I could do it.

By the afternoon, I realised that my father was no longer the main object, not quite. If, at some level, I would always be thinking about him, then it was also true that it was time to concentrate on those who had never met me, and did not even know I existed. That is, it was time to look beyond him and approach my Icelandic siblings and tell them that they had a brother in Australia.

I didn't know much about them. I'd heard that one sister, Bryndís, lived in Paris, and that the eldest, Fríða, had recently returned to Iceland after many years in Spain. There was Anna, who was living in a village in the countryside, and a brother, Björn, who'd followed our father into the import business. And then a fifth sibling, another brother, Ólafur, who I heard had died in an accident some years before.

When I left the café, I knew that I couldn't go back to Iceland again without breaking the secret. It would cost me too much to keep living in that way. I had my siblings' names, and only the barest outline of their lives. But that was enough, for, as my father knew well, in Iceland everyone knows everyone. And people are easy to find. Just about everyone's occupation and address are listed in the phone book.

That August, I flew to Reykjavík and stayed with old family friends, who set up a guest room for me, and each night over dinner gently encouraged me to look up my family. I noticed that to others, it seemed almost impossible not to. That to others, I had some basic rights in the matter: to know my family, and to be known for who I was.

I wasn't as sure. Did I really have the right to step across the lives of others in that way, and disrupt how a family understood itself, its past? For a month, I threw myself into my work instead. I had a reading desk at the medieval manuscript centre in Reykjavík, the Árni Magnússon Institute. It was named after one of the first

Icelanders to collect and protect the manuscripts that contained the saga stories. He'd given his life to literature. Maybe literature would be enough for me, as well.

For much of the time, it was. But in the evenings, after a day of quiet research, I would walk back home along the Reykjavík shoreline, and a space would open up to think about the other Iceland that existed here. Like the sagas, much was in the past. And yet, like the ancient stories, there was always the chance that what had been unsaid would speak into the present.

One night, about a month after I'd arrived, I came in from my walk home and wrote a group of letters. The first was to my father. I told him that I'd decided to break the promise I'd made nine years before, on that day when we had gone for our drive together.

> *Gísli,*
> *I would like you to know that I am going to be open about the*
> *fact that you are my father. This is a secret that should never have*
> *been created. It was very wrong of you to keep me hidden, and I*
> *will not live in secret any more.*
> *Kári*

I took the bus to his apartment and slipped this letter under the door, then left as quickly as I could. I was worried he might open the door while I was still there. When I stepped outside the building, I began to yell with joy and relief, as though calling to the wind to witness what I'd done. The secret was over.

The remaining letters were to my siblings. They had no idea about me, and so I had to explain that I was their brother, born in Iceland, but that Mum and I had promised Gísli that we wouldn't reveal his identity as my father.

They responded straight away: they met up and rang me the same night they got the letter, and we arranged to meet – all of us except Bryndís, who was still in Paris.

When my eldest sister Fríða met me for the first time, she held my face in her hands and said, 'Oh, Dad.'

To her, it was that obvious that I was his. And theirs.

I looked into their eyes that night and felt that I was also looking into my own. I'd always known that Gísli was my father, but what shocked me now was that I suddenly belonged not only to him and my mother, but also to an entire family tree. Within a matter of hours, my place in the world had changed forever.

My siblings, for their part, were endlessly curious. How could they not be? It was as though they were meeting their father anew, learning things about him that they hadn't thought possible. But they were also insistent that this was the beginning of something, not merely a moment to re-evaluate up the past. The family had had its share of losses. My siblings had lost a brother; they were determined to see me as a gain.

THE FOLLOWING SUNDAY, I was invited to a family lunch. It would be held at a nearby village, Hveragerdi, where Anna, my third sister, lived. She invited everyone: my siblings and all their partners and children, as well as my father and his wife.

Fríða and her partner collected me from outside the house where I was staying, and we drove to lunch. She was heavily pregnant at the time, and I can't imagine she was comfortable. The baby was due that very day. Maybe the reason why she was so calm about my arrival was that she was expecting her own. Two of my other siblings, Bryndís and Björn, had only recently had children too.

Despite all that was happening in her own life, the gathering seemed to be Fríða's idea. She wanted everything to be out in the open. She was sure that in the end it would work out. How could our father not take the chance to know me, especially when pressed to do so by his other children?

I told her that I wasn't sure, but then my experience of him was so different from hers. My instinct by then was to let him be, to accept that it was too late.

When we arrived at the house, my siblings noticed my hesitancy and joined forces in looking after me. My brother Björn sat next to me and asked about my PhD project, how on Earth it was that I'd managed to study the sagas all the way over in Australia.

'It's not as strange as it sounds,' I said. 'People love the sagas all over the world.'

'Do you read them in Icelandic?' he asked.

I had lost a lot of the language by then. 'Yes,' I said, 'although I sometimes cheat too, and pull out the Penguin Classics edition.'

'Well, we'll have to speak only Icelandic with you, then. That way you won't ever need to cheat.'

Björn and the others looked over at my father's wife, Ólöf. She'd never known about her husband's affair, and until that week had had no hint of my existence. But that day she handled it almost impossibly well. She said I was welcome into the family.

In the years ahead, that welcome would be harder for her to maintain, understandably I think. She found it harder to see me. It must have been difficult to separate her husband's deception from me, the product of it.

But all that day, she and the family were very generous to me; they pushed the day forward with their good will. Not all families could have responded in this way. I fell in love with them completely.

The more difficult matter was what to say to my father. For my whole life, he had hidden from me, afraid of how I might affect his family. Now, with the door to him strangely and so suddenly opened, it seemed too late to say very much at all. He was unwell: he'd recently been diagnosed with Parkinson's disease. So for most of lunch we merely exchanged the odd glance and smile.

Fríða, I noticed, didn't think that was enough. She was determined that the two of us talk properly. 'My God,' I heard her say to Anna, 'it's his son. He *has* to speak to him.'

When it was obvious that we weren't going to get anywhere on our own, Fríða pulled the two of us aside and sat us down on two chairs at the far end of the living room. It was a slightly raised section of the room, and it felt like we were settling down to an interview. But what would we talk about?

Gísli began by asking how Mum was. I said she was well, and still living in Australia. He smiled and for a moment looked away. Perhaps he was imagining her as he'd known her: a pretty young woman with black hair that ran all the way down her back. Her sudden arrival in the Reykjavík office that had thrown his life into disarray.

'How did you break your nose?' he asked.

'I'm not sure. I think I fell when I was little.'

'Here in Iceland?'

'Yes.'

'And they didn't straighten it for you?'

'I don't know.'

'You could get them to do it while you're here.'

I looked at Gísli, and again he looked away, towards the family activity in the kitchen – the dishes being collected and new ones put out for coffee and cake. Was this it, then? A conversation about my mother and my nose?

His grandchildren, nephews I was meeting for the first time, were running across the living room, skipping over the step where the floor was raised. What an odd moment in their lives, I thought: the arrival of a new uncle, out of nowhere. The two of us sitting here, waiting for something, working out what should be said in such a moment.

'Mum loved Iceland,' I said.

'Yes, she fell in love with the country,' Gísli replied. 'Maybe she should have stayed here.' A pause. 'And now you're back.'

'Yes.'

'To live?'

'Just for a visit. I'm here for my studies.'

He nodded, and seemed to be coming back a little. 'What do you do?'

'I'm in literary studies. I'm here to do research on the Icelandic sagas.'

'Oh?'

'Maybe one day I'd like to write.'

After some thought, he smiled and said, 'That makes sense.'

'Really?'

'You know you're descended from Snorri Sturluson, don't you?'

Into the Landscape, into the Light

S NORRI STURLUSON IS, I discover, Iceland's national hero and the greatest of the saga authors. He was also a poet, a historian and a national leader during Iceland's most turbulent century, and he met with a horribly violent death in 1241. Every Icelander knows his work and his name is everywhere: the island has a shrine, a statue, a street and a beer dedicated to him.

Snorri is believed to have written *Egil's Saga*, one of the most loved family sagas. He also wrote the epic history of the Norwegian kings, *Heimskringla*, and the *Prose Edda*, the compendium of Norse myths that remains the richest source of information we have on Thor, Odin and Loki, the creation of the Norse universe and its apocalypse on the day called Ragnarok. Today, Snorri Sturluson's name scarcely reaches beyond Scandinavia, but his reach is global: so much of what we know today of the Vikings – their gods, their adventures and their inner lives – comes from the pen of this man, living in a faraway island on the rim of the Arctic Circle in the Middle Ages.

Snorri Sturluson, illustration by Christian Krogh,
from Heimskringla, *1899 edition*

Snorri was an outstanding lawyer and wordsmith in a nation that prized such skills above all others. His talents as a poet and storyteller, harnessed to his political ambitions, made him the most powerful Icelandic chieftain of his time. Iceland was a commonwealth without a king, but if there was to be a single pre-eminent figure, Snorri was determined it would be him. Allies, enemies, lovers and family members were forced to revolve around his brilliance like lesser satellites.

Yet Snorri did not fit the classic mould of the war-painted Viking chieftain who leads his men into battle, sword in hand. He was a well-padded, charming lawyer, skilled at manipulating others into wielding the axe on his behalf. He saw himself not as a warrior, but as a king without a crown, and so he shrank from physical violence, often travelling at the centre of an army of kinsmen. This earned him a reputation as a coward, but Snorri enjoyed power, poetry and life too much to want to die young on the point of a sword.

'Snorri', his nephew wrote, 'was a very good businessman and a man of many pleasures'. In conversation, he was beguiling and witty, a compulsive gossip. Holding court at his great keep at Reykholt, he could be a princely host at great Viking feasts – lavishing his guests with beef, mutton and horsemeat served on silver platters, and wine poured into golden bowls; providing riotous entertainment with music, dancing and bouts of wrestling. And yet, as a power politician, Snorri could be ruthlessly mean, wielding his sharp legal intellect to carve out every last petty advantage from a lawsuit settlement. Although masterful and persuasive at legal argument, he was often a poor judge of people. In the pursuit of money and power he needlessly bruised egos, and all too often he would pick the losing side in his larger battles, which would, in the end, destroy him.

WE'RE IN KÁRI'S KITCHEN in Brisbane when he tells me of his possible bloodline connection to Snorri, and I'm taken aback. It's like being told your friend might be the great-grandson of Tolstoy.

'But is it true?' I ask him.

'Maybe. Probably. I can't be sure.' He smiles. 'I *want* it to be true.' He thinks for a moment. 'When my father told me about Snorri,' he says slowly, 'it felt like a gift. Like he was handing me a family heirloom. It was a really lovely moment and I'm grateful to him for it.'

I'm not sure what to say. I'm wondering if that gift from Gísli might be a beautifully wrapped box with not much inside it. A bit of half-remembered family folklore to cover an awkward moment.

Still, I am intrigued. The Vikings were meticulous in recording their family lineages, and as a result, Iceland has the most comprehensive, far-reaching genealogical records in the world.

Today's Icelanders can trace their lines of descent all the way back to the first settlers. The records have been digitised and are held at an institution in Reykjavík called Íslendingabók, which takes its name from *The Book of Icelanders*.

'So,' I ask, 'did you ever go to Íslendingabók to confirm the connection to Snorri?'

Kári smiles wistfully. 'I did try. Once. This was after Gísli died. I got the address for Íslendingabók in Reykjavík, and I really did mean to go there. But ...' he starts to laugh, 'you might find this hard to believe, Richard, but when I got there I couldn't find it.'

'I don't understand.'

'Well, it's a little embarrassing. When I got to the street number, all I saw was a boring-looking computer business, so I gave up and went home. I thought I'd got the wrong address. But later I discovered I'd been at the right place after all. Íslendingabók *was* the computer business. I just wasn't expecting it to be in such an unlikely location.'

'So did you go back?'

Kári shrugs. 'I was leaving the next day. I've never really followed it up. To be honest, mustering up the courage to declare my existence to my Icelandic family was very satisfying and wonderful, but really draining. Then when I came back to Australia, I was flat out with family life, I had my work and my writing and I was just too busy. I told myself I'd go looking for Snorri again one day.'

'Can't you just log in to the Íslendingabók website from here and see if it links your name to Snorri's?'

'The privacy protocols won't let me. Gísli's name was never entered on my birth certificate, so there's no official link from me to him in the database. My name is in there, but it's not connected to the rest of the family. Without the link to Gísli, I can't follow the chain of ancestry back to Snorri... if it exists.'

I have another idea: 'How about your half-sisters Bryndís and Fríða? Could they look it up for you, using their access to Íslendingabók?'

I'm trying to crack open the safe but Kári's already spun every available combination on the dial.

'I did ask them to do that.' he says patiently. 'And it turns out there *is* a connection between Snorri and my siblings. But the computer tracks the connection through the shortest path, which is through their mother. It doesn't say if there's a link to Snorri through Gísli.'

The next step seems obvious, to me at least.

'So why don't we make this our second mission in Iceland? To see if this bloodline connection to Snorri and the sagas really exists? If we show up in person, I bet we can get someone at Íslendingabók to help us.'

'Okay …' Kári replies warily.

THE NEXT DAY we sit down together and Kári proposes an itinerary. He sketches a rough map of Iceland on a blank sheet of paper. The island is shaped like a stonefish: the east coast forms the head, with the Westfjords serving as a bony tail. The outline, drawn from memory, is unusually detailed. How many hours has Kári spent gazing at maps of Iceland?

The interior of the island, the highlands, is a frozen, uninhabitable wasteland of lava fields, jagged mountains and gravel, so all our destinations are dotted around the green coastal fringes of the island. Kári suggests we base ourselves in Reykjavík, in the southwest, then travel out to the saga lands in the south, the west and the north of the island. This journey, he promises, will take us through a multitude of landscapes – from the grassy dales of Snaefellsnes, to the waterfalls and glaciers along the south coast, to the heroic mountain ridges of the Westfjords.

Our plan is to record the stories of three different people from the sagas. The first one, Gunnar, from the pages of *Njál's Saga*, will take us to the gorge of Thingvellir and then to the farmlands of Hlídarendi in the south. Then we'll go to the western dales for the story of Gudrún from *Laxdaela Saga*. Finally, the tale of Gísli the Outlaw, from *Gísli's Saga*, will bring us to the remote fjords in the northwest.

'And while we're in Reykjavík,' I say, 'we'll be hunting down the bloodline connection to Snorri.'

'That's the plan,' Kári says.

LATER THAT NIGHT, a web search leads me to the homepage of the Snorri Sturluson Museum, located at his old estate at Reykholt, where he lived for much of his life, and where he was murdered in 1241. Directly in front of Reykholt's austere research centre, I see a statue of the great saga author on a plinth, looking upright and scholarly. The image doesn't align with the gregarious character Kári's been describing to me, the power politician who fathered five children by four different women. Who *is* this man we're looking for?

I discuss this with Kári the next day, and he recommends I look at *Sturlunga Saga*, the history of Snorri's powerful clan, the Sturlungs. *Sturlunga Saga* is seen as a fairly reliable account; it was largely written by Snorri's nephew, who knew Snorri well, but was not overawed by his charismatic uncle.

Through the library system, I'm able to get hold of a rare copy of the sole English translation of *Sturlunga Saga*. Leafing through the book, I see Snorri's story is told in fits and starts throughout the narrative, interspersed with accounts of the lives of other family members and other goings-on in Iceland at the time.

I slot the book into my luggage, alongside the recording gear. I want to see the picture that emerges when I extract these fragments of Snorri's life and piece them together.

Lava Fields

KÁRI HAS FLOWN to Iceland ahead of me. I stop over in the UK to stay with some old friends, Rachel and Simon, who live in a sixteenth-century house in Cambridgeshire with a painted concrete cow in the garden. My flight to Reykjavík is booked with a budget carrier called WOW Air. Rachel is impressed by the name: 'Do you think the crew will be, like: "Wow, we took off! Wow, we landed!?"'

The flight is fine, and four hours later I'm pulling my bag through the gates of Keflavík Airport, with a bottle of duty-free whisky tucked under my arm. Kári is easy to spot in the arrivals lounge, being almost a head taller than everyone else.

'Welcome to Iceland, Richard!' he says in that warm and slightly formal manner of his.

Outside the terminal, the air is warm, but there's a stiff breeze that cuts through my thin jacket. It's high summer, and Iceland's Arctic latitude means the low-hanging sun will keep rolling across the sky until 11pm, when it will slip below the horizon, introducing a long, fuzzy twilight that will linger for five hours or so, until daylight resumes at full strength at four in the morning.

THE HIGHWAY FROM THE AIRPORT to Reykjavík cuts through a weird moonscape: the lava fields of Keflavík. There's plenty of geothermal activity rumbling beneath us, but on the primordial surface, nothing moves. From the road I see no trees, no houses, just a rocky crust, covered in lichen and moss. The land looks much as it did when the Vikings came ashore here eleven centuries ago.

On the flight, I'd been thinking that we've been using the word 'Viking' quite freely, so I ask Kári how we should define a Viking.

'Well, in its narrowest definition,' he replies slowly, 'the word "Viking" applies to the Norse pagans who sailed out of their little fishing villages to plunder and to trade, and eventually to settle in foreign lands. They think it comes from the Norse word *vík*, which means "inlet", or "little bay". There are more than a few coastal towns here in Iceland with "vík" in their names. But in a broader sense, "Viking" refers to a whole culture that came out of those settlements, and spread from Greenland to England to Russia. There are still traces of "Viking-ness", if that's the word, in those places today. It's a culture that stresses the value of honour and law and poetry and kinship, along with its guilty pleasures, like feasting and drinking and fighting. And family too: women were as much a part of Viking culture as men.'

Kári is scrolling though the local stations on the car radio, flipping past the talk shows in search of music. I hear plenty of animated discussion in Icelandic.

'So even Iceland has talk radio.'

'Of course. And now that you're here,' he says, 'don't be surprised if they ask you for an interview. The local paper and the TV stations might call you too.'

'Why on Earth would they want to talk to *me*?'

'It's a small place. Word gets around. When they discover there's a foreign media person making a documentary here, they'll want to talk to you about it. You could end up being quite famous in Iceland, Richard!' Kári smiles. I can't tell if he's pulling my leg or not.

I tell him how relaxed and happy he looks.

'I always feel like this in Iceland,' he says with a sigh. 'I was a boy when I left here, but when I came back in my early twenties I was shocked by how comfortable I felt. Straight away there was this, this physical feeling of … of rightness. Like I could fit right into the landscape. I could fit into the light. It's hard to explain.'

'You're talking about Iceland like it's an old girlfriend you never got over.'

'Oh, yeah. It *is* a bit like that. There's a saying here that you can be homesick for Iceland even when you're in Iceland.'*

Kári looks at the road ahead for a while and then he says, 'You know, I actually want to die in Iceland. I've thought about this quite a lot and I do want to be buried here.'

'That's a lovely idea, Kári,' I say. 'But can you put those plans on hold while I'm here? I don't want to be the one who has to call Olanda and break the terrible news to her.'

'That won't be necessary, Richard.' He laughs. 'If I'm going down, I'm dragging you down with me.'

---

*   Later Kári admitted this was his phrase, no one else's.

CHAPTER FOUR

(Kári)

The Ghosts of Reykjavík

I'M HOPEFUL THAT RICHARD'S death won't be needed on this trip. But I seem to be dragging him into the darker corners of my own life. It's not fair: why should he, a good friend but one I've known for only five years, be made accomplice to this search, and to all my entanglements in Iceland – my father, Snorri, and the sagas?

That said, he hasn't made much of an effort to escape. After we finished the interview on his radio show, he walked me to the lift on my way out. We stood there for a while, talking about Iceland, the Vikings, and our families. The lift door opened and closed a few times, and then a few times more. Half an hour later, we finally left off, although we hadn't really finished.

When I see him now, it's as though we're still trying to complete that conversation. But perhaps our friendship is built on the understanding that we most probably never will.

'Iceland at last!' he says, as we drive into Reykjavík.

'You're here.'

The first sight of the town always takes my breath away. I'm back in the place that in a sense owns me, but it is also somewhere that remains ever so slightly out of reach. Maybe that's part of its allure: I'm never in full possession of it.

Today, it looks about as mild and as bright as it can. Clear, too. We get a wonderfully full view of the city as it follows the peninsula on which it sits, narrowing to the west, stretched out like an arm to the sea – towards Greenland, then Canada. In every way an island capital, and as much as anything, a place that connects to the sea.

We slow down into city streets. I open the window a little. A breeze carries the coolness of the water, which feels close, and the faint smell of seaweed, wet rocks, and seeds from the high grasses that line the shore.

We're heading to the west part of town, just outside the centre, to an attic apartment we're renting. I pull off the road to ring ahead to Einar, the owner, who says to show ourselves in. Upstairs, we find him opening the balcony doors, letting in the morning air.

'Welcome, Richard,' he says, smiling. 'Come onto the balcony. Feel this sunshine!' He looks at me and adds, '*Velkominn heim*, Kári', 'Welcome home.'

We stay on the balcony while he points out the way around: to the shops, the pool, a nearby bike path. Our view is northwest towards a calm sea and the wide bend of the fjords. We can even make out the white shadows of Snaefellsjökull, a glacial volcano 100 kilometres away – from here, a silken triangle suspended over the horizon.

Einar leaves us to settle in. Onto the dining room table, we unload a jumble of laptops and phones, recording equipment, saga editions, notebooks, and a bottle of scotch. Richard begins to load a SIM card into his phone.

'What should we do today?' he asks. 'Are you going to show me around?'

'Yes, yes,' I reply. 'Of course. Let's go for a walk. What do you want to see first? The museum, the new concert hall?'

He looks up from his phone. 'I don't know.' A pause. And then, 'Actually, I think I want to see *your* Reykjavík. I mean, the places where you go when you come back, the places you loved when you were a kid.'

'I'm not sure how exciting that'll be.'

'I don't care. We can always visit museums later.'

Old Reykjavík

I DON'T REALLY KNOW where to take Richard first, but I do know that we should end somewhere by the sea, maybe around the old harbour area. This is where the town first began as a Viking settlement, but also where it shapes itself towards some kind of final point, its full stop. And where I feel as though I am back again.

'You've got a plan?' asks Richard.

'Something like that,' I say. 'I'll walk you down to the harbour.'

'Sounds good.'

'Let's get going now, then, while the sun's out. We won't get many days like this.'

'I'm in your hands,' he says.

➤➤➤

HALLDÓR LAXNESS WAS a major literary figure of modern Iceland who won the Nobel Prize for literature in 1955. One of his best-known novels is *Independent People*, about the struggles of crofter farming, and the unhappy attempts that the main character makes to pay for his own piece of land.

The book spans many years. In its way, it's an epic tale of how an individual confronts those with more power and wealth. But I've always loved the work's quietest and most intimate scenes. In one, a young boy wakes up and looks out from under his bed covers. The rest of the house is still asleep, and it's dead quiet. But from his bed he can see the kitchen, all the pots and pans, the cooking utensils. As he wakes up, he begins to imagine them talking, gossiping and arguing. The emptiness of the house is filled with his imagination, the secret life of pots.

For me, this is Reykjavík, or at least the Reykjavík of my own boyhood: a magical world that I always felt was completely alive even when it was quiet, even in the dead of winter when you'd often find yourself alone, the world around you still asleep. In the narrow streets, I joined in the conversations between uneven houses with bright, corrugated-iron walls; harbour warehouses with broken windows and rusted gates; bikes pushed up against front steps; alleyways that sneaked in behind rows of houses, where snow piled up against wooden fences and garden sheds.

My imperfect expression for this now, to Richard as we leave the apartment, is that the town is just the right size. You can walk everywhere. Things are always close. But maybe what I really mean is that it feels like home, and that it still seems to serve my imagination the way it did when I was a boy.

'This sounds a bit crazy,' I say, 'but I do feel like these streets are my friends.'

'Don't worry,' Richard replies. 'I don't mind crazy.'

We cross a main street near the flat, and take a shortcut through the old town cemetery, then head out the other side of it towards Tjarnargata, Pond Street. This skirts Tjörnin, a body of water that is bigger than a pond, but not quite the size of a lake. In winter, Tjörnin freezes over, and gets used as a shortcut from one side of town to the other. And on the coldest days, the town council even lights up one side for ice skaters, and kids from the local school pour out to use it as a shiny, slippery football field.

'I remember an ad that used to run on TV when I was a kid,' I say to Richard, 'that showed you what to do if the ice broke under someone and they fell in. You were meant to lie down on the ice, distribute your weight, then slide out until you reached the person.'

'Distribute your weight? Does that work?'

'I don't know. But whenever the ad was on I did have visions of getting pulled *in*, rather than pulling the drowning person *out*.'

'I bet they didn't show that scenario in the ad.'

'There was another one too, about what to do during an earthquake.'

'Right. Did you have to distribute your weight then, as well?'

'I seem to remember that you go outside and stand next to the building.'

'Oh. Sounds like a great way to get crushed. I'd run as far from the building as I could.'

'I don't think it works like that. The buildings are designed to fall straight down, not topple into the street.'

'Okay, so while the building is crashing down you stand still and admire the perfect Icelandic engineering around you.'

'Yes.' We're both laughing. 'Or run.'

We stop to look at the pond. On one side, elegant three- and four-storey homes from the nineteenth century, with lovely white-framed windows, look across the pond towards Laekjartorg, Lake Square, a busy intersection framed by boutique shops, an art gallery, a church and also the rather mixed assembly of buildings – some concrete, some iron-clad – that belong to Reykjavík Grammar School, the oldest secondary school in the country.

'It's very pretty,' says Richard.

He's charmed. Like me, he likes the size of the town, how we can walk downtown from the apartment. But he notices something else too. 'It's more modest than I imagined,' he says. 'I think I was expecting something like Swedish prosperity, but it's more hardscrabble than that. You see it in the buildings, how tight it all is. The pebblecrete apartment blocks. It reminds me of Ireland.'

'Yes, it's less uniform in style than other Scandinavian capitals.'

'It looks like things have just gone up where and when they've needed to. That's what happens in port towns, isn't it? Everything gets jammed in around the waterfront wherever it can fit.'

'I guess so,' I say.

Actually, port towns also have a way of accepting strays and unexpected changes. As something more than a collection of farms and harbour buildings, the town is quite young, less than 250 years old. But it's had more than its share of boom and bust years, and each one appears as a kind of bark ring, representing a different architectural style.

A few streets back from the pond you find some of the oldest buildings, merchant homes constructed over the past two centuries. They are modest and uneven in design, but in the way of broken pieces of jewellery. We follow these streets as they run in their rather random criss-cross pattern. They climb up a hill, on the top of which sits Hallgrímskirkja, a vast, concrete Lutheran cathedral that stands over the city a little more ferociously than one might expect of a modern church.

Hallgrímskirkja

I remember when it was being built, and how we followed the very slow progress of the construction. Everyone hated it while the scaffolding was still up: it was going to be too big, too expensive, too ugly. But when the structure was finally revealed, it made sense; it was a little severe, but you felt the poetry in it too.

I explain all this to Richard. 'In the end,' I say, 'I think people recognised themselves in it. Icelanders are known for being reserved at first, even a bit severe, like the church. But after a while you realise that it's not a hostile reserve, more a kind of waiting.'

Richard looks around us. Everywhere, people are out enjoying the fine weather. The atmosphere couldn't really be any more open and expansive. 'Everyone looks pretty friendly to me,' he says.

'Mainly foreigners,' I reply. 'The ones who are smiling, anyway.'

'Icelanders don't smile?'

'Can I tell you about another advertisement?'

'Let me guess: a safety notice about smiling?'

'Well, yes, sort of – anyway, this one was more recent, just before the tourism boom, which I guess was getting started about fifteen years ago. The boom prompted a state-run TV campaign that tried to change the national expression, if you like. It urged Icelanders to smile more, which used to be seen as a sign of weakness.'

'Smiling?'

'It's ridiculous, I know. But there's also some charm to Icelanders' reserve, because it doesn't take much to get underneath the sternness. Like all this around us: a slightly austere world, but inside this incredible warmth, too. Anyway, the ads showed a few everyday situations – shopping, waiting for a bus, picking up the kids – and each demonstrated that it was perfectly possible to be friendly. Give a greeting, reply to questions, don't frown, and so on.'

Richard is incredulous. 'It can't have been that bad.'

'One Easter,' I continue '– actually it was just like every other Easter – the town shut down for the weekend. I mean, completely shut down. Nothing was open. This was around the time the boom started. That night, there was a story on the news about foreigners trying to find food. There was footage of these poor people wandering the streets, asking what they should do. When the journalist interviewed them, they said they'd be happy to eat anything.'

Richard's laughing, and I'm not sure he believes me. 'I'm sorry, but how is that possible? Don't you people care about visitors?'

'No one realised.'

'So what happened to the tourists? Did they get fed?'

'In the end. A couple of shop owners agreed to open up for a few hours. They had to.'

'Otherwise the tourists would have starved.'

'No doubt.'

We leave the cathedral, and idle past craft shops until we reach Laugavegur, the main street of this old downtown area. It dips back down towards the pond, and eventually we see a blue corner filled with birds and excited children feeding them. Arctic terns fly dart-like across the shallows.

The scene is model-like, as though the real thing is stored somewhere else: an original of narrow downtown lanes, crowded shop windows, a town square with pockets of light and shadow, a small parliament building, a chapel next to it, ground-floor bars, and a corner shop where the town chemist used to be.

We walk past them, and I can almost imagine what it would be like to hold it all in my hand, a miniature of the streets I knew as a child.

An Extra Copy

WHEN I WAS EIGHT, I began looking for part-time jobs around town. I spent the summers selling newspapers, during long days that folded across a lightly shaded midnight. There was a small army of us who did this; we split up at the top of the main street, Laugavegur, looking for our own corners and side streets to mine.

I didn't like to stay still in one spot, as some others did, banking on the passing trade in order to clear their cargoes of news and Reykjavík gossip. Instead, I traced the back streets of old homes and uneven fences dividing small yards. There was something very solitary about these hours, but I liked the time alone, and how familiar the streets began to feel.

I walked everywhere. And so there was a chance that my father and I would bump into each other one day, and that fate would make nonsense of all the secrecy that surrounded me. For I would surely call out to him, now that I knew what he looked like.

Once, he'd driven past Mum and me as we walked home. Mum had pointed to the car. 'That's your father there,' she said.

It was a nice car, if a little showy. I couldn't see inside to where my father sat, but in my mind I saw him watching us, and maybe wanting to stop. From then on, I always kept an eye out for his car. It seemed impossible that we wouldn't meet again soon.

Maybe I'd see my siblings too – the half-brothers and sisters of whom I'd heard but who didn't know about me. I often thought about them; they were older, and lived in a different part of town. But maybe they also sold newspapers, or had other jobs. Most kids in Iceland worked, especially during the summer holidays, which were wonderfully long. Maybe I would meet them downtown.

That didn't happen. And there was no chance meeting with my father Gísli. Over time, I realised it would take a more concerted effort than merely wandering the downtown streets on my own.

So one day, I walked to his office, which was just outside the centre in a more open area of car yards and importers' showrooms. I went in. I found him and asked if he'd like to buy a newspaper. I stood at the door and waited, like he had when he visited us. He, too, seemed at loss as to what to say. Then his business partner, Ragnar, came and stood beside him. He asked who'd come to visit them. With that, my father smiled at me and said no. He had the paper delivered at home.

It was a shock. It hadn't occurred to me that he'd refuse. I understand now why he did, but there's a part of me that still feels as humiliated and ridiculous as I did then. He was afraid, I can see that. To buy an extra newspaper would have revealed his secret, for why would anyone buy two copies of the same paper unless there was some special reason to do so? The world simply couldn't know that reason. That my father was a married man with a family of his own to protect.

I walked back out onto the street and resumed my paper run. Away from the offices, and back towards the town centre – to its corners and tapering alleyways, which more than ever I saw as my true home.

When I told Mum about what had happened, she swore. 'The rotten bugger!' I'd never heard her swear before, and very seldom since. Would it have been so bad to have an extra copy?

I didn't visit him again during my walks through Reykjavík. But the streets were loyal, good friends. They got emptier as the summer passed and the first dullness in the sky appeared, around September, when the northern lights also began and school resumed. Then I'd return my two newspaper satchels, one across each shoulder, to the head office, and take my leave.

THIRTY YEARS ON, walking here with Richard, those days seem both very close and also to be receding. The miniature is slipping through my hands, but the sensation of it remains.

I still ask myself what I wanted when I visited him, why I put myself at his mercy. Simply him, yes: a father. But more than that too. Even at an early age, I wanted him to *give* me something, a token, even if only payment for a newspaper. Something that would help me understand, and perhaps calm my feelings – my early, intuitive sense of illegitimacy.

I wanted a sign that, in his eyes as in my mother's, I belonged. I wanted something back.

Songs for the Sentimental Icelander

AS YOU LEAVE THE POND, the streets tighten even more. It's as though the closer you get to the sea, the more huddled the buildings.

'There's a local joke,' I tell Richard, 'that says Iceland has only three weather conditions: wind, rain and cold. If any one of these three elements is missing, we call it beautiful weather.'

Even today, with the sun high, a cold breeze picks its way through the gaps between the buildings. There is no rain, but as we near the sea the smell changes, becomes wetter: the oil and rust of an old dock, wet rope, seawater against rock walls.

'I could go a bite to eat,' Richard says.

We find a table at a crowded, lively fish and chip shop close to the oldest port warehouses. A pretty waitress in a black apron brings us haddock served in metal baskets, and asks about our day, smiling.

'Another of your stern Icelanders?' Richard asks.

'Well, those ad campaigns obviously worked. Now Icelanders smile, and presumably know what to do in an earthquake.'

Richard watches the pedestrian traffic outside, eyes the tables around us. 'Would all these people have read the sagas?' he asks. 'Are they made to read them at school?'

'Yes,' I say. 'Icelanders begin reading the sagas at school, when they're eleven or twelve.'

'When did you leave, again?'

'Ten.'

'Probably a good thing, wasn't it – I mean, not being *made* to read them?'

'Yeah, I'm not sure how typical I am. I'm not sure I'd have taken to them the way I did if we'd stayed here. Most people are probably relieved when they stop reading them at school. But it's also much stronger than a childhood obligation. You know – you find a connection to a character that you don't expect, and suddenly the work changes completely.'

'The sagas still matter to people.'

'Deeply. That's why it's not odd when someone's obsessed with them, the way I am. The sagas aren't obscure or elitist. And because the Icelandic language hasn't changed very much since the time they were written, you can read them in almost their original form.'

'And so they're more familiar than you might expect?'

'Yes, they can be. Depending on how you come at them.'

AFTER WE ARRIVED in England when I was ten, Mum mentioned to me that I was named after one of the saga characters, Kári from the epic work *Njál's Saga*. She said she'd loved the sound of the name, which she pronounces like cowrie, the shell. It's not quite how it's said in Iceland, but close.

For a long time, that was all I knew about the sagas. It was only when I began university, across the other side of the world in Brisbane, that I encountered them in full. In my very first class, my tutor Martin Duwell looked up from a class list he was holding and said, '*Kári*. Isn't that an Icelandic name?'

'Yes,' I replied.

Martin had read all the sagas, and taught a survey of the Viking myths, and of a body of stories called the family sagas. These, I discovered, were the stories that medieval Icelanders had written about themselves, and in their native language rather than in Latin, which in the Middle Ages was the default language of learning.

I became captivated by them – not just the story of my namesake who lived in the pages of *Njál's Saga*, but all the extraordinary tales, the complex and often very broken characters, and the sweet, strange taste of Iceland you found they carried in their hopes and desires. The sagas came from another world, I knew. They were quite foreign, in a way. And yet it seemed to me that they also held the very place I'd come from, and to which I needed to return.

More or less straight away, I committed my education to the sagas. I was an Arts/Law student, but in reality, from then onwards I was a student of Icelandic literature, thousands of kilometres from their source. Just as port towns sometimes welcome stray arrivals, it seems they also have a way of sending stories across the seas.

These stories reminded me that I was still in love with Iceland, and so I listened to them as closely as I could.

MY FATHER DIED in September 2010, after a series of illnesses that took him far out of reach before he passed away. The conversation we had about Snorri turned out to be our last, and I didn't ever get to ask him how he knew about the connection, or whether it was really true.

By the time he died, I was convinced that we were very separate beings. I'd decided that I didn't need him, and that the missed chance of a relationship didn't matter. Over the years since we'd met, I'd come to know my siblings very well: the welcome they gave me at that first Sunday lunch was strengthened whenever I returned to Iceland. This came to matter more than Gísli.

But Fríða, I know, regretted that I wasn't getting to know him. She couldn't see what was standing in the way of our relationship now that my identity was out in the open. Perhaps she underestimated the power of habits. Gísli had felt bad about the affair for three decades, and was as accustomed to the secret as I was. To the end his greatest loyalty remained to his wife, and to an ideal of family unity that couldn't quite accommodate my full arrival in his life.

BUT THEN ONE winter a couple of years ago, I came back to see his grave. I knew he was buried with Ólafur, my fifth sibling, who'd died before I had the chance to meet him.

It was a Sunday morning, and I walked through thick, undisturbed snow. On my left, Reykjavík was still under the cover of a blue night, and orange streetlights. On the other side of the bay, the distant town of Akranes answered with its own lights, but beyond them the mountains escaped all colour, revealing only whiteness.

I'd drawn myself a map of the graveyard, one I copied from the internet, but I didn't follow any particular path. Eventually, I found myself up to my waist in snow, pounding my way through the deep. I came out in an area of low mounds at a side entrance to the cemetery. There, I met my only companion on the walk, a man on his own, closing a gate behind him further along the cemetery fence. He noticed me, and for a moment we watched each other along the street. Then he finished closing the gate and walked on.

My father's grave was covered in thick snow. A light pulsed through the blue dawn. I felt that I was meeting him in the perfect stillness of a winter morning: the air so balanced and delicate that even the most snow-laden branches showed no sign of releasing their burden.

'I'm here, Gísli,' I said. 'I came to say goodbye.'

I waited, then began to go, but something clawed me back, a need that I hadn't expected at all. I turned around and said, 'I love you.'

I walked back into town. With the snowfall, the sound of tyres on the roads was muted and the traffic downtown was slow. Reykjavík is even prettier when it's like this; it's so lovely to walk in. But eventually I stopped in one of the streets of my childhood and watched the thick flakes fall around me.

It was an immeasurably calm moment. But through it all, I also felt the distant tremor of an anger, something like an earthquake far in the hills, and with it a desperate desire to escape. To leave him behind.

It was too late. My father had crept up beside me again, and I didn't know what to do about it.

WHEN RICHARD ASKS ME why Snorri matters, I can find all kinds of disclaimers to say that he doesn't. Of course he doesn't *really* matter, I say.

But the truth is that direct descent from Snorri means much more than any of that. I care almost too much. Somehow, Snorri has become part of my family, although maybe the same way my father is part of my family, through the wish for more than I know. Snorri has become part of Reykjavík – *my* Reykjavík of imagination and wonder.

Mistakes

AFTER LUNCH, we take the last steps of our walk to the harbour. From the fish and chip place, it's about ten minutes to the outermost buildings of the town's peninsula. Some of these have been renovated and repurposed as shops and cafés. Beside them, though, are warehouses filled with goods, stevedoring offices, and ship mechanics. It's a good mix, as uneven in tone and purpose as the town has always been.

'The ports have names for the sea.' This is a well-known line from a poem that W.H. Auden wrote about Iceland. The line has a story of its own, one that is somehow very fitting for Iceland, and the sagas too. An insight into mistakes, and what to do about them.

Auden travelled to Iceland in 1936 with his friend Louis MacNeice, the Irish poet. Out of their journey together came a travelogue called *Letters from Iceland*, a lightly jumbled and very lovely compendium of poetry, stray thoughts and letters back to Europe.

Auden was obsessed with Northern Europe, and with Germanic culture. But he despaired at what was happening in Germany, and in the book he mocks the Nazis he and MacNeice encounter on the road in Iceland, including Hermann Göring's brother, whom they kept bumping into.

The Nazis saw Iceland as the cradle of Germanic culture, and the sagas as preserving an earlier, purer ethos of heroism to which they could aspire. Listening to them speak about Iceland and the sagas in this way, Auden realised that even here, on an island as distant and northerly as this, you were followed by the ugly politics of the modern world. There was no escape.

And so his poem 'Journey to Iceland' became one about islands, and their separateness or otherwise. Like the sagas, islands somehow lie apart from the rest of the world, but not completely.

Auden sent his final, handwritten draft to the publisher for printing. One line was 'The poets have names for the sea'. When the typescript came back, Auden noticed that the line had changed. 'Poets' had mistakenly become 'ports'.

To a friend, he wrote, 'The mistake seems better than the original idea.' So he kept it. 'The ports have names for the sea.'

What a glimpse this is into Auden's spirit – that of a writer able to read with an open mind, letting mistakes take their course. It's the opposite of the certainty promised by fascism, but it's very much how the sagas exist.

They're not clear-cut or ideological. Their characters are more like the ghosts of Reykjavík, people who are complex and often mistaken, often very broken. The true heroism of the sagas doesn't lie in certainty or even bravery, but in how they try to understand humankind, and our regrets.

That's what I've wanted to show Richard, today in Reykjavík. That it's a beautiful town, but also a bit torn at the edges, and worn away by the wind and the cold sea air. You might even call it a mistake, for there shouldn't really be a town like this, on the edge of an island at the edge of the world. But then again, mistakes are not always the worst things to happen.

A Parliament of Vikings

Drinking in the Laundromat

EARLY THE NEXT MORNING I get up early to have another good look at Reykjavík on my own. I can't quite believe I'm in Iceland and I want to go outside and make sure it's real. I've always enjoyed doing this – wandering the streets of a new city, aimlessly and alone, as it unselfconsciously reveals itself through an odd shop, a secret laneway, an architect's folly.

Icelandic kids play on the streets unsupervised, something I don't see too often in Australia any more. On the corner outside our apartment I encounter a huddle of ten-year-old boys with close-cropped hair, giggling furtively. Clearly they're up to something. When I walk past, one of them wheels around and glares at me defiantly. I arch my eyebrows imperiously, as if to say, 'I know what you're up to', even though I don't. The kid pulls a face and raises his eyebrows too, mocking me. There's nothing to do but smile and move on.

Reykjavík, despite its small size, has the raffish energy of a busy port town. The Viking gods are honoured, ironically, in the streets below the skyscraper cathedral – Thórsgata, Ódinsgata, Freyjugata. There are other streets – Njálsgata, Kárastígur – named after saga characters. Inevitably, I find a Snorrabraut – Snorri Street, a disappointingly non-descript traffic artery.

Laugavegur, the main commercial strip, is crowded with cafés, and bars painted in jaunty colours like vermillion and spearmint green. Even the grey pebblecrete is brightened with yellow-painted lintels. The city itself, it seems, has signed up to that 'put-on-a-happy-face' campaign Kári was telling me about.

Snorri Street, Reykjavík

I've arranged to meet him at a café on Skólavördustígur. He's seated outside, braving the stiff breeze and reading a novel. His big frame dwarfs the little aluminium table and chair. I order a coffee and we watch the world go by.

The streets are crowded with cheerful, good-looking tourists who all seem to be wearing the same brand of brightly coloured puffer jackets. The mass influx of visitors goes some way to explaining why the city feels so prosperous. The crash of 2008 hit Iceland particularly hard, but, unlike Greece, Iceland was not part of the Eurozone, so the value of its currency was slashed. Almost overnight, tourism in Iceland went from being an expensive proposition to an absolute bargain.

Across the island, the boom in visitor numbers has transformed dying villages into major tourist centres. In summer, the visitor numbers now dwarf the local population. Kári is a little startled by how much Reykjavík has changed to accommodate the masses of holiday-makers.

'But isn't it better,' I ask, 'that the streets are prosperous and lively, rather than hollowed out and depressed? Wouldn't it break your heart to see Reykjavík shuttered and half-empty?'

'I suppose so. But part of me misses the miserableness.'

After coffee, we walk up the hill to Eymundsson's bookstore, which has a substantial amount of shelf space devoted to Icelandic authors. In a nation of only 330,000 people, how many local authors can there be?

'Everyone here writes and reads each other's books,' Kári explains. 'Iceland has the highest percentage of published authors in the world. There's a saying here: "*Að ganga með bók í maganum*" – "Every Icelander walks around with a book in their stomach."'

I HAVE PLENTY of questions and Kári has answers for all of them. It's as though he has the complete set of *Encyclopaedia Icelandica* in his head and all he has to do is put a hand to a book to draw down a fact, a figure or a story.

'Nobody loves this island as much as you do,' I tell him. 'They should make you President of Iceland.'

'But I don't really care for politics, Richard,' he laughs.

'I didn't say prime minister, I said president. Head of state. A figurehead, like the queen. You'd go around the country, talking to Icelanders about their incomparable land and culture, appeal to the better angels of their nature and make them feel lucky to be Icelandic.'

'Well it's nice of you to say so, but I'm not actually a citizen of Iceland any more. I think you need to be a citizen before they let you become president.'

IN THE SUMMER, the nightlife in Reykjavík doesn't really fire up until 11pm, when the daylight finally fades to twilight. Kári and I step out for a drink and we find a grand old art deco building on the main drag called the Laundromat. Downstairs is an actual coin-operated laundromat, but the ground floor has a handsome bar with shelves of worn paperbacks and excellent beer on tap. The idea is that you drink while you wait for the machines to finish with your laundry, although I'm sure that more than a few patrons would have staggered home with their washing still in the dryer.

Kári and I sit at the bar and are delighted to order two bottles of Snorri Pale Ale, a craft beer named after the great man. The bottle comes with helpful tasting notes: 'A refreshing golden ale with hints of citrus and sweet juniper, flavoured with Icelandic organic thyme, giving it a fresh, floral finish'. Again, it seems I've been misled. Kári had warned me before we left that Icelanders were people of modest means and simple tastes, stern Lutherans who frowned upon fine food and artisanal beer.

'I'm as shocked as you are,' he says. 'Shall we drink it anyway?'

TWO HOURS AND many beers later we're both in a very good mood indeed. We raise a toast to Snorri, and engage in charming banter with the woman behind the counter, although, on reflection, she might have chosen to describe our conversation as repetitive and self-congratulatory.

Kári suggests we have some Brennivín, the caraway-flavoured

spirit considered to be Iceland's national drink. We drain our glasses and I tell him how much I like it.

'Well, yes, it's easy to enjoy Brennivín, Richard,' Kári says dismissively. 'It's much more important that you taste and enjoy *hákarl*, the national *dish* of Iceland. And,' he says with a slight edge of coercion in his voice, 'while you're here you're definitely going to try it.'

'What is it?'

'Fermented shark.'

'What do you mean by "fermented"?'

'Well, rotten.'

'Your national dish is rotten shark?'

'Greenland shark. The shark is dragged ashore,' he says dreamily, 'and they gut it and behead it. Then they lay it down in a shallow trench, and cover it in sand and gravel. The meat of the Greenland shark is toxic, so they have to place heavy rocks on top to squeeze out the toxic fluids. Then they just leave it alone.'

'For how long?'

'They leave it to ferment in its own bacteria for around two months. The fermentation actually cures the meat and makes it edible.'

'What does it smell like?'

'It smells like ammonia, and it tastes like very rancid cheese. I'm making it sound worse than it really is.'

'Yeah, you know what? I reckon I'll give the rotten shark a miss this time, buddy.'

Kári is shocked and offended. 'But you have to try it! It's an important cultural experience. You won't really understand Iceland until you have *hákarl*.'

I ask our barmaid if she's tried this fermented shark.

'Yes, I have,' she says.

'Well what did you think of it?'

She glares at me. 'It's disgusting. And you should definitely have it.'

THE STAFF ARE STACKING CHAIRS and we belatedly realise it's time we took our leave of the Laundromat. It's long past midnight, but there are still people streaming everywhere on the streets. We decide to sober up by joining the queue at a red and white fast-food stand for a couple of *pylsur* – Iceland's famous hotdogs.

'We'll need two each,' says Kári. 'I'm surprised that you're game to try them, Richard, given your incredible bigotry against traditional Icelandic food.'

He hands me two small steamed buns, each bearing a sausage made of Icelandic lamb mixed with beef and pork. Both dogs are covered with a stripe of sweet brown mustard and ketchup, and a sprinkling of fried onions and finely chopped raw onion. The special sauce that completes this culinary masterpiece is a remoulade of mayonnaise, capers and herbs.

'Not bad,' I concede. Inwardly my heart is singing. 'Actually, Kári, this is the greatest thing in fast food since the invention of the burrito. And yet Icelanders, it seems, would rather talk all day about *hákarl*. It's perverse. It reminds me of the way so many Japanese insist that their love of whale meat makes them special.'

'Yes,' he says. 'Icelanders are a bit prone to the idea of Icelandic exceptionalism. People here often say things like, "We Icelanders love fishing", or "We Icelanders like our ice cream", as if no one else in the world likes fishing or ice cream. It's a fallacy, but it's mostly harmless. I have to be careful not to lapse into it myself.'

We walk back to the apartment, passing alongside Tjörnin pond. At the far end is a cemetery. Kári has a charming ignorance of trashy horror films, so when he suggests we take a 3 a.m. shortcut through the graveyard, he does so quite innocently.

This is the oldest cemetery in Reykjavík. There are special plots for drowned sailors from France and the Faroe Islands. Kári tells me his grandmother Fríða – Gísli's mother – is buried somewhere here, but in the gloom he can't find the headstone. While he wanders around searching for the grave, I'm fixated by the otherworldly, shadowless twilight that dimly illuminates the cemetery, shifting its colours towards the ultra-violet. The gravel path has a metallic purple hue, while the lawn is lemon-lime. But despite the eerie light and the late hour, the atmosphere in this graveyard is more sweet than sinister.

Icelandic tradition holds that when a cemetery is consecrated, the first person to be buried in it becomes its guardian, or 'lightbringer'. And so when Gudrún Oddsdóttir, the wife of a magistrate, was laid to rest here in 1838, it was said that her body did not rot like that of a Greenland shark; instead, she was preserved to keep watch over the other dead folk brought in to people the cemetery, so she could lead them gently into the afterlife.

Asking

KÁRI TAKES MY POINT when I say we should look to confirm his connection to Snorri Sturluson sooner rather than later. And so, after a day wasted nursing our hangovers, he and I set off purposefully for the offices of Íslendingabók, the institute that holds Iceland's genealogical records.

This time, I joke, we will not be so easily put off by the misleading street frontage. But Kári is quiet on the drive into the city centre, and when we pull up on Thverholt Street, he asks for a moment before we go in.

'You know, if there's any part of this trip that I dread, it's this.'

'I don't understand. You want to find out about Snorri, don't you?'

'Yes. Yes, I do.'

'So why the dread?'

'It's the exposure of it. If we go in there and they tell me I'm not meant to have access, or that I'm not in the system … And it's about having to explain who I am, and my situation. You get sick of always having to tell people your father isn't listed above your name. I'm tired of always having to establish myself. And this is *the* place where I want to be known for who I am. I want the database and the records to be an honest document about my identity. But it feels dangerous to ask for that.'

'Because of what, illegitimacy? Or not being a legitimate, full Icelander?'

'Yes, it's the two combined. I think that's why Snorri is so important to me. It's because that link to Snorri stands in for my long absence from Iceland, and also from that side of my family. It's hard to ask for those things when you don't feel entitled to them.'

'If you listen to that dread, and we don't go in there, and we don't find out the truth, won't there be a price to pay for that, too?'

'There is a price for silence. And it's heavier than the price for awkwardness and feeling somehow inappropriate, that I'm somehow not behaving in the way that my position dictates. I don't want to feel that shame of uncertainty. I don't want that to be how I live. But on the other hand there's a big part of me saying, "Really, you're going to keep going with this? Let it go. Are you still talking about this stuff?"'

'But if we do go in there, and we do get an answer, then that will be an end to it, won't it?'

'Not quite. Because what's the answer I want? Snorri isn't quite all of it. The answer I want is something impossible. I want the records to be right. I want there to be a correction. I'm pretty sure it's too late. My father's dead.'

'What do you mean, "correction"?'

'I'd like the documents about me to reflect the reality. When my father said I was descended from Snorri, that was the closest he ever came to setting the record straight. He said it in front of the family. When I look for Snorri now, I'm looking for that moment again. I'm still waiting to hear him say: "You are my son."'

'Well, then. Despite your feelings of dread, are you ready to go in?

Kári groans. 'I'm at that point, Richard, where I'm not just ready, I *have* to get it done. It's like an exam. I'm at a point now where I'm over-prepared, and I just need to sit down and do the test.'

KÁRI'S MOOD LIGHTENS and we march up Thverholt Street, to a ratty office front. He mumbles something in Icelandic into the intercom, the door buzzes and we enter. Inside, Kári has a short, polite conversation with the woman behind the counter. She scribbles something on a piece of paper and hands it to him. Kári folds it into his pocket and smiles at me sheepishly.

'What did she say?'

'She says the Book of Icelanders isn't here any more. They've moved to the offices of Decode.'

HALF AN HOUR LATER we're in an industrial park on the outskirts of Reykjavík, outside a gleaming building of glass, concrete and steel. This is the corporate headquarters of Decode, the biotech institute that uses Iceland's genealogical records and population data to unlock the secrets of the human genome. Its mission is to identify genetic markers for common illnesses like cancer and heart disease. The Decode logo features two picto-humans linked by a DNA spiral.

The automatic doors open with a swish.

'Shouldn't we have made an appointment?'

'It's not the Icelandic way, Richard.'

'So our strategy is to front up and throw ourselves on their mercy?'

'I wouldn't put it like that, but yes.'

At the reception desk, we're told that the two researchers we need are on vacation, but they'll be back in two weeks. Perhaps we could come back then?

So that's it. For now, anyway. Unless we're prepared to track down these researchers on holiday, and to ask them to abandon their families and return to Reykjavík to help us – which we're not – we'll just have to wait out the fortnight. Two weeks from today is the day before we're set to leave Iceland, so we'll be cutting it fine.

It's all very anti-climactic, and we go back to our apartment frustrated and disappointed. We retreat to our respective rooms to call our families on the far side of the world.

Then we pack the recording gear and prepare for an evening trip to Thingvellir, the closest thing Iceland has to a sacred site.

Thingvellir

With laws shall our land be built up. But with lawlessness laid waste.

—Njál's Saga

THE GREAT FISSURE between the North American and Eurasian tectonic plates zigzags across Iceland diagonally, from the southwest corner of the island to the northeast, like the crack in a broken dinner plate. Around fifty kilometres inland, the tectonic fissure opens out to form a spectacular rift valley, with a deep blue-water lake teeming with

Arctic fish. The rift is flanked by several volcanoes, which over time have ejected streams of lava into the valley, creating layered shelves of rock that form a gorge fit for a procession of giants. The startling grandeur of the rift valley made it the perfect site for a Viking parliament.

Iceland's settlers brought their habits of assembly with them from Norway. A farmer would declare his allegiance to a local chieftain for protection against rival clans, and to receive help when food or hay was in short supply. In return, the farmer would pay taxes and agree to accompany the chieftain into battle, if need be.

Thingvellir Gorge

The bond between farmer and chieftain was not considered sacred, as it was in much of medieval Europe. Both could choose to terminate the relationship, and the farmer could switch allegiance to another chieftain, but it was nearly always more practical to stick with the local leader for protection.

A quarrel with a rival farm or family could easily erupt into an intractable blood feud, so it was often better for both parties to go to a chieftain to settle their differences through adjudication. And so the chieftains of an area would gather every spring at a local *thing*, or assembly, to present the lawsuits of their followers for settlement.

Within sixty years of the arrival of the Vikings, all of Iceland's farmlands had been occupied, and the population had swollen to 40,000. Iceland's chieftains realised there was a need for a national assembly, an *althing*, to make laws for the whole of the island. A man named Grímur Goatfoot was asked to ride all over Iceland to find a suitable site.

When Grímur rode his horse down into the rift valley with the crystal lake, he knew he'd found it. The valley was astonishingly beautiful, and accessible from most parts of the island. There was fresh water, fish, and forest wood for kindling. Conveniently, the owner of these rich lands had just been found guilty of murder and been stripped of his holdings, so the whole area could be set aside as common land.

THE VALLEY WAS named Thingvellir – Assembly Fields – and in 930 the first Althing of the Icelanders was proclaimed under the Law Rock, a boulder perched above a natural amphitheatre.

Each year, in the tenth week of summer, the thirty-six chieftains of Iceland would ride into Thingvellir with their families and followers. They would assemble booths of timber and tent cloth along the banks of the stream that ran through the middle of the gorge.

The high season at Thingvellir attracted hundreds, sometimes thousands of people from all over the island. It was a riotous festival, with plenty of beer-drinking, gambling and wrestling. People would trade, tell stories, exchange gossip, flirt and fall in love. It was the one time of year when everyone in Iceland could get a good look at each other. Marriages were arranged, divorces were settled. Carrying weapons was absolutely forbidden and the spilling of blood through violence was considered a defilement of the land.

Presiding over the Althing was the lawspeaker, the only national political figure on the island. At each meeting of the assembly, the lawspeaker would stand high on the Law Rock and recite, from memory, a third of all the laws of Iceland, so that every single law would be recited over a three-year period.

Once this ritual was completed, the chieftains would get down to debating, making laws, appointing judges and settling lawsuits. There was no executive, no police and no army: if the Althing found in favour of someone who had filed a lawsuit, then that person had to enforce the punishment of the guilty party, or to collect the compensation awarded to him. If he lacked the strength or courage to confront his opponent and extract the payment, then he would be dishonoured.

The season at the Althing encouraged conviviality, and oaths of blood-brotherhood were often exchanged, but the dangerous politics of Viking honour kept wearing away at Icelandic society. Not everyone could be equally honourable, and so those who achieved great things, who won money, fame and respect, inevitably came under attack from those who wanted those same prizes. Attacks could come through legal disputes, land grabs, sport, insults – but always the economy of honour meant that someone had to lose. And suffer.

THE FOUNDING OF THE ALTHING at Thingvellir in 930 marks the beginning of a golden age for Iceland: the period of the commonwealth, when Icelanders began to create their own stories and to strike out into the wider world, from the Holy Land to the Americas. There was a growing confidence, a quickening of the spirit, and a deepening sense of their own distinctiveness, which led them to prize their independence all the more. But the island was still under pressure from the Kingdom of Norway, particularly concerning the vexed issue of religion. The settlers had brought the old Norse gods with them to Iceland; many temples to Thor had been erected across the island. But when Norway became Christianised, its kings demanded that Icelanders follow suit.

The issue came to a head in 1000 AD, in the last summer of the Christian millennium, when Iceland's chieftains assembled at Thingvellir to debate whether they should accept the religion and the law of the Christians. The advocates for Christianity made their case from the Law Rock, and the pagans made theirs. The arguments flew back and forth, growing in intensity, until both factions declared themselves to be under separate laws from each other and stormed out of the assembly.

It was a dangerous moment. The chieftains withdrew to their tents, wondering if their commonwealth would break apart, and push them all into civil war.

That night, the leader of the Christians decided to visit the lawspeaker in his tent to ask him to decide the matter. The lawspeaker, Thorgeir Thorkelsson, was a pagan, but was well-respected on both sides.

Thorgeir took himself away, and lay down under a blanket for a day and a night to ponder the question. When he emerged, blinking into the light, he called everyone to the Law Rock to announce his decision.

Thorgeir began by reminding everyone of the dangers of living under separate laws. 'It will prove true,' he said, 'that if we tear apart the laws, we will also tear apart the peace.' Therefore, he said, they must first pledge themselves to abide by the compromise he'd arrived at, whatever that might be. The chieftains nodded their assent.

Iceland, he declared, would become Christian. *However*, the worship of the old gods would still be acceptable, so long as it was done in secret. The old practices of eating horseflesh and exposing unwanted infants to the cold would still be permitted, even though such things were abhorrent to Christians.

Thorgeir, who had once been a pagan priest, also announced that he himself would be a good Christian from now on, and he hurled his pagan idols into a waterfall, now known as Godafoss – the Waterfall of the Gods.

'*THING*-VUH-LEER?'

'Not quite,' says Kári. '*Thing*-vett'llr. There's a kind of a guttural trill at the end. You close your tongue and push your breath over the top of it.'

Thingvellir is just an hour's drive from Reykjavík. It's high summer and the country is as green and lush as it's ever going to be. We drive across open, flat plains framed by a row of distant mountains.

Looking at Iceland's landscape is like peering at the natural world through a slightly distorted prism: clouds are twisted, the bluff faces of steep cliffs are stretched too high. The scattered trees are leaning over, buffeted by the high-speed winds blowing across the plains.

We come into Thingvellir at around eight o'clock in the evening. The sun has only just started to dip and the valley is bathed in a golden glow. We follow the path that runs down into the gorge, between two slate-grey walls of lava rock. In between the folds of basalt are patches of green moss and sprays of wildflowers. A little stream courses through the gorge. This is a naturally grand and ceremonious place. It's like entering the ruins of some lost civilisation.

Jutting up over the narrow gorge is the Lögberg – the Law Rock – where Snorri Sturluson once presided as lawspeaker. His name is listed on a placard, which notes his two terms in office, nearly 800 years ago.

Further along the path there are cascades and a waterfall. Tourists are leaving the national park to catch the last bus back to Reykjavík, and we have this magnificent place all to ourselves. The chatter of human voices dissipates, and Thingvellir falls quiet, with only the trickle of the stream and the call of a distant bird in the air. The atmosphere is mild and still.

Kári points to a rectangle of foundation stones, where a Viking booth once stood. Behind the stones is a narrow path, the same path where Gunnar of Hlídarendi came walking one day a thousand years ago, and caught sight of the most beautiful woman he'd ever seen.

The River Axe, Thingvellir, at 10pm in high summer

The Saga of Gunnar and Hallgerd

GUNNAR
A Viking warrior and farmer in the south of Iceland

HALLGERD
The daughter of a chieftain in the mid-west

NJÁL
Gunnar's best friend, a great lawyer

OTKEL
A neighbour of Gunnar's

GUNNAR OF HLÍDARENDI was the most promising and able young man of his day. He was tall with fair hair, and he was athletic in all things: they say he could jump as far backwards as he could forwards. He was a great runner. He swam like a seal. When he wanted to mount his horse, he'd run up behind it with his halberd and pole-vault himself into the saddle. He was popular too: slow to make friends, but unbreakably loyal to those who were close. And he was an expert bowman, more accurate and deadly with the weapon than any other man in Iceland – although it was also said of Gunnar that he hated to kill.

When he was a young man, Gunnar travelled to Norway, where he performed great acts of courage and daring. He returned to Iceland with wealth and honour. In the summer, he made the journey to Thingvellir to take part in the annual parliament. People couldn't stop looking at him, for he seemed to have everything. He was handsome, and he had travelled widely.

Gunnar arrived at Thingvellir wearing a beautiful cloak that he'd acquired on his travels, and a golden bracelet given to him by Hakon, an earl in Norway. He walked along the gap in the rifts, past the stream, and then he saw the most beautiful woman he'd ever seen.

Her name was Hallgerd. She wore a red dress decorated with ornaments, and a coat trimmed with lace. Her hair was long and fair.

Gunnar approached her and asked if she would sit down with him for a moment. He began to tell her about his travels, and she listened to him as he spoke. Eventually, he asked, 'Are you married?'

'You can't possibly be interested in that,' replied Hallgerd.

'What if I am?'

'Then you should go and speak to my father and my uncle.'

Gunnar went to see them. They welcomed him and listened to his plea for Hallgerd's hand in marriage. Then they said to him: 'Gunnar, we like you. You're a good man. We don't think you should marry Hallgerd.'

There were reasons for this. Hallgerd had already been married twice before, and both marriages had ended badly. In the first, she'd been forced to wed a man she didn't love. They argued, and Hallgerd's husband hit her across the face. When she told her foster-father, a man who cared perhaps too much for Hallgerd, he found a new resting place for his axe in the back of her husband's head.

She had then married a man whom she *did* love. But they too argued, and once again Hallgerd was struck by her husband. When Hallgerd's foster-father saw her upset, she noticed his anger and told him to leave the matter be. It was between her and her husband. But against her wishes, he again found a new resting place for his axe.

Hallgerd had lost two husbands, one she hadn't minded losing and one she grieved over. But Gunnar knew what he wanted. Something very basic had passed between them, and they needed each other.

Against the advice of her kinsmen, Gunnar married Hallgerd, and took his new bride back to Hlídarendi, his farm in the south of Iceland.

Hlídarendi

IT WAS NEVER going to be easy for Hallgerd to settle into her new home, and the district to which Gunnar introduced her. Here was a new woman, and a rather proud one. There was some resistance to her arrival on the part of Gunnar's friends and family. Of course, they knew about Hallgerd's reputation, and what had happened to her first two husbands.

Gunnar's best friend was a lawyer named Njál. The two men were very different – Gunnar a man of action, Njál much more given to words. But their friendship suited both men; they complemented one another, and understood each other's very different strengths. Njál could already tell that Hallgerd's arrival would not bring good luck to Gunnar, and he disapproved of the union. Yet he invited Gunnar and Hallgerd to a feast at his farm, not far from Hlídarendi.

The day of the feast came, and Gunnar and Hallgerd rode across the pastures and flats that lay between the two farms. But as soon as they arrived there was trouble. It came down to the seating arrangements. Hallgerd wasn't given the seat of honour that she'd expected.

'I'm not sitting at the end like some old wench!' said Hallgerd.

'I'll decide that,' said Njál's wife Bergthóra.

When Bergthóra came back later with a basin of water for washing, Hallgerd saw her hostess's hands and said, 'Your fingernails are rotten.'

Bergthóra replied, 'At least I haven't killed off any husbands.'

The women hated each other instantly, and not long after the feast they began a feud. First of all, they conducted it through their slaves, whom they pressed into killing one another. But gradually the feud escalated, until it got quite close to Gunnar and Njál: their kinsmen were dragged into the dispute, and for a moment it looked like the households would have to fight it out. Thanks mainly to Njál's foresight and good will, though, the friends were able to stop it from going too much further. Njál put his friendship with Gunnar ahead of the demands of the feud. For a while at least, there was peace in the district.

But Hallgerd had made her mark.

DURING PERIODS OF AUSTERITY, the farmers in the district relied on each other for help, and there came a time when Gunnar needed help. There was a shortage of hay, and his livestock were in danger. Gunnar knew that his neighbour, Otkel, had a surplus of hay. So he visited Otkel to buy some. But Otkel, jealous of his most famous neighbour Gunnar, and wanting to steal some of his honour for himself, refused the request.

When Hallgerd found out about this, she was furious. She sent another of her slaves to Otkel's farm, and told him to raid the house and bring back something for her larder. The slave returned with cheese.

The next time Gunnar had visitors, Hallgerd brought out the cheese and served it to Gunnar's friends.

Gunnar reeled back. 'Where did you get this cheese?'

She answered, 'Don't concern yourself with domestic matters.'

In front of the others, he hit her across the face.

Hallgerd said, 'I will remember that blow.'

GUNNAR'S REPUTATION AS a warrior and now as a local leader began to cause him problems. People in the district grew jealous, and some started to band together to bring him down. Some slandered him, while others tried to bait him into fights.

Eventually a big fight did break out not far from his farm, beside the River Rangá, and Gunnar was forced to kill a number of his enemies. Between them, he and his brother Kolskegg killed eight men, including Otkel, the farmer who'd denied him the purchase of hay.

At its close, Gunnar turned to his brother and asked, 'Why do I find it harder to kill than other men do?' He was good at fighting, but he hated it.

He began to rely more and more on the advice of his best friend Njál. He consulted Njál on most matters, especially how to deal with the growing hostility towards him.

Njál gave him one very particular piece of advice: 'Never kill twice in the same family.'

'I would hope never to do that,' said Gunnar.

'But if you do,' continued Njál, 'then you must accept any settlement that is made for you by men of good will.'

Gunnar gave his word that he would.

His enemies, meanwhile, kept at him. Because Gunnar had killed Otkel, Otkel's son was honour-bound to come after Gunnar. Eventually, he also fell to Gunnar's sword. Against his own nature and wishes, Gunnar *had* killed twice in the same family, and the matter was referred to the Althing for arbitration and settlement.

Gunnar hadn't really been to blame for the killings. His enemies had provoked and attacked him constantly. But all the same, the men of good will came up with this settlement: Gunnar would have to leave Iceland for three years of exile, after which he could return.

Njál told him that if he accepted this settlement, he would eventually prosper again, and live a long and honourable life in Iceland. And so Gunnar agreed. He and his brother would leave for three years.

On the day set down for their departure, the brothers rode down the slope of Hlídarendi. But then Gunnar's horse tripped and he was forced to jump clear. He turned around and looked back at his farm.

He said, *'Fögur er hlíðin*. The slopes are beautiful. I will not go.'

His brother was shocked. 'Don't please your enemies by doing this!' he said. 'I won't stay with you in Iceland.'

Gunnar rode back to the farm, on his own.

Hallgerd was very pleased to see him back.

GUNNAR'S ENEMIES NOW had to attack. Gunnar had broken the settlement, and the next move was theirs. They approached Hlídarendi and began their assault.

It didn't start well. Gunnar had his bow, and he was able to keep the attackers at bay. They made one charge on the house, but were forced to retreat. Then they made a second attempt, this time trying to get into the house from the top. Gunnar was able to thrust his halberd up through the turf roof, and again push them back.

The attackers gave up and began to ride away. But then Gunnar made a mistake. He spotted one of the attackers' arrows on the side of the house. He thought it would be fun to use it against his enemies, humiliating them as they retreated. He leant out of the window to fetch the arrow.

'Leave it,' said his mother, who saw what he was about to do. 'You don't need it.'

Gunnar ignored her and reached for the arrow. As he did, one of the attackers saw the glint of the gold band on his arm. They thought, *if Gunnar needs one of our arrows, he must be running out of his own.*

'The slopes are beautiful': Hlídarendi

They resumed their attack, and this time with much more force and conviction. They hitched thick rope around the base of the turf roof and heaved it off. Now they could attack properly from above.

Still, Gunnar had his bow and could defend himself with it. But eventually the bow string broke.

He turned to Hallgerd, and saw her long hair.

'Give me some of your hair,' he said.

'Does very much depend upon it?' she asked.

'I need it to repair my bow. My *life* depends upon it.'

'In that case, let me remind you of the time you hit me. I refuse.'

With that, the attackers came in. They hacked at Gunnar. He killed two men and wounded another eight, but he was tiring and they had the numbers. Finally he tripped, and then, too weary to stand, fell down at the feet of his enemies.

They crowded around him, and each of them stabbed him.

Gunnar of Hlídarendi was dead, killed in front of his beautiful wife.

Fiery Play Around the Head

HLÍDARENDI IS STILL a working property. As we look on, a tractor crunches into gear and begins moving hay into one of the sheds.

To the right of the farm, a dirt track winds steeply to a small chapel made of timber and corrugated metal. It's boarded up, abandoned; sheep are squatting on the front steps for shelter and the porch is covered in animal shit.

The white paint on the church is cracked and scratched black. In 2010, the nearby volcano Eyjafjallajökull exploded and rained a shower of scalding ashes onto the farm and the church. The eruption shut down airports across Europe for several weeks and generated powerful electrical storms. Broadcasters like me all over the world struggled and failed to pronounce the name of the volcano correctly, which amused Icelanders no end.

As I peer into the church window, I ask Kári what happened to Hallgerd after Gunnar died at her feet.

'She was forced out of Hlídarendi by Gunnar's mother, who hated her for not helping Gunnar. She said: "*Illa fer þér og mun þín skömm lengi uppi.*" "That was a terrible thing to do, and your shame will be long-lasting."

'Hallgerd moved in with a daughter she'd had by one of her earlier marriages. She spent her last years in solitude on a farm near Reykjavík. There's a public swimming pool and a hot-dog stand there now. I used to meet Mum there every day when I was a kid and go swimming.'

'So why do you think Hallgerd does that? Why does she refuse to give Gunnar a lock of her hair? Is it spite, or something else?'

'I think that in that moment, Hallgerd's honour was just as important as Gunnar's.'

THE TRACTOR HAS gone silent. The farmer has gone inside the farmhouse for his lunch. Turning our back on the church, we walk further up the grassy slope.

Australians are taught from childhood to be careful walking through long grass, lest you arouse a sleeping brown snake. But there are no snakes in Iceland and the grass is long and soft. After a minute I stretch my arms out and flop down on the meadow like it's a grassy mattress. I look up at the distant clouds and feel the cool Icelandic sunshine on my face and repeat the line from the saga: 'The slopes are beautiful. I will not go.'

'Actually,' says Kári from further up the hill, 'that's one of the most famous lines from the sagas. Over the centuries those words have come to represent how important it is to love this country, and to stay here for that love. Because Iceland is a hard place to live in. And I've always felt that if you want to stay here, you really do have to make a choice to stay here.'

'Is that why every time you get into a cab, the driver asks you when you're coming back here to live?'

'Exactly. When you return, everyone asks you: "When did you leave?" and "When are you coming back?" For Icelanders, it's a given that you will want to come back. And it would be better if it were sooner rather than later.'

Ash-burnt church at Hlídarendi

WE DRIVE BACK to Reykjavík, and later that day we call on Guðrún Nordal, the director of the Árni Magnússon Institute. The institute preserves and protects the manuscripts of the sagas, which are treasured as the foundational documents of the nation – as essential to the Icelanders' sense of who they are as the Declaration of Independence is to Americans. Kári met Guðrún some years ago while writing his thesis on medieval Icelandic literature.

Kári and I are welcomed and brought into the institute's reading room, furnished simply and elegantly in Scandinavian blond wood. Guðrún greets us and embraces Kári.

I ask her if the saga manuscripts at the institute are stored ten miles underground in a nuclear-proof bomb shelter. She laughs and says, 'Something like that, yes.'

'Are they very fragile?' I ask.

'They've been preserved remarkably well,' she says brightly. 'However, most of our manuscripts are dark in colour, because they were kept in farmhouses with open fires, and there was a lot of smoke. These books were not kept behind lock and key. They were read and enjoyed through the centuries.'

I'm keen to find out what she thinks Gunnar means when he says, 'The slopes are beautiful. I will not go.'

'Oh, this has been debated for so long,' she says. 'Novels have been written about this, and there's been so much romantic nonsense about the beauty of the countryside, but Gunnar's statement is not actually about that.'

'What is it about, then?'

'Well,' she says, 'Gunnar is talking about the fields and the freshly mown grass. Everything is so prosperous. Hlídarendi is his domain … and he's not just going to *leave* it.'

'Oh! So you think that when Gunnar says "I will not go", it's not because the land is so lovely … it's because it's *his*?'

'Yes. It's his, and he's not going to let them drive him away.'

Guðrún laughs mischievously. 'Of course I could say something else tomorrow.'

The Papar

KÁRI IS UP early the next morning, packing our gear into the back of the car, humming a Lee Dorsey tune, *'Ever-ry thang I do gohn be fun-ky … from now on. Yeah.'* An hour later, we're driving along the southern stretch of Iceland's Route 1 when Kári impulsively turns off the highway onto a country road. He pulls over to check a battered old motorist's guide for directions, and then we bump along more country lanes, each one narrower than the last, until we pull up at a farmhouse. A woman in Wellington boots answers the door. She converses with Kári in Icelandic for a moment then points to a hayshed nearby, only the hayshed is more like a hobbit house, a wooden door embedded into the side of a grassy hillock.

I pull open the door and we enter a cave, with hay bales stacked neatly near the entrance. We flick on the torches on our iPhones to look at the cave walls, and make out markings scratched into the soft rock, and the outline of a cross with flared points that looks very Celtic.

This cave was once a dwelling of the Papar, the Irish monks who came to Iceland a century before the Vikings, sailing up from the North Sea in small boats made of wicker and leather.

The presence of these mysterious Irishmen is recorded in the opening passage of *The Book of Settlements*:

> Before Iceland was peopled from Norway there were in it the men whom the Northmen called Papar; they were Christian men, and it is held that they must have come over sea from the west, for there were found left by them Irish books, bells, and croziers.

The Papar disappeared not long after Viking settlement. The only physical evidence they left behind are markings on the walls of caves like this one. Did a priest once sing a Latin mass here to a tiny congregation of half-starved hermits?

I step outside and look around at the open plains that roll down to the coast. Where on Earth did these monks imagine themselves to be, having sailed all the way to this land at the top of the world? There would have been mornings when they stepped outside the cave into a bright summer silence, broken only by the song of a distant bird and the wind through the grass. In such moments it would have been easy to think the kingdom of heaven was very near. But in the harshness of winter, or in the choking aftermath of a volcano, it would have been another story. And what terror did they know when they saw, for the first time, a party of tall, tattooed heathens striding purposefully towards them?

Papar cave, south coast

The Shadow of the Volcano

'KÁRI?'

'Yes, Richard?'

We're back on Route 1, zooming along the plains of the south coast.

'Audun had to go to Greenland to get his polar bear. Are there no polar bears in Iceland?'

'No, there aren't,' he says, sorry to be disappointing his child-like companion. And I am duly disappointed.

'But they do show up occasionally,' he continues brightly. 'Every once in a while, a massive platform of sea ice will snap off from Greenland and just float across to Iceland on the ocean currents, with a stranded polar bear on its surface. When the ice shelf crashes into the coast, the bear just strolls off and starts wandering around.'

'What happens when someone realises they have a polar bear on their property?'

'Well, then it becomes big news all over Iceland. The bear is in all the papers and on TV. Then the question arises: what are we going to do with it?

'Why can't they let it stay?'

'Iceland's habitat isn't right. And no one wants a polar bear mauling their sheep.'

'Or their shepherds for that matter, I suppose.'

'Right. So there's always this agonised national debate about what to do with the bear. Someone will say, "Why can't we just airlift it back to Greenland?", and then someone else will say, "That will cost hundreds of thousands of dollars and it might kill the bear! We should spend it on schools instead!" Then the decision is made to shoot it, and lots of people are upset for a while, and life goes back to normal for a decade until the next polar bear steps ashore.'

We're coming off the highway, turning into a low plain of grassy fields. There are no polar bears in sight – just a pretty farm and a timber church with a graveyard beside it. This farm is called Oddi, and Snorri Sturluson spent most of his childhood here. The farmhouse and the church were built in another era, long after Snorri's time.

Inside the little church, the atmosphere is perfectly still, the quiet broken only by the sound of our footsteps and the wind pummelling the windows. Next to the altar is a hand-carved baptismal font, delicately painted in pale red, green and yellow, with a doll-like Icelandic bird at its apex. I recognise the bird – I've seen it several times over the past few days in the fields along the south coast, emitting an odd chittering song as it soars across the sky.

Back outside the church, Kári points over my shoulder to Mount Hekla, one of Iceland's most active volcanoes. Hekla means 'Hooded

Cloak'; its cone is broad and flat, weighed down by a glacier on its crown. Kári says he can dimly recall the eruption of Hekla in 1980, when he was a boy.

A particularly violent eruption occurred in September 1845. Local farmers were alerted to the impending disaster by a groaning within the Earth. Then, with a tremendous crash, two gigantic gashes broke open on the sides of the cone. Torrents of lava streamed down the flanks of the mountain into the neighbouring rivers, which became so scaldingly hot that many fish were boiled alive. Flocks of sheep fled in terror from the heaths adjoining Hekla, some burnt to death before they could escape.

Hekla's first recorded eruption was in 1104, when its cap exploded and showered half of Iceland in ash. The disaster made Hekla famous across medieval Europe. Cistercian monks in France believed the gateway to hell could be located in the abyss beneath the volcano's maw. Hekla was named as the prison of Judas Iscariot, the traitor, condemned for his sins to drown for all eternity in its cauldron of boiling magma.

Mount Hekla, gateway to hell, illustration from Olaus Magnus, History of the Northern Peoples, *1555*

SNORRI STURLUSON grew up on the farm here at Oddi, in the shadow of Mount Hekla. He was born in 1179 into the Sturlung family, a clan of ambitious upstarts. At the age of four, he was brought here to be fostered by the family of a powerful chieftain named Jón Loptsson. Fostering children between families was a common practice in Iceland at the time, to guarantee and strengthen bonds of allegiance and trust. The island was difficult to cross, even in summer, so Snorri's separation from his parents was profound and it must have affected him deeply.

Jón Loptsson gave Snorri the best education available in Iceland at the time, and he was taught Latin, poetry and history. When he came into adulthood, Snorri discovered his mother had squandered his small inheritance. Still, his education and family connections put him in high social standing.

At the age of twenty Snorri married a wealthy woman named Herdís, and was given a property and a chieftaincy in the marriage settlement. They had a daughter, Hallbera, and then a son, Jón, who became Snorri's favourite; he gave the boy the affectionate nickname of *murtur*, or little trout, because he was so small.

In 1202, Snorri and his young family moved to a farm called Borg, in the west of Iceland. Snorri was a shrewd and capable manager, and he built up the estate with milk cows, sheep and horses. With his newfound wealth and status he was soon able to acquire Stafholt, another farm nearby, and he began to gather more property and chieftaincies through persuasion, purchase or intimidation. He was sent to represent his local area at the Althing at Thingvellir, where his skill as a lawyer and wordsmith propelled him to the forefront of public life. By the time he was thirty, he was the richest and most powerful man in Iceland.

Snorri was an irrepressible philanderer, and his marriage to Herdís soon broke down. In 1206, when he moved from Borg to a larger estate further inland at Reykholt, he did so without his wife and children. He would go on to have two more daughters and a son, with three more women.

JUST BEFORE SNORRI abandoned the farm at Borg, one of his servants reported a startling dream. Borg had once been the home of the hatchet-faced warrior-poet Egil Skallagrímsson, one of Snorri's ancestors (whose saga he would later write). In the servant's dream, the shade of Egil stood scowling over his bed and asked if it was true that Egil's kinsman Snorri was planning to leave Borg.

'It is true,' replied the servant.

'Then he does a shameful thing,' said the ghost. 'He should not scorn this land.' The apparition then uttered some lines of verse, warning that a reluctance to draw the sword now would result in much greater bloodshed later:

Men now spare the sword,
Snow-white is blood to see,
An age of quarrels will now begin,
Sharp blade won land for me,
Sharp blade won land for me.

The 'snow-white' coward's blood was Snorri's. And the coming 'age of quarrels' would foreshadow the destruction of Iceland's independence.

ICELAND HAD COME into nationhood quite naturally as a republic, with laws created by gatherings of local chieftains that applied to everyone on the island. But in Snorri's time, this old egalitarian system was being bent out of shape – primarily, I've discovered, by Snorri himself. Local chieftaincies were being consolidated into the hands of just a few elite families like the Sturlungs, who began to fight each other for supremacy. The old republic began to crack under the weight of the clan leaders' ruthless ambition.

As Iceland became more unequal and its wealth more concentrated, men and women of property walked away from their rough, homespun ways and adopted more sophisticated European manners and customs. Educated Icelanders were becoming more worldly, more closely tied to the Christian culture on the Scandinavian mainland. Pious Icelanders set out on pilgrimages, travelling vast distances to the holy cities of Rome and Jerusalem, gaping in wonder at the great churches and ancient ruins.

Iceland, in Snorri's time, was also in a state of moral confusion, caught between the sermons of Christianity and the old Viking code of honour. Icelanders scratching out a living on an unforgiving island were expected to live by the sword, and yet pray for their enemies.

Two centuries had passed since that momentous year of 1000 AD when the lawspeaker came out from under his blanket to declare that Christianity would be the island's official religion. Christian worship was now deeply entrenched, and church leaders had accumulated greater power at the expense of the chieftains. Bishops and priests now asserted that the principle of the separation of church and state made them exempt from laws made at the Althing, that they could only be judged under church law.

Amidst all these tensions between the old and new ways of living, the rivalries between the great clans of Iceland were deepening, becoming harder to resolve. Clan leaders would often appeal to Norway to intercede on their behalf. Iceland lacked timber to build ships, making the island dependent on Norwegian shipping for their trade. Iceland, which had cherished its independence for so long, was learning to live in the shadow of the bigger, richer nation across the water. Chieftains began to jostle for the attention of the Norwegian king.

Haakon and Skuli

AT REYKHOLT, Snorri made several improvements to the estate: a defensive wall was constructed, alongside a cleverly designed outdoor bath filled with hot water piped in from an underground thermal spring. Snorri, as an educated man commanding a great fortune and the loyalty of many kinsmen, was frequently called on to adjudicate in legal matters, and in 1215 he was elected lawspeaker of Iceland, the most senior position in the Icelandic commonwealth. He was just thirty-six years old.

Having reached the summit of wealth and power in Iceland, Snorri now tried to catch the eye of Norway. He crafted several poems dedicated to powerful figures at the Norwegian court, which were warmly received. In 1218 his strategic flattery paid off when he received a royal invitation from the new king, Haakon IV, to visit Norway. At once he stood aside as lawspeaker and sailed across the North Sea, determined to impress his hosts with his skill as a poet and historian.

Snorri's first port of call was Bergen, a prosperous market town on Norway's rugged west coast. It was the first time Snorri had set foot in any kind of urban settlement, and he must have marvelled at the busy streets, the closely packed timber houses and the twin-towered stone church of St Mary. After a short stay, he again took to his ship, which looped around Norway's south coast, then took him up to the royal fortress town of Tunsberg.*

---

*   The modern-day town of Tønsberg, 75 kilometres south of Oslo.

NORWAY, UNDER THE RULE of its young king Haakon IV, was poised to enter a golden age. At the time of Snorri's arrival, Haakon was just a boy of fourteen. But as the commander of a powerful fleet of ships, he would one day become a significant player in continental European politics, a figure to be courted by other great powers. At different points in his long reign, Haakon would be offered the high kingship of Ireland, the command of the French crusader fleet, and the crown of the Holy Roman Empire.

Nonetheless, the young king's elevation to the throne in 1217 had been strongly contested. The clergy and elements of the aristocracy had voiced doubts about his legitimacy, citing rumours that he might have born from an adulterous liaison. To rebut these scandalous charges, Haakon's mother, Queen Inga, agreed to be subject to the 'ordeal of the iron', where she was required to grasp a red-hot iron poker and carry it for a distance of ten feet. Her stoic endurance of this hideous ordeal mollified the clergy and persuaded them that Haakon was God's candidate for the throne after all.

Haakon IV was small in stature, and described as 'merry-tongued' and curious. At the start of his reign, he struck up a friendship with another boy-king, Henry III of England, and the two monarchs exchanged letters and gifts. Haakon sent Henry thirteen Icelandic gyrfalcons, an elk and, years later, a polar bear.* In return, Henry gave Haakon several editions of chivalric romances like *Tristan and Isolde*, which were wildly popular in England and France at the time. Haakon ordered them to be translated into Norse so they might be more widely enjoyed.

In going to Norway, Snorri might have been hoping to be appointed by Haakon as the first *jarl*, or earl, of Iceland. Yet it was

---

* The polar bear was kept on the grounds of the Tower of London, where it was allowed to fish from the Thames.

difficult for an Icelander, even one as accomplished as Snorri, to command a king's attention. Iceland had no navy, and little in the way of tradable goods to compel respect. Ambitious Icelanders had to rely on persuasive conversation and a command of poetry to catch the king's ear. Poets did have some cachet in the Norwegian court; they were seen as slightly otherworldly creatures, with the power to confer a degree of immortality on their subjects. In 1030, just before the Battle of Stiklestad, King Ólaf II took care to place three poets behind his shield wall, so they might survive to record his noble death in verse.

Soon after his arrival in Tunsberg, Snorri befriended Earl Skuli, the king's principal advisor. Skuli had been the other main candidate for the throne, and in return for accepting Haakon's rule, a third of Norway had been given over to him. Both Snorri and Skuli were ambitious men of a similar age and they hit it off straight away. Skuli invited Snorri to stay with him for the winter.

The following summer, Snorri travelled east to Gautland in Sweden, to deliver a poem he'd written for Lady Kristín, the widow of a prominent earl. The poem had been commissioned by her late husband, and its title *Andvaka* – 'Sleeplessness' – refers to her beauty, which had kept him awake at night. Kristín was moved and delighted by the poem and gave Snorri many fine gifts. She was now married to Askell, the lawspeaker of the province, who could share his knowledge of Swedish law and history with Snorri.

In the autumn of 1219, Snorri returned to Norway to join Earl Skuli at his northern estate in Trondheim. He may well have attended the royal wedding of Skuli's daughter Margret to King Haakon in September that year. Snorri at last seems to have made an impression on Haakon at this time with his quick wit and mastery of skaldic verse.* The young king was pleased enough to award Snorri the honorary title of *skutilsvein*, or cup-bearer. Snorri, for his part, was greatly impressed with the indoor toilet in the king's royal hall.

DESPITE HIS POPULARITY in Norway, Snorri had arrived at a dangerous moment, when Norwegian attitudes towards Iceland were hardening.

Snorri's foster-brother Saemund, acting on a grudge, had led a band of warriors to extort a large sum of gold from the merchants of Bergen. Both Haakon and Earl Skuli were of a mind to come down hard on this naked act of piracy, by sending their fleet to assault and intimidate Iceland, and force it to submit to the Norwegian crown. Haakon ordered his ships and men to be mustered in preparation for an attack.

Norway had been trying half-heartedly to assert some kind of dominion over Iceland's affairs ever since King Ólaf had sent a messenger to the Althing in 1024, inviting Icelanders to become his subjects and accept his protection. Back then the offer had been politely but firmly declined. In the centuries that followed, Norway's leaders had been too absorbed in their internal power struggles to be very mindful of their wayward Icelandic cousins across the water. But the country had stabilised under Haakon, and the young king saw Saemund's attack as an opportunity to bring Iceland to heel.

Snorri, seeing the crisis unfold, moved quickly. He reached out to the moderates in the court, who thought sending the fleet was an over-reaction and would simply harden hostility to Norwegian rule. Iceland, he said, would prove impossible to govern without the consent of the Icelanders.

---

*   A form of Norse poetry, constructed almost like a puzzle, with extraordinarily complex forms of metre, rhyme and metaphor.

Snorri eventually persuaded Haakon and Skuli that they would be wiser to make an alliance with the leading families of Iceland, who he said were pragmatic and would be sympathetic to royal overtures, particularly if they came from Snorri acting on the king's behalf. In this way, he said, Haakon could gain control of Iceland without risking his fleet or his army. At Skuli's urging, Haakon now made Snorri a *lendr maðr*, a landed man, an honour never before accorded to an Icelander, and gave him his blessing to return to Iceland and make the case for Norwegian rule.

Seal of King Haakon VI
(a gift to Haakon from Henry III of England)

EARL SKULI GAVE SNORRI 'fifteen noble gifts' and a ship, and Snorri sailed for home across the Norwegian Sea. It was late in the year and the weather was rough. The ship lost its mast and was wrecked on the Westman Islands, off Iceland's south coast. Snorri, his bodyguard and their caskets of Norwegian treasure had to be ferried to the mainland.

Snorri's homecoming was welcomed with cheers. He uttered some lines of verse, singing the praises of his new friend Earl Skuli as a tough but fair leader of men:

Hard-mouthed was Skuli,
Magnanimous to all,
A stallion of power
Among earls.

For once, though, Snorri's verse failed to win over his audience. The rebellious clans in the south of Iceland smirked at Snorri's tribute to his 'hard-mouthed' friend. A southerner named Thórodd was said to have paid a local wordsmith 'a whole sheep' to write this parody:

We have an earl
Who rules all others!
Unpleasant to kiss –
Hard-mouthed our Skuli!

Snorri stayed over in the south for a few nights at Skálholt, the seat of the bishops of the south, with eleven of his men, but their swaggering, self-satisfied behaviour irritated the locals. The leader of the southerners, a chieftain named Björn, confronted Snorri and bluntly accused him of treason against Iceland. Snorri vehemently denied the accusation, but Björn refused to take him at his word and the two men parted in anger.

Snorri spent the winter of 1220 mulling over the unhappy state of affairs. It's not clear whether Snorri had ever truly intended to act on his promise to King Haakon, to persuade his fellow Icelanders to give themselves over to the dominion of Norway. In any event, now that he was back on Icelandic soil he spoke no more in favour of it. He distracted himself by planning further renovations to the estate at Reykholt, ordering the construction of new timber houses, a great hall and a study for himself.

The following year, Snorri resumed his role as lawspeaker of the Althing. His oldest son, Jón Little Trout, was now eighteen, and Snorri sent him to Norway for an extended stay with his good friend Earl Skuli, to acquaint him with the larger world of Norwegian court politics.

But Snorri was grooming Jón as a lieutenant, not a successor. He was still full of restless energy and there was no end to his ambitions.

The Clever King of Hleidr

BY 1223 – three years after his return from Norway – Snorri had entered his mid-forties and was ready to settle into a stable, long-term partnership. That summer, while riding to Oddi, he stayed overnight at a farm called Keldur, where he was introduced to a young woman named Sólveig. Snorri found her 'altogether delightful to talk to' and they rode out together the next morning. Along the road, they ran into Sólveig's cousin, Hallveig Ormsdóttir. Hallveig was recently widowed and had two young sons. Snorri flirted with her by teasing her about the unfashionable blue woollen cloak she was wearing, which was fastened awkwardly to her head like a kind of hat.

Whatever designs Snorri might have had on the charming Sólveig, they came to nothing when she suddenly became betrothed to his ruthless nephew Sturla. Snorri sulked over the arrangement, and was not invited to the wedding feast later that year. He turned his attentions instead to the widow in the unfashionable cape he'd encountered on the road. Hallveig was the better match for him anyway. She was well-known for her good judgement and character. And it certainly didn't hurt that she also happened to be the wealthiest woman in Iceland. In time, Snorri persuaded her to become his partner and live with him at Reykholt.

Snorri was not on good terms with either of Iceland's bishops, and never bothered to seek an official annulment of his marriage to Herdís. So when Hallveig moved in with him, she did so as his common-law wife. Such arrangements were not unusual in Iceland at the time.

The union of Snorri's power with Hallveig's wealth was mutually advantageous, but his affection and respect for her were genuine. Hallveig bore several of Snorri's children, but none survived into adulthood. He would have to focus his dynastic plans on his existing offspring.

SNORRI HAD THREE daughters: Hallbera, Thórdís and Ingibjörg. When they came of age, he arranged strategic marriages for each of them to powerful chieftains, hoping to bind these men to him.

When Hallbera turned seventeen, Snorri arranged for her to marry a chieftain with the unpromising name of Árni the Quarrelsome. Árni was much older than her, but he was said to be a good friend of King Haakon. The groom agreed to hand over one of his estates to Snorri as a *brúðkaup* – a bride price, or dowry – and he consented to live with Hallbera at Reykholt.

Then there was Thórdís, headstrong and independent-minded. Of all the children, Thórdís most closely resembled her father. In 1224, Snorri arranged a marriage with Thorvald of Vatnsfjördur, another older man, who already had teenage sons. Thorvald was a chieftain in the Westfjords and a former enemy. The marriage sealed a new alliance between the two men.

The youngest daughter, Ingibjörg, was said to be particularly lovely. When she turned sixteen, Snorri arranged for her to marry Gizur Thorvaldsson, the fifteen-year-old son of a chieftain from the south. This marriage seemed the most promising: Gizur was clever and talented, a natural leader, and he appeared very much in love with his beautiful bride.

Snorri, whose power base was in the west of the island, was able through these strategic marriages to extend his reach into the north, the northwest and the south. The alliances also served to box in the man who was shaping up as his chief rival on the island: Sturla Sighvatsson, his nephew.

STURLA WAS THE SON of Snorri's older brother Sighvat. Strong, forthright and handsome, Sturla was much more the classic Viking warrior-chief than Snorri would ever be. He was physically courageous, prepared to personally lead his followers into battle and to swing the axe into his enemies with his own hand.

If Sturla wanted something, he was inclined to simply walk over and take it. At the age of eighteen, he had discovered the neighbouring property possessed a special sword named Byrnie-Biter* that had come all the way from Constantinople. Sturla had demanded the neighbour sell it to him, and when he refused, Sturla rode over to his farm, broke into the house and took it. He brought the sword out onto the porch to take a look at it, but a visiting priest came out and told him not to unsheathe it. The farmer and his family rushed onto the porch and demanded Sturla hand it back. Sturla coolly said he merely wanted to 'borrow' it for a while, and a brawl broke out. The farmer twisted the sword out of his grasp, but Sturla pulled out his axe from under his arm and cracked open the farmer's head with it. Sturla shrugged at the bleeding and unconscious farmer, and rode off. In time a settlement was reached with the farmer's family, but Sturla was slow in paying it.

The hostility between Snorri and Sturla was inflamed when the Sturlung family *goðorð*, or chieftaincy, was given to Sturla on

---

*   A byrnie is a tunic of chain-mail.

his marriage to Sólveig in 1223, over the head of Snorri's strong objections. Four years later, Snorri successfully connived to have two-thirds of the *goðorð* taken from Sturla and given to Jón Little Trout instead.

Sturla had regarded this chieftaincy as his birthright and he bitterly resented having it wrested from his grasp by his greedy uncle, who already had seven chieftaincies to his name.

BY 1228, SNORRI was at the summit of his power. One evening, as he relaxed with friends in his outdoor bath, his guests hailed him and told him there was no chieftain like him in all of Iceland. 'No one can compete with you!' they said. 'You have so many kinsmen.' Snorri basked in the flattery, but his attendant, who had been standing guard at the bath, was unable to hold his tongue; he shot Snorri a verse that warned him his end might come to him not through Sturla, but through his ambitious sons-in-law:

> *You have similar in-laws*
> *As had in the past –*
> *Injustice always proves*
> *Ill – the clever king of Hleidr.**

Already, a few of Snorri's foundation stones had begun to come loose. He'd arranged his daughters' marriages strategically, but had given little thought to their happiness. Hallbera had never wanted to marry Árni the Quarrelsome, and had divorced him after six years. Snorri, quick to find the upside of any misfortune, had turned the divorce settlement to his advantage, naming Árni as the guilty party,

---

*   The 'clever king of Hleidr' referred to here is the legendary Danish king Hrólf Kraki, who killed his step-father for refusing to pay a promised reward.

demanding and receiving a large portion of Árni's wealth and half his chieftaincy in the settlement.

For all his cleverness, Snorri seems to have been oblivious to the dangers of using and discarding such men. Árni would nurse his grudge against Snorri for the rest of his life.

In 1227, Snorri had organised a second marriage for Hallbera, this time to a promising younger man named Kolbein from the north. But this marriage also failed to take hold, and after two years Kolbein abruptly abandoned her. Hallbera, weary of men and marriage, retreated to the old family estate at Borg.

THAT SAME YEAR, the marriage of Snorri's second daughter Thórdís was also brought to an end, but in far more brutal circumstances. Snorri himself was largely to blame: his overweening need to stamp his authority on the countryside – and to slap down his nephew Sturla – had led him to overreach himself and invite a terrible retribution. After he had stripped Sturla of the family chieftaincy, Snorri had come swooping down into the family lands in the western dales with 300 kinsmen to extract oaths of allegiance from the local farmers. Even the tenant farmers at Sturla's own property of Saudafell were obliged to pledge their support for Snorri.

Riding alongside him had been his son-in-law Thorvald of Vatnsfjördur, who had once been close to Sturla, but was now Snorri's chief ally. As they left the dales, Thorvald was told to watch out for his enemies. He dismissed the warning with a wave of his hand.

Sturla, who had been advised to clear out of the area for a while, seethed at his loss of face and the treachery of his former friend. He had formed an alliance with two younger men who had also come to detest Thorvald and were stalking him from a distance. The following Sunday they received word their quarry was staying overnight at a farm called Gillastadur.

At dawn, while Thorvald lay asleep in his bed closet with Thórdís, one of the farmhands stepped outside the house, yawned, then noticed the cattle had been moved. Turning his head, he spotted five men crouching by the side wall. One was holding a flaming brand. The farmhand dashed back inside and cried out: 'The house is under attack!'

Thorvald and Thórdís tumbled out of their bed closet just as smoke began to fill the house. One of Sturla's men was suddenly at the back entrance. A servant tried to fight him off, but was speared in the throat and in the belly.

The thick smoke was choking everyone inside now. Thórdís collapsed. A farmhand kicked a hole in the turf wall and dragged her out to safety.

The blaze roared through the longhouse. Within minutes, it burnt to the ground. Thorvald's charred remains were found among the smoking ruins of the kitchen.

The attackers stole some horses and weapons, then rode off in triumph to report the success of their mission to Sturla.

Thórdís was now a widow. But rather than wait for her father to line up another suitor, she made a bid for independence. She handed over the family estate at Vatnsfjördur to Thorvald's teenage sons, and relocated to a property in the distant northwest, outside her father's influence. Thórdís took two lovers and had a child by each of them, but she never remarried.

STURLA SENT AN EMISSARY to Snorri to ask for a truce for the killing of Snorri's son-in-law, which was accepted. Sturla also tried to smooth things over with Thorvald's teenage sons by offering them compensation for the attack, but he was rebuked, and the teenage brothers now plotted their own revenge.

They rounded up a war party of fifty young men, made up mostly of their teenage friends, and on 13 January 1229, they galloped down to Sturla's farmstead at Saudafell. Sturla wasn't there; he was at another farm on business, but had left behind his wife Sólveig, their baby daughter and the servants.

The howling mob charged into Sturla's home. For a moment, they were taken aback by the richness of the furnishings – the fine tapestries in the hall, the shields and armour. Then they ran wild, smashing the furniture, and slashing at the women and servants with axes and swords. The local priest was there and tried to fend off their blows with a cushion. Ysja, an elderly servant, was sadistically attacked: the young men cut off her breasts and she soon bled to death. Then they seized Sturla's valuables – his gold-tipped spears, ceremonial axes and horses. As the terror of the night gave way to morning, they rode off into the mountains, crowing over their successful raid.

After they left, Sólveig called the remaining servants to her and told them to round up some men to chase after the attackers. But her mother stopped her cold.

'Two things are certain,' the old woman said. 'Sturla will reserve revenge for himself. And no good can come of it unless he *does* take it himself.'

STURLA WAS IN HIS BATH when breathless messengers arrived with news of the attack on his farmstead at Saudafell.

'Is Sólveig all right?' he asked.

'Sólveig is unharmed,' they said.

After that Sturla said nothing for a while. His allies urged him to summon his men and give chase, but he said he wouldn't be rushed into anything. Instead, he came home to assess the damage.

Three people were dead or dying. Another fifteen were wounded or maimed. His home was wrecked.

News of the cruel and cowardly raid on Saudafell spread quickly, and was received with widespread disgust. Many assumed Snorri had contrived the whole thing, goading the sons of Thorvald into the attack in retaliation for the murder of their father. Verses were composed laying responsibility for the raid at his feet:

> Snorri has avenged his Thorvald,
> His poetry is his power.
> Fiery play around the head
> Of his daughter's husband, dead.

'His poetry is his power' was meant as an insult. It was unseemly for Snorri to have taken his revenge against Sturla by proxy. He was mocked as a coward:

> Men murdered old Ysja
> Ill work to spill peace,
> Although they'd have failed
> Had they not followed Snorri,
> That powerful warrior
> Who has clearly avenged
> His kinsmen – in ditties!
> There's your honour, Snorri!

Sturla summoned his men, and broached with them the idea of assassinating Snorri, but the men in the hall fell silent and uneasy. A few spoke up against it, and the idea was dropped.

SNORRI RODE OUT to the Althing that year with an entourage of more than 700 men, making it clear to everyone at the assembly he was still the dominant figure in Iceland. His booth, made of turf, stone and timber, was absurdly titled 'Valhalla'.

Snorri was unwell and remained inside for much of the season at Thingvellir, so his son Jón Little Trout, who had returned from Norway, spoke on his behalf at the assembly. A lawsuit was mounted against Thorvald's sons for the raid on Saudafell, which fizzled out. But Sturla did manage to persuade the Althing to return to him one-third of the family chieftaincy that he'd lost to Jón and Snorri.

THEN, ALL OF Snorri's dynastic plans crumbled into a heap.

Jón Little Trout was now twenty-six years old and eager to marry a woman named Helga. He came into his father's booth at the Althing to ask him for the estate at Stafholt as a bride price for the wedding. Snorri said he would be happy to arrange the marriage but he refused to hand over Stafholt. Jón would be more useful to him, he said, if he stayed on managing the estate at Borg. Fed up with living by his father's grace and favour, Jón stormed out and bought passage on a ship to Norway. Realising his mistake, Snorri relented and hastily sent a message to Jón, telling him he could have Stafholt after all, but Jón stubbornly refused to change his plans and sailed to Norway anyway.

Hallbera, Snorri's eldest daughter, was still living at Borg, but her health was declining. In the summer of 1231 Snorri sent a physician to examine her. He recommended a hot bath, which he said would cure her if she could endure it. When Hallbera stepped out of her bath, she clutched her chest, collapsed and died. She was just thirty years old.

Then, several months later, Snorri received news from Norway that Jón Little Trout was dead too.

The account of how he'd met his death was somewhat confusing.

After a year in Norway, Jón had run short of money. He'd asked permission from Haakon to return to Iceland, but the king refused. Stranded in Bergen, Jón was forced to share a room with his brother-in-law Gizur (married to Ingibjörg), and a friend, Ólaf, both of whom happened to be in Norway at the time. Gizur, the most promising of Snorri's sons-in-law, was intent on forging his own links with Haakon and his court.

Jón and Gizur were invited to the king's court for Christmas celebrations and both young men became very drunk. When they returned to their garret apartment, Jón saw that his bed had not been made, and he insulted the servants. Ólaf spoke up in the servants' defence, and Jón snatched up a piece of firewood and clubbed him with it. Gizur moved to restrain Jón, while Ólaf, in his fury, picked up his hand-axe and smashed Jón on the head.

At first the wound didn't seem too bad and Jón wriggled free from Gizur's grip. Ólaf, terrified, ran off into the night, while Gizur stayed behind to help bind Jón's wounded head. In the morning, Jón and Gizur searched for Ólaf through the snowy streets of Bergen but couldn't find him.

Later that afternoon, Jón complained of pains in his head. He lay down on his bed and never got up again. He died a few weeks later, in January 1231.

Gizur had gathered up Jón's belongings and brought them back to Iceland. At Reykholt he related the sorry circumstances of Jón's death. Gizur, who was somewhat glib and untrustworthy, knew he was under suspicion of having had a hand in the matter, so he swore an oath to his father-in-law that he had in no way plotted with Ólaf to kill Jón, and that he had done his best to stop the fight.

Snorri, stony-faced with grief, said he would accept Gizur's account. But Snorri's youngest daughter Ingibjörg simply couldn't forgive Gizur, her husband, for the death of her older brother.

Swallowing his own suspicions about Gizur, Snorri tried to hold the marriage together by giving the couple more money. Nonetheless, despite her husband's still-strong affection, Ingibjörg walked away from the broken marriage and returned to the family estate at Reykholt.

Snorri's dynastic planning was now completely undone: his heir and eldest daughter were dead, and the marriage alliances he had so carefully arranged for his other daughters had come to nothing. And would eventually come to worse than nothing.

CHAPTER EIGHT
(Kári)

The Sweetest Light of My Eyes

T HE NEXT DAY is day six of our journey. We've rented a small cabin in the south, within sight of the slopes of Hlídarendi. The cabin is simple, homely and cluttered with cracked leather couches and arguably a bit too much of the colour brown: the coffee cups and rugs seem to be fading to the same sunburnt sepia as the photos hanging in the kitchen. I like it, though, even the odd little knick-knacks – wall plates depicting the history of Copenhagen, his and hers Bavarian beer jugs, a miniature bell set from the former Yugoslavia.

We arrive in the morning, and sit drinking coffee on a back deck almost within reach of the Rangá, a winding salmon river that crosses the plains towards Gunnar's farm, where he fought the battle side by side with his brother, and, in the stillness after the fight, wondered why he hated killing more than other men did. Further to the west, across light steps of fields of hay, is Oddi, the farm where Snorri Sturluson was fostered and first took his place at the table of sagas, myths, and poetry.

We also have a view of Eyjafjallajökull, the volcano that became the ultimate pronunciation challenge for journalists all over the world. Eventually, someone had the idea of calling it E15, after the number of letters. But it's actually a very pretty name, much nicer than E15. Broken down into its parts, Eyja-fjalla-jökull means 'island mountain glacier'.

Richard, I have discovered, fancies himself as having a good ear for new languages. The first time he heard me speaking Icelandic on the phone, just after we arrived, he turned to me and said, 'You have no idea how fucking cool that is.'

Straight away, he wanted to learn it.

Now, as we sit looking at the volcano, he insists on a tutorial on how to say Eyjafjallajökull.

'Just say it slowly,' he tells me.

I do.

'Add-dja-feeatla-kjukle,' he tries.

'No, that's not it.'

'That's exactly what you just said.'

I repeat the correct pronunciation.

'Eggja-feetler-jerkutl,' he says.

'It's better,' I tell him, 'but still miles off.'

'Fuck off, then.'

I'VE BOOKED US A TABLE for lunch at a lobster restaurant in the coastal village of Stokkseyri. We're given a window table, and order white wine and then a serving of the local langoustines. They're small but very sweet, cooked in garlic and butter and then brought to the table in a copper pot.

Two children are playing out the back of the restaurant. I think they're brother and sister. The girl is a little older, twelve or thirteen, almost too old for the game of chase they're playing. Her heart's not quite in it, but she's enjoying the boy's happiness, and letting herself pretend to be his age again.

Richard and I are both fathers of children. Mine are in primary school, his just going into high school. But they get along well. When Richard and his wife Khym visit, their kids seem happy to play games with ours, and my two boys watch them almost obsessively, looking for a glimpse of the world as it will exist in a few years' time.

Finnur, our older son, has just turned ten. He's already well used to being told that he looks just like me, but he doesn't seem to mind the comparison. We have a lot of other things in common, too. We love swimming and football, and language; Finnur is forever being asked to give speeches for his class at school.

But our younger boy Magnús is, in a way, the more bookish of the two, and even now, aged seven, can spend many quiet hours reading. In my mind, I can hear what he'd say if I read that sentence out to him: 'Hey, I like swimming and football just as much as Finnur!' Yes, that's true. And they're both tall, beautiful boys.

My siblings have children too – all older than mine. When I visit Iceland with the family, more than anything else the boys want to spend time with their cousins. They do lose track of their names a little; there are seven to remember, and all rather unfamiliar to Australian-Icelandic ears. Perhaps it's a bit like encountering a list of saga characters for the first time.

My sister Bryndís's two girls – both young women now – lavish the boys with attention, and in return they bristle with young, gentlemanly pride. They explain things that I'm not sure their older relations are too concerned about: the Under 10s soccer schedule; how often, on average, we go out for dinner at the local Thai restaurant. But these exchanges, the countless smaller stories of family life, build something else.

The boys know *my* story, and accept it as simply part of who I am. But even here, in Iceland, I think they barely sense its full reality: that there is an Iceland of forty years ago where their grandmother was a young mother very much on her own, and where I wasn't placed in the world anywhere near as surely as I am in theirs. Now and then, they even forget that I didn't know my father, and ask me questions about him that I don't have the answers to, and never will.

But I'd like to be able to answer just one. If they ever ask me whether it's true, as he said, that we're descended from the greatest ever Icelandic writer, I'd like to be able to tell them one way or the other. I want to give them that, and not leave it for them to sort out later.

RICHARD AND I finish our lunch while talking about *Njál's Saga*, and then about how we'll spend the next couple of days. We've done all the recording we need to do in the south – more quickly than we'd expected. We now have a bit of extra time to look around, or work on the radio edits in the quiet of the cabin.

By the time we pay our bill, the lunchtime crowd has left, and the village has emptied, too. Busyness here comes in rushes – a busload of tourists; families in hire cars; us chasing old stories, and good food.

We may have had a little too much of the latter; we need a walk. We leave through the restaurant's back door, exiting into the garden area, then clamber up the ocean wall of uneven rocks onto which the garden backs. There's a path along the wall, which we follow out of the village, towards the last houses and the start of the farmlands.

By the time we trail back, we notice that the wind has strengthened. It's low tide; beneath the wall, the black beach paints a thick marker line around the coast.

'I can't get my bearings at the moment,' says Richard. 'How far are we from Hlídarendi?'

'Not that far. The road here took us a bit of a roundabout way. Hlidarerndi's about fifty kilometres away, Njál's farm maybe a bit less. I think it would have been more direct on horseback, too.'

'A saga about neighbours.'

'And about a tiny country of farmers that's still living by a warrior code. Some people holding on to the past, while others are doing their best to escape it.'

A cottage in Stokkseyri village

Fathers and Sons

GUNNAR HAD DIED a warrior's death, but he was slow to take his place at Valhalla, the hall where he would partake of the banquet promised to Vikings who died in battle.

His body was placed in a burial mound. That should have been that. But one day a shepherd and a servant woman were walking past and heard him inside, chanting poetry.

When Gunnar's best friend Njál was told about this, he asked his oldest son, Skarphédin, to visit Hlídarendi to see what he could discover. He rode to the farm, and then with one of Gunnar's sons he crossed the home pastures to the burial mound. All night, they sat and waited.

Finally the mound opened. Gunnar sat upright, facing the moon. There were lights burning inside. He looked content, but, just as the shepherd and servant had said, was reciting verse:

This shield-holding ghost would sooner
Wear his helmet high
Than falter in the fray,
Rather die for battle-freyja.*

When Skarphédin heard the verse, he said, 'Gunnar stayed true to the life of a warrior. He is telling us to live the same way. That is why he has stayed on.'

Njál was less sure. When Christianity arrived in Iceland in the year 1000, eight years after Gunnar's death, Njál was a very willing convert. For him, its teachings of good will to all, and the shared honour of Christ's compassion, were much more appealing than heroism. Christianity seemed to offer the chance to bend the course of disputes, and heal the wounds of the past.

He and his wife Bergthóra had three boys, very different in temperament. Njál also had children with other women, mistresses

---

*   A reference to the *valkyrie* who will select Gunnar as a hero who has died in battle.

whom his wife knew about and somehow managed to bear – adopting Christianity had not changed his relationships with them. But the terrible truth about Njál was that he loved none of these children as much as he loved another boy, a child called Höskuld, whom he would foster and to whom he would dedicate all his hopes.

SKARPHÉDIN, NJÁL'S OLDEST SON and the one who'd seen Gunnar turning in his mound, often ruled the household. Skarphédin was a difficult man, hard-tempered and violent, and not at all given to Njál's way of seeing the world.

He made enemies easily, and had come to hate one of Gunnar's kinsmen, a man called Thráin. They had exchanged insults and threats, and it seemed only a matter of time before they would fight. The heroic code demanded it: a resolution in blood.

To the east of Njál's farm lies a wide estuary. In winter, its many streams begin to freeze from the edges in, but just as often the water keeps running through the middle.

One winter night, Njál's sons heard that Thráin was riding towards their farm, and approaching the estuary. Early the next morning, while it was still pitch-dark, they took their weapons down from their wall hangings.

Skarphédin's axe chimed against the wall.

'Where are you going?' Njál asked.

'To find some sheep,' said Skarphédin. 'Go back to sleep.'

The Njálssons rode to the estuary and lay in wait near the frozen streams. As Thráin and his men neared from the other side, Skarphédin began to run at the river. He lifted his axe into the air and jumped over the still-running stream, landing on the ice on the other side.

He began to slide across the ice, heading straight for Thráin. When he reached him, Skarphédin drove his axe into Thráin's head. It split open down to his jaw, and his molars spilt across the ice.

Skarphédin picked them up and put them into his pocket.

NJÁL COULD NOT CONTROL his sons, but it would fall to him to patch together a settlement afterwards. As the next assembly, Thráin's kinsmen were given a large monetary settlement for his death. But Njál knew that more would be needed to stop the feud from escalating. His sons wanted control of the district, and Thráin's family were not going to accept it.

Then Njál met Höskuld, Thráin's son. Like everyone else, he saw how lovely the boy was – gentle and open, and kind to everyone. Njál came to love him, and would spend time talking to him whenever he could. They also spoke about the fighting that had happened, and Höskuld's father Thráin.

Njál asked Höskuld whether he knew that Skarphédin had killed his father.

'Yes, he was killed by your son. But we don't need to talk about it. The matter is settled and compensation has been paid.'

'Your answer is better than my question,' said Njál. He was stunned by the boy's forbearance and good will: wasn't this a perfect example of the good will that was advocated by the Christian God? 'You'll grow up to be a good man,' he said to Höskuld.

Njál asked Höskuld's mother whether he could adopt the boy as his foster-son. In reply, she asked if Njál would honour him as much as he did his own sons, and Njál gave her that promise. He loved the boy, and would seek only the best for him. And yet Njál knew that he was risking Höskuld's life by bringing him so close to Skarphédin, his father's killer.

To begin with, Skarphédin and Njál's other sons welcomed Höskuld into the family. The Njálssons took Höskuld with them wherever they went, and Höskuld loved being with them. He told Skarphédin that he would never seek blood vengeance for his father's death, and for the time being Skarphédin believed him.

The years passed, and Höskuld reached manhood. Njál offered to help him find a wife. Höskuld said that, as always, he'd be happy to follow Njál's advice.

Njál already had someone in mind. Her name was Hildigun, a very beautiful young woman who lived to the east. She was known for her intelligence and strength of character.

Njál and Höskuld rode to speak to her most powerful kinsman, the chieftain Flosi, whose approval would be needed for the match to go ahead. Njál put forward his proposal, and both Flosi and Hildigun answered favourably. Höskuld married and moved to his wife's farm.

LATE ONE NIGHT, there was banging on the door of Njál's farm. Njál got out of bed to find his mistress standing outside. She had terrible news. Their son together had been ambushed and killed by Höskuld's kinsmen, those in his family who couldn't be persuaded to adopt his own forbearance. Years after his death, blood revenge for Höskuld's father had finally begun.

'What will you do about it?' she asked.

'My sons will know what to do,' Njál answered.

The Njálssons again brought down their weapons from the wall, and took blood vengeance for the killing of their half-brother with a an attack on Hoskuld's kinsmen.

For a while, there was some calm. But Njál could see that, now that Höskuld had left his farm, he couldn't control the events of his foster-son's life. A rumour began to spread through the district. It said Höskuld had never been happy with the settlement for his father's killing, and had always wanted Skarphédin dead.

Höskuld refused to act to correct the rumours. He would not hear it said that his foster-brothers would believe the false reports.

He was wrong. One morning just after sunrise, Skarphédin and his brothers rode to the farm where Höskuld and Hildigun lived. There, they crouched behind a stone wall and waited.

Höskuld came out to do his morning work, and walked along the home field wall. As he passed where the Njálssons were hiding, Skarphédin stood up. He and Höskuld stood on either side of the wall for a moment, looking into each other's eyes.

Höskuld turned away and started to walk back to the house.

Skarphédin jumped the wall and followed him. He didn't say anything, or call out. But he caught up to Höskuld, and landed his axe in the back of Höskuld's head. Skarphédin's two brothers ran up to the body, and each of them stabbed Höskuld where he lay dead on the ground.

WHEN NJÁL HEARD about what his sons had done, he said it was as though the sweetest light of his eyes had been extinguished. But his foster-son would not have wanted a blood price for his death. He would not have wanted anyone else to exact revenge.

Flosi, the chieftain who'd given away Hildigun's hand in marriage, came to see her. She prepared a meal for him and his men, and had the servants place rich fabric hangings on the walls. With great ceremony, she then walked Flosi to a high seat.

Flosi pushed the high seat over. 'I'm not a king. Don't mock me.'

'I only want to show you honour,' said Hildigun.

When the men finished their meal, Hildigun returned. She stood in front of Flosi with her hair pushed across her face. Then she brushed her hair aside. She was crying.

'You have every right to grieve,' Flosi said. 'Your husband was a good man.'

'But what will you do for him?' she asked. 'He would have taken blood vengeance for you by now.'

Flosi was silent.

Hildigun walked over to a chest that was kept at the side of the room. From it, she took out a cloak, the same cloak Höskuld had been wearing when he was killed, which was still caked with his blood. She walked behind Flosi and lay the cloak over his shoulders. Dried blood began to flake off and fall into his lap.

Flosi reeled back in disgust. 'Monster!' he cried. His face turned red as blood. He and his men went to their horses and rode away.

FLOSI NOW TOOK UP THE CASE against the Njálssons, and prosecuted the matter at Thingvellir. Njál confided in him that he was distressed by the death of Höskuld. He said he would rather have lost any of his own sons than Höskuld, and put forward an offer of a vast sum of money as compensation.

Flosi saw that Njál was heartbroken, and accepted the offer of settlement. The money was collected and prepared for exchange. At the last minute, Njál placed a silk cloak over the top of the silver.

Flosi and his followers arrived to collect the money. As the two groups stood facing each other, Flosi looked at the money. It was all there. But something else, too. He noticed the cloak on the top.

He picked it up. 'Who added this?'

There was no answer.

Flosi asked a second time. 'Who put the cloak over this silver?'

There was silence. Njál wouldn't say.

Flosi waited. He was certain some offence was intended by the addition of this gift. Was he being mocked? He held the cloak, gripped it in his hand. 'There is no settlement in this case.'

SHORTLY AFTERWARDS, NJÁL, Bergthóra and their sons were attacked – at the farm where Njál and his family lived, and where they'd often entertained Gunnar and Hallgerd. Flosi assembled a large band of followers and rode to Njál's farm to avenge the death of Höskuld. Njál and his sons came outside to meet the group.

'What do you think will happen?' Njál asked Skarphédin.

'It's a big enough force, and they're well equipped. But they'll have a hard time against us.'

Njál said, 'I think we should go inside and defend ourselves from there, the way Gunnar did. Our house is as strong as his.'

'That's not the right way to look at it,' said Skarphédin. 'Gunnar was attacked by honourable men. The ones we face will do anything to kill us. They'll trap us inside and set fire to the house.'

'Yet again, you don't know how to show me respect.'

'We'll do what you say, then,' said Skarphédin. 'If you want to see your sons burnt to death, then let's burn.'

Njál walked back inside, and his sons followed.

The attackers resorted to fire almost straight away. They lit piles of chickweed, and fanned the flames until the fire took hold of the thick beams inside the house. The entire household was trapped.

As the beams began to crash down onto them, the women and the children were offered clemency and allowed out.

Njál, too, was told that he could leave. He refused. He said he was too old to avenge his sons. His wife Bergthóra said she would stay with him. They walked to their room, and asked a servant to cover them in a hide blanket.

One of their grandsons, Thórd, was standing with them. He said he didn't want to be separated from his grandparents.

While Thórd's father, a man called Kári, tried to shoot at the attackers from among the flames, the boy lay down with Njál and Bergthóra. They put him between them, and together the three of them perished in the smoke. Their bodies were later discovered in exactly the same place as they'd lain down. There was only one visible wound on any of the bodies: at some point, the boy had brought his hand out from under the blanket, and a single finger had been burnt off.

Only one man escaped the flames that day. It was Kári, Njál's son-in-law, and the source of my own name. Because he had lost his young son in the fire, it fell to Kári to avenge the attack on the family, and then to create a lasting peace in the district.

It took him many years, and it wasn't until much blood had been spilt that he was able to forgive the attackers.

But forgiveness came.

One day, Kári the avenger was sailing along the south coast, not far from where Richard and I had lunch, when his ship hit trouble and he was forced to beach. The ship was wrecked, and Kári and the others were drenched and freezing cold.

The nearest farm belonged to Flosi, the very man who'd led the attack on Njál's farm. Kári knocked on the door. When Flosi saw his old enemy, he held him in his arms, offered him shelter, and begged for an end to their dispute.

Kári, worn out by the shipwreck and also, no doubt, by years of conflict, relented. The two sides were finally at peace.

SINCE THEN, THE waters of the south coast have come to be known for their destructive power. This is a hazardous place to sail. Unlike other parts of the island, there's a lack of natural harbours, and the breakers are ill-tempered and unpredictable.

That night, I sit outside in the orange light of a long dusk thinking about Hallgerd and Gunnar, and why over the years I've been so intensely drawn to their lives. They are so different from me, and from my situation. And yet I notice a spirit in their story that helps me to understand mine.

Many readers are shocked by the sagas' bloodlust. Usually, the violence has had its genesis in the past, as in Kári's pursuit of his son's killers. Sometimes, it's shown to be inherited, or a result of things that happen before the main action of the saga.

As a girl, Hallgerd was beautiful and much loved by her father. And yet when she was of marriageable age, her father made her marry a man she didn't know, and didn't want. Her second husband, the man she did love, was killed by her over-protective foster-father. By the time Gunnar struck her, I expect she'd had enough of being pushed around by men. A wave, formed early in her life, was at last ready to break.

That's why I don't judge Hallgerd, or Gunnar. Or even Njál, who accepted the loss of his own sons and grandson as part of the price that he felt must be paid – for Höskuld, and also perhaps so that the relentless feuding in the district might end.

Each character is responding to a situation in which violence seems necessary and ceaseless. And somehow, the saga asks for something better than judgement from us as readers. It prompts us to see the strangeness of the characters' behaviour in the light of their desires, their complexity as human beings.

Is it too much of a stretch to apply this to Gísli, my father? Maybe. He wasn't bound by a Viking culture that passed into history a thousand years ago. But his sense of family and personal duty affected him just as powerfully as the Viking notion of honour. It guided many of his actions – his ambition at work, his care for his children, a kindness to others that often appeared as charm – and in the end it also created a terrible gap between what he wanted and what he had.

Gísli loved his wife and the family they made together. As a result, it was impossible for him to include me in it. I need to remember that, just as we must remember that Gunnar and Hallgerd were torn by the conflict of personal desire and the hopes of those they loved.

THE NEXT MORNING, Richard says he needs to spend some time in the cabin, to write and do first edits of the recordings we've made so far. Much of that work falls to him: he's been in radio for years, and I'm just a beginner. But I'm restless; around mid-morning I leave him to his laptop and headphones, and head out for a drive.

I'm not sure where I want to go, but I really like the car we've got, and I enjoy driving on country roads. Our hire car was meant to be a modest sedan, but when I went to pick it up and started speaking Icelandic to the lady at reception, she asked the usual questions I get. Why was I back? How long had I been away? Didn't I miss Iceland? By the time I left the car hire office, we had a large four-wheel drive at no extra cost.

When I get to the end of our side road, I take a right onto the main highway, and follow its arcing, eastward sweep towards Markarfljót, the estuary where Skarphédin skated his way to revenge. The slopes taper towards the southern coastline, and then I seem to reach the

corner that marks the very base of the island. After that, I find the
other Iceland – one of vast waterfalls, caves and broken cliff tops,
where the heathland descends along deep veins of water erosion to
narrow pastures and stranded rocks. This is the Iceland that doesn't
seem to welcome us, maybe doesn't even want us here, but which we
seek all the more as a result.

Today, I find myself looking for Seljavellir, Seal Pastures, and a
glacial valley that sits directly under the Eyjafjallajökull volcano.
There used to be a camp ground next to the farm there, and a small
swimming pool next to it. And another, much older pool, a short
hike up the valley. I heard that it was all destroyed by the volcano,
but haven't been back since.

The old pool at Seljavellir

It takes me a while to find the turn-off. I don't have a map, and the
farmhouses are hard to tell apart – white-walled and red-roofed,
and most often pressed up against the base of the mountains. I drive
past the turn-off twice, and finally realise that the camp ground has
vanished. I park the car, and find the little pool still there, but locked
up and filled with mud and ash.

I want to know how it is further up, where the old pool was, and maybe beyond, where a gorge climbs towards the volcano. I stumble along the rock path at the opening of the valley.

Suddenly, I find myself joined by a young Frenchman with an open face, smiling. 'Going to the pool?' he asks.

'Yes.'

'Oh, great. Can I walk with you? I don't know the way.'

There are a few people on the path ahead of us; it would be difficult to get lost. But I say, 'Of course', and we begin to chat. As we walk together, he shakes me out of a feeling of solitude that had settled while I was driving.

His name is Michel, and he speaks English with a French-American accent. He tells me that he can't believe he's in Iceland. Can *I* believe it? he asks.

I'm half-Icelandic, I confess.

'Wow,' he says. 'You're lucky.'

I notice he's carrying a very large backpack. 'Oh, yeah, that's right,' he says. 'This is it. The lot. I'm catching a plane in three hours. I hope I have time.'

'To France?'

'New York.' After a moment, he adds, 'Banking.'

We fall into a companionable silence. The track is cradled into the side of the valley, and then among the gaps left between the wide boulders of the river bank. I can't stop thinking about how little time Michel has given himself to catch his plane when he says, as though answering my thoughts, 'We're close now? The pool, I mean.'

'Not too far.'

'I really have to have a swim. And then I can get back to Reykjavík.'

It's a two-hour drive. 'I'd make it a short swim, if I were you.'

But I'm entirely on his side. I recognise how he's trying to squeeze every last minute out of Iceland, how this place turns us into excited children again. We round a bend, and the pool comes into view: a narrow cement box painted white; at the far end, a broken-down change room crumbling into the mountain side.

'It looks like there's been a lot of damage,' says Michel.

In fact, it hasn't changed at all; the damage is just age, not the explosion or the ash. I feel strangely elated by that, by the dereliction, and that it hasn't been fixed up, or made more attractive to visitors. A sweet, ugly little pool in the countryside remains wonderfully unchanged.

'I'm going to run on,' says Michel.

'Good luck,' I say. 'I hope you catch your plane.'

He runs ahead, turns and smiles.

He doesn't care about the flight.

PAST THE POOL, the valley suddenly narrows, and a few hundred metres on I'm alone on the track. I miss the companionship of Michel, and am joined instead by the feeling of aimlessness I had when I first left the cabin.

I think about heading back, sitting in the cabin and reading. But something pulls me on. 'Spirits,' I joke to myself out loud. *Landvættir* in Icelandic, the spirit guardians of the land.

The hills sharpen towards the high, dark gorge that I've come to see. Here, the pebble path I've been following ends at the river bank. There's a track rising to the left; it's slimy and narrow – almost a little stream it's so wet. But I figure it must be a new path.

It's steeper, though, and before long I'm looking directly down over the river, which from up here is glacial white. I'm on a ledge, very exposed. As the path steepens still more, I have to use my hands to scramble up. Then finally it dawns on me. It's not a path at all; it's a sheep track. I've come much too far. I glance behind me, and feel the first strike of vertigo. I'm stuck.

I sit down, can't move, and don't know what to do.

The ravines in Seljavellir

For a few minutes I do nothing. I'm waiting for something. Then I look up. The cliffs above me are as black as ash, their posture as straight as mine is cowed. But the river is quieter up here, and there are birds. I haven't heard them until now. Two of them crosshatch a route between the gap in the rocks, up to where it widens at the top. Watching their flight, I notice that the ravine is actually a step to another valley as wide and calm as the one behind me.

I begin a very slow slide down on my bum.

By the time I get back to pool, Michel is gone; he must be racing to the airport. An hour later, I'm at the cabin again. I don't mention what happened on the track to Richard. There's some exposure in the story, as in the moment, that I don't fully understand. Something about my father, and not knowing how far to go in this new search for him that I seem to have taken on. Whether the willingness to accept him as he was, in all his complexity, amounts to a need to include him in my life again.

Part

II

The Poets' Mead

I T'S DAY SEVEN of our journey, our final day in this cabin on the south coast. Kári has come back from his drive, and is now out for a late afternoon walk, and so I have the place to myself again.

I put aside my laptop and stretch out on the cabin's spongy old sofa to read Snorri Sturluson's *Prose Edda*. Of the three great works attributed to Snorri, it's the *Prose Edda* that resounds longest and loudest throughout the centuries. It's the best source we have for the Norse myths, the stories the Vikings once told each other to explain the creation of the world in fire and ice, and to prophesy its inevitable doom.* English-speaking people all over the world unconsciously chant the names of the gods from the pages of the *Prose Edda* every day: Tyr, also known as Tiw, gives us Tuesday; Odin, also called Woden, lends his name to Wednesday; Thor's day is Thursday and Friday belongs to Frigg.

---

* Scholars are uncertain as to the origin of the word 'Edda'; it may be a corruption of 'Oddi', the farm where Snorri was brought up, a longstanding centre of learning. Others believe it simply meant 'mythology'.

Cover of the Prose Edda, *1666 edition:*
Heimdall blows his horn; Thor grasps his hammer;
Huginn and Muninn flank Odin's shoulders

In Snorri's telling, the Norse gods are like humans, but with the volume turned up to eleven: they are stronger, cleverer, faster and trickier. They have all the best toys, too: a lethal hammer that never misses its mark, a super-fast horse with eight legs, and a collapsible ship that you can fold up and slip into your pocket. The Norse gods fight too much and drink too much; their victories are sublime, their torments last an eternity.

The main tribe of gods, known as the Aesir, have the powers of super-heroes: they can walk across the sky, command the thunder and drink up the ocean. But they are mortal too; even Odin, their one-eyed king, dreads Ragnarok, the long-foretold day when he and all the Aesir will die.

The *Prose Edda* is a delight, written in the same direct, uncluttered language of the family sagas, but these tales are giddy and fun. It's not known for certain when Snorri wrote the *Prose Edda*, but the account of his life offers a clue.

In 1229, after the burning of Thorvald and the murderous attack on Saudafell, an uneasy peace fell upon Iceland. Snorri and his nephew Sturla were reconciled for a short while. *Sturlunga Saga* records:

> *Things now began to go better between Snorri and Sturla; Sturla*
> *spent some considerable time at Reykholt and gave much thought*
> *to having copies made of the saga books which Snorri was writing.*

Perhaps it was during this interlude that Snorri put together the *Prose Edda*. As it was with the family sagas, putting the Norse myths to the page was an act of conservation as much as anything. In Snorri's time, these myths were slipping out of memory, and worship of the old heathen gods was deemed by the church to be heretical. Snorri's clever trick in the *Prose Edda* is to rescue the Norse myths and make them acceptable by nesting them inside a larger Christian universe.

In Snorri's telling, the Aesir are not gods at all, but legendary people from ancient Troy, empowered with magical abilities, who wander out of 'Turkland' into Northern Europe and become famous chieftains by dint of their magical brilliance. After they die, their graves become sacred sites; men and women begin to call upon their spirits for help in times of need. In this way, the names of these mortals become venerated and they attain god-like status in the Viking mind.

THE FIRST BOOK of Snorri's *Prose Edda* presents the Norse myth of the creation and destruction of the universe. It reads like it was hammered out on an anvil. The story is told to a Swedish king named Gylfi, but it's all a sneaky illusion, which is why the book's title is 'Gylfiginning', 'The Tricking of Gylfi'.

Fire and Ice

A long time ago, there was a king named Gylfi, who ruled the land that people now call Sweden.

One day a wandering woman caught his eye. He offered her, in return for her favours, a plot of land in his kingdom; but he stipulated that the land should be only so big that a plough pulled by four oxen could turn up its soil in a single day and night.

She agreed to the bargain and they enjoyed a night of pleasure together. But this woman, named Gefjun, was secretly a daughter of the Aesir.

Gefjun flew north to the land of the giants and gathered four mighty oxen (the beasts were her own children, born from a coupling with a giant). She harnessed the great oxen to the plough, and it cut so wide and so deep that a great mound of soil formed from its blade. And the oxen, their eight bright eyes gleaming like headlamps, hauled this mountain of soil into the water to form a new island, which she named Seeland.

Gylfi saw how he'd been tricked, but he was no fool and had some knowledge of sorcery. He wondered if all the Aesir were so deceptive. He resolved to walk all the way to Asgard, the home of the gods, to find out. Gylfi tried to conceal his identity by travelling as an old man, but of course the Aesir had no difficulty in seeing through his disguise and they prepared an elaborate deception.

Gylfi wandered far from home, but the Aesir diverted him onto a path that led to what appeared to be a village. In the village he saw a great hall, with an impossibly high roof tiled in golden shields, just as the roof of Valhalla, the hall of dead warriors, was said to be thatched.

In the doorway, he saw a man juggling seven swords. Gylfi asked him where he might find lodgings for the night.

'What is your name?' asked the juggler.

Gylfi gave a false name: 'Ganglieri.'

The juggler brought Gylfi through the heavy door, which slammed shut with a mighty thud behind them. Inside the great hall Gylfi saw a riotous spectacle: clusters of people eating, drinking, playing games and fighting.

Presiding over the action were three great and mysterious figures in high seats, each one stacked above the last. Gylfi asked who the figures were.

'In the lower seat,' said the sword-juggler, 'is our king whose name is "High". Above him sits "Just-As-High". And the king in the highest seat is called "Third".'

Gylfi now stood before High, who frowned and warned him he should ask a question that was clever, otherwise he would not leave the great hall alive.

'Then please tell me,' Gylfi gamely asked, 'who is the greatest and oldest of the gods?'

High's voice rang out through the hall: 'We call him the All-Father, but he has many names. He is known as Lord, and as Thruster. He is sometimes called Wise One, or Wish-Granter. He is also known as Spear-Shaker, Weather-Ruler and Glad of War. He lives through all ages and governs all things. He made man and gave him a living spirit that cannot die.'

Now Gylfi asked where the All-Father was before the creation of heaven and hell.

'Back then,' said High, 'he was with the frost giants.'

'SO TELL ME,' said Gylfi, 'what was at the beginning of things?'

This is what the three kings told him.

'There was once an age when nothing existed. Nothing. No sand or sea. No grass nor the cold stream of the ocean waves. Only a yawning void.

'Underneath the void was Muspellheim, the fire realm. It burnt bright and hot, just as it does today. No being can live there except Surt, the Black One, who stands guard over it with a flaming sword. One day in the future, Surt will kill the gods and set the whole world on fire with that sword.

'High above the yawning void was Niflheim, the dark world, where all the coldness comes from. At the heart of Niflheim was a roaring cauldron, which spilt over, and many rivers came streaming from it.

'These storm-rivers rushed out far from the cauldron and hardened, like slag from a furnace, and turned icy cold. There was venom in the waters and it froze upon the surface.

'Hot blasts of wind from below melted the poison ice-crust. It dripped down and formed into the first frost giant, a colossal creature, whose name was Ymir.'

NOW THE SECOND KING, Just-as-High, spoke.

'Ymir dwelt alone in the grassless void. And as he slept, a sweat came upon him, and from the folds of his left armpit he gave birth to a man and a woman. His other hand rubbed against his foot and it gave birth to a son – another frost giant – and from here came all the frost giants.

'Ymir was nourished from the milk of a great cow, whose milk streamed in four rivers from its udders. The cow, in turn, was nourished by licking away at a salty ice-block.

'By the evening, a man's hair was exposed from within the ice-block. On the next day the man's head came forth, and on the third day the whole man was revealed.

'This man fathered more children, who in turn had three sons: Odin, the chief of the Aesir, and his brothers Vili and Ve.

'The three brothers saw the hoar-frost of Niflheim above them, and the furnace of Muspellheim below. But the void between these realms was as mild as a windless sky. Still, there was no shape to it. To give it form and meaning, the brothers realised they would have to murder Ymir. They stabbed Ymir in many places until he was dead. Then they pulled apart his corpse and set to work building everything from the ruin of his body.

'From Ymir's blood they created the sea, which they laid out in a ring around the Earth. They built the mountains from his bones and draped them with his flesh. His enormous teeth were smashed and shattered and made into the gravel, rocks and stones.

'Then Odin and his brothers tore out Ymir's skull, and made from it the roof of heaven. They hoisted it up over the Earth, and in each of its four corners they placed a dwarf; the four dwarves' names are East, West, North and South.

'Then they snatched some burning embers from Muspellheim and flung them in the void to illuminate the night sky.

'Finally, the brothers pulled out Ymir's brain and flung it into the sky to create the bitter-mooded clouds.'

NOW THE KING in the uppermost throne, whose name was Third, spoke:

'Odin and his brothers now made a walled citadel in the middle of the world and called it Midgard. But who was to live there? The brothers walked along the grey shore and found two tree trunks, which they fashioned into the first man and the first woman. Their names were Ash and Elm. The two humans were placed inside the realm of Midgard, and from them came all the people of the Earth.

'Then the brothers constructed a fortress for the gods, which they called Asgard, with high walls and towers. From his high seat there, Odin can see and understand everything that goes on in Midgard below. At the dawn of each day, he sends out his ravens Huginn and Muninn – Thought and Memory – to fly all over the world and bring back information to him. Odin remembers everything they tell him.

The three kings, High, Just-as-High and Third, spin their tale for Gylfi: from an eighteenth-century Icelandic manuscript

'Odin's wisdom is boundless, and he knows he is powerless to prevent his own doom on the day of Ragnarok, when all the gods will be destroyed. His doom is certain. This knowledge haunts him and taints all his pleasures.'

NEXT GYLFI ASKED the three kings what lies at the centre of all creation. 'Yggdrasil,' they said at once. 'Yggdrasil, the world-tree.'

'Yggdrasil,' said High, 'binds the nine worlds together. Its branches reach the top of heaven and its roots touch the lower depths.

'High up in its limbs there is an eagle. Between that eagle's eyes is a hawk. At the base is a foul dragon named Nidhogg that gnaws at one of the roots of the tree. The squirrel Ratatosk runs up and down the trunk, passing spiteful messages between the dragon and the eagle, trying to set one against the other.

'Under the branches of Yggdrasil is the walled city of Asgard, the home of the Aesir. From there, the rainbow bridge, Bifrost, leads down to Midgard, where the humans dwell.

'There is another root of Yggdrasil that leads down to a well, the well of Mimir the frost giant. All the knowledge in the world lives in its waters. Mimir drinks from this well every day, scooping up its waters in the Gjallarhorn.

'One day Odin came to the well and asked to drink from it. But Mimir demanded that Odin first sacrifice an eye to the well. Odin didn't hesitate – he wrenched out his eye and plopped it in the water. Then he filled the Gjallarhorn and drank deeply. This was the price of wisdom: to see everything, Odin had to lose an eye.

'Odin took the Gjallarhorn and gave it to Heimdall, the watcher of the gods, who dwells at the top of the Bifrost. Heimdall hears everything: he hears the grass grow on the far side of the world, and the wool grow on the sheep's back. One day he will sound the Gjallarhorn, to signal the beginning of Ragnarok.

'Odin's wife is named Frigg. Like her husband, she is extremely wise and has the gift of prophecy. From them comes the family of gods known as the Aesir.

'ODIN AND FRIGG had a son named Thor. He is the strongest of all the Aesir. Thor is the god of the skies. He commands the lashing rain, and the thunder that crashes through the storm. Thor rides across the sky in a chariot pulled by goats. Each night, he eats the goats and places their bones on their skin, and the next day they are restored to life.

'Thor possesses two things that make him unbeatable in battle. He has a magical belt called Mengingjard, and when he buckles it around his waist, his strength is doubled. His greatest treasure, however, is Mjölnir, his mighty hammer. Mjölnir is unbreakable. When thrown, it always hits its mark, and always returns to his grasp.

'Another of the Aesir is Loki, also known as the Source of All Lies and the Disgrace of All Gods and Men.

'Loki is a trickster, a shape-changer, and is exceedingly sly. He is beautiful to look at, but his nature is treacherous and he enjoys mischief for its own sake. He is sometimes called Loki Skywalker, because he wears shoes that carry him through the air. He is forever creating problems for the Aesir, and then using his trickery to pull them out of it.

'Loki once coupled with a giantess named Angrboda, the Bringer of Sorrow, and she gave birth to three monsters. First there was Hel, whose face is half blue and half flesh; then there was the Fenriswolf; and finally Jormungandur, the Midgard Serpent.

'Odin knew these children of Loki would bring terrible danger to the world, and so he ordered these monsters to be brought to him. When he saw the Midgard Serpent, Odin flung it into the outer sea. The serpent lurked and grew in the deep and in time it became so big and fat and long it encircled the whole world, long enough to bite its own tail.

'Then Odin took Hel and threw her down to Niflheim, the dark world, to rule over those who die inglorious deaths from sickness and old age. In this place Hel has become sad and cruel. She lives in an icy mansion with many rooms. Her hall is blasted with snow and sleet. Her dinner plates are empty. The knives are dull and the servants are lazy. Her threshold is a stumbling block and she sleeps on a sickbed.'

'And what of the Fenriswolf?' asked Gylfi.

'The Fenriswolf is the most dangerous of Loki's monsters. At first, when Fenris was a cub, the Aesir raised him like a pet. Tyr, the god of battle, would play with Fenris and feed him. But the wolf grew bigger every day, and the gods came to fear that the creature would one day destroy them all. So Odin sent a messenger to Svartalfheim, the realm of the master-smith dwarves, to ask them to forge a special fetter to hold the wolf-monster.

'The clever dwarves fashioned a powerful leash from six impossible ingredients:

> 'The sound of a cat's
> footstep, the beard of a
> woman, the roots of
> a mountain, the sinews
> of a bear, the breath of
> a fish, and the
> spittle of a
> bird.

'The chain that emerged from the dwarves' forge was the strongest in the world, yet as slender, smooth and soft as a ribbon.

'The Aesir showed the Fenriswolf the ribbon and offered to test its strength. They told Fenris that surely such a narrow, silky band could not bind him. Fenris suspected a trick. The wolf-monster agreed to be bound by it, but only if Tyr, who had shown him such kindness, would place his hand inside his mouth as a pledge against deceit. Tyr placed his hand into the maw of Fenris as the Aesir tied the ribbon to the wolf-monster's leg. When Fenris discovered he could not break it, he growled and bit down hard, and Tyr lost his hand. From that day, Tyr would no longer be able to swear an oath or hold a sword with that arm.

'Still, the beast was fettered. The loose end of the ribbon was tied to a great rock and plunged into the earth, yanking the Fenriswolf down with it. There he waits to this day, growing bigger and stronger, until Ragnarok, when he will be set loose to take his vengeance on the Aesir.'

'If that is true,' said Gylfi, 'then why didn't the gods simply slaughter the Fenriswolf while they could?'

'Are you mad?' said the three kings. 'The Aesir would never defile the floor of Asgard with a splash of wolf's blood.'

Loki's Neck

THE LATTER PART of the *Prose Edda* is called the 'Skáldskaparmál', which means 'Language of Poetry'. It takes the form of a dialogue between two figures who strike up a conversation while seated at a feast in the halls of Asgard. Everything is noble and splendid. The hall is lit by dazzling light radiating from Odin's swords. Magnificent painted shields hang from the walls. Strong mead is served and everyone is drunk and merry.

The question is asked: how is it that gold is sometimes called 'Sif's hair'? The phrase, it is said, originates in one of Loki's pranks:

ONE NIGHT, as Thor lay asleep with his beautiful wife Sif, Loki sneaked into their room and shaved Sif's head. When Thor awoke, he knew at once who was responsible. He found Loki, grabbed him by the neck and told him to replace her hair, otherwise he would break every bone in Loki's body. Loki swore he would persuade the dwarves to forge a new crown of hair from gold that would grow like any other hair.

So Loki came to Svartalfheim and announced a competition: he would pit two teams of master-smith dwarves against each other to make spectacular gifts for the Aesir. Odin, Thor and Frey, the god of the fruit of the earth, would be the judges.

The first team, known as the sons of Ivaldi, set to work at their forge. The second team was led by a dwarf named Brokk, who told Loki if he and his brother Etri won, he wanted Loki's head as a prize.

Deep in his underground forge, Brokk pumped at the bellows, while Etri poured in the gold. Then a fat fly buzzed in and tormented Brokk, biting him on his hand, neck and eyelids, sending a stream of blood into his eyes. Brokk took his hand from the bellows momentarily to swat at the fly, which nearly ruined all their work.

NOW IT WAS TIME to present the gifts to the Aesir.

For Odin, the sons of Ivaldi had made a spear called Gungnir that always flew through its target.

Frey was given Skídbladnir, a massive ship that could be folded up like a piece of cloth and put inside your pocket.

Sif was delighted to receive a new crown of golden hair, which grew fast to her scalp.

Then it was Brokk's turn.

To Odin he gave a gold ring that gave birth to eight more gold rings every ninth night.

To Frey he gave a giant boar forged with bristles of gold that could pull a chariot across the sky.

And to Thor he gave the weapon known as Mjölnir, a war hammer that always hit its mark, and would always fly back to Thor's grasp. Mjölnir's only flaw was its handle, which was slightly shorter than Brokk had intended: an imperfection caused by that moment in the forge when he had been distracted.

Thor and Odin marvelled at the power of this weapon. No one cared about the short handle, and so Brokk's team was declared the winner.

Brokk reached for his axe with a smile, to claim Loki's head as his prize.

Loki offered to pay him off with gold.

'No chance of that!' said Brokk.

'Well … catch me, then!' said the trickster, and took off into the sky in his winged shoes.

Thor flew up and dragged Loki back to Brokk.

Loki screamed: 'Wait! Wait! If you do this, you will be in breach of our agreement!'

'How so?' asked Brokk.

'It's true you have a right to my head … *but not to my neck.*'

'But … how can I cut off his head,' cried Brokk, appealing to Odin, 'without his neck?'

None of the Aesir could think of an answer. So Brokk had to content himself with sewing Loki's lips together.

➤➤➤

THOR THE WEATHER god was naturally the favourite of the farmers and fishing folk of Iceland, but Snorri subversively portrays Thor as a bit of a meathead, the man with the hammer for whom every problem is a nail. Thor doesn't need to think too hard when he can just smash his way through every obstacle.

Throughout the *Prose Edda*, Snorri makes clear his deeper affection for the wicked Loki, who can think five steps ahead of the rest of the Aesir. It's not hard to imagine Snorri outfoxing his opponents in the Althing with such a slippery formulation as 'You have a right to my head but not my neck': a clever lawyer's trick if there ever was one. Loki's bad behaviour has all sorts of welcome, if unintended, consequences. His pranks bring exciting new technologies like Mjölnir and Skídbladnir into the otherwise static world of the Aesir. At the very least his misdeeds generate amusing stories to be enjoyed by gods and mortals alike.

And yet it is Odin, the one-eyed king of the Aesir, who is surely the figure Snorri most admires: magisterial and wise, seeing things that ordinary men cannot. At times in the *Prose Edda*, Odin can be as sneaky as Loki. Snorri tells us how Odin used trickery to steal the most precious elixir in the world, the Mead of Poetry.

AT THE END OF A WAR between the two tribes of gods, the Aesir and the Vanir,* they declared a truce by spitting into the same vat. From this spittle they fashioned a creature named

---

* A rival collection of gods associated with nature and wisdom, who would eventually be incorporated into the Aesir.

Kvasir, who was the wisest human who ever lived. Kvasir was so wise there was no question he could not answer.

Then one day, two dwarves, whose names were Deceiver and Screamer, took Kvasir aside and murdered him. They drew out his blood, poured it into a vat and mixed it with honey. This concoction was fermented into a special mead, the Poets' Mead; whoever drank it would receive the gift of poetic inspiration.

The Aesir began to ask questions about the death of Kvasir. The dwarves lied and said Kvasir had choked to death on his own knowledge, for lack of good questions to draw it out of him.

A GIANT NAMED GILLING came to visit the dwarves one day, accompanied by his wife. But instead of showing him proper hospitality, the evil dwarves took him out to sea in a rowboat and drowned him.

They rowed back to shore, and they told Gilling's wife her husband had drowned at sea. Gilling's wife became inconsolable. The dwarves tired of her wailing and dropped a millstone onto her head.

But Gilling had a son named Suttung, and when he learnt of the death of his father, he seized the murderous dwarves and strapped them to a rock at low tide.

When the waters began to lap at their waists, the dwarves screamed and begged for mercy, and offered to give Suttung the Poets' Mead in compensation for his father's death.

Suttung took the mead and hid it inside a mountain, and set his daughter Gunnlod to stand guard over it.

ONE DAY, ODIN WAS TRAVELLING past a farm, disguised as a wandering field-hand, when he saw nine slaves reaping their harvest with scythes.

He offered to sharpen their scythes with his whetstone, and when he did, the scythes cut so well the slaves wanted to buy the whetstone from him.

Odin said they could have it, but only at a high price, and so he threw the whetstone into the air, and each slave scrambled to take it from the other, cutting each other's throats until they were all dead, and now there was no one to reap the field.

That night Odin stayed in the farmhouse nearby with the giant Baugi, who happened to be Suttung's brother. Baugi complained that he was going broke because all his slaves were dead. Odin, still in disguise, offered to do the work of nine men if the giant would give him a draught of Suttung's mead. Baugi said the mead wasn't his to give, but he would do his best to help him get some.

Odin, being one of the Aesir, completed the work easily. He asked Baugi for his reward, and the two went to visit Suttung.

Baugi told his brother of his agreement, but Suttung refused to hand over a single drop of the mead. Odin whispered to Baugi that they should try to steal it, and Baugi nodded.

Odin gave Baugi a powerful drill and told him to bore a hole into the mountain, where Suttung had stored the mead within three great vats. Baugi drilled into the side of the mountain several times without success, and Odin suspected he meant to betray him. When the drilling was at last completed, Odin turned into a snake and slithered into the hole. As he did so, Baugi tried to smash him with the drill, but missed.

Odin crawled inside the mountain, where he found Gunnlod. He slept with her for three nights before she gave permission for him to take three drinks of the mead.

With each gigantic gulp, Odin drained each vat of every last drop. Then he turned himself into an eagle and flew away as quickly as he could.

Suttung saw Odin fly off with his mead, and so he too put on his eagle shape to give chase.

When the Aesir saw Odin flying fast towards Asgard, with Suttung close behind, they put out some vats. As he flew over the walls, Odin swooped down and spat out the mead into the huge containers. As he did so, Suttung came up so close behind him that Odin blew the last of the mead out of his arse and it landed in a disgusting mess.

This final portion was less precious than the other mead, and became known as the Bad Poets' Mead. Anyone was welcome to it, but few cared to drink it.

AND WITH THAT, Snorri Sturluson was able to explain where all the bad art in the world had come from, and what those second-rate poets had been consuming all this time.

No one can be entirely certain how much of the *Prose Edda* was compiled from old Norse mythology, and how much springs entirely from Snorri's imagination. Much of the book chimes with an earlier work known as the *Poetic Edda*, written by an unknown author. Perhaps both works draw on a common source now lost to us.

The tales in the *Prose Edda* don't click together neatly. For Snorri, the important thing was to gather up the great big mess of legends and conserve them on the page, even if they don't always seem to be talking to each other. He was writing in an age when medieval scholars in Byzantium, Rome and Baghdad were diligently compiling great encyclopaedias, fearing that the wisdom they recorded might otherwise seep out of the world and be lost forever. The library shelves of palaces and monasteries were being stocked with compendiums of old poetry, travellers' accounts of faraway places, biographies of the saints, mathematical treatises and observations of the natural world, carefully transcribed and indexed.

Snorri, in the spirit of this era, used the *Prose Edda* to record the art of 'kenning' – the use of roundabout, allusive phrases, embedded in Norse poetry. In this poetic language a battle is 'a wind of weapons'; a serpent becomes a 'valley-trout'; a ship is 'the horse of a sea king'; a sword becomes a 'blood icicle'.

Yggdrasil, the world-tree, has several kennings concealed in its name: *ygg* means 'terrible one' and is yet another of Odin's nicknames. *Drasill* means horse. Odin is known as the god of the gallows, and so 'Odin's Horse' might refer to a hanging tree, because the man dangling on the noose jerks and bobs like a ghastly parody of a rider on his steed.

Ragnarok

LIKE THE BIBLE of the Christians, the *Prose Edda* has both a creation myth and an apocalypse. The final fate of the Aesir is revealed to Gylfi at the end of 'Gylfiginning' by the three kings in the great hall:

'NOTHING CAN ESCAPE RAGNAROK,' said High. 'Not one of the Aesir will be left at the end of it. Its arrival is certain.

'Ragnarok will be heralded by three summerless winters.

'Yggdrasil will shudder and groan.

'Brothers will kill brothers and there will be no kinship in the world.

'A wolf will swallow the sun and another will swallow the moon.

'The stars will wink out, one by one.

'The seas will surge, carrying the Midgard Serpent to the shore, who will thrash about, spraying its putrid venom into the skies and the sea.

'Earthquakes will course through the ground and smash the fetter of the Fenriswolf, who will have grown as big as the Earth. The wolf-monster will want vengeance against the Aesir who bound him into captivity so long ago.

'The Naglfar, the great ship made from the fingernails and toenails of the dead, will slip its moorings and be carried along with the storm-waves. Loki will pilot the Naglfar, and its crew will be the frost giants.

'Surt, with his blazing sword, will come striding down the Bifrost, followed by the legions of Muspellheim. They will come in such numbers the Bifrost will shatter behind them.

'Then Heimdall the watcher will stand and sound his horn, the Gjallarhorn, which will split the air in two and wake the gods.

'All of them – the gods, monsters and giants – will meet on a vast plain called Vigrid, and the final battle will commence.

'ODIN AND THOR don their shining helmets and suits of ring-mail, and fly forward into the attack.

'The Fenriswolf comes trotting into battle with a heavy gait, his dripping maw gaping so wide that the top of his snout will touch the heavens and the lower jaw will drag on the Earth. He would open them still wider, but there is no more room.

'Odin will charge at Fenris with his spear, Gungnir, but Fenris will simply engulf him with a single bite. And that will be the death Odin has long foreseen and dreaded.

'Then Vidar, the silent god, arrives. Vidar is almost as strong as Thor, and on one foot he has a thick shoe, fashioned from all the scraps of leather cut away from the toes and heels of all the shoes that have been made down the ages. He will place his foot inside the wolf's lower jaw and with one hand he will rip its mouth apart. And that will be the end of the Fenriswolf.

'Loki will battle with Heimdall the watcher. The fighting will be fierce because they hate each other so much, and each will kill the other.

'Thor, mightiest of the gods, will fly to the Midgard Serpent and pound its writhing body with his hammer; but in doing so he will be spattered and poisoned with its venom. Thor will smash Mjölnir into the great serpent's head. Then he will stagger backwards and drop dead.

'Then Surt, the Black One, will stalk across the ruined battlefield strewn with the bodies of the gods, the frost giants, and the numberless hordes of Hel. Surt will blast the Earth with fire from his sword, incinerating the whole world.

'FOR A TIME,' said Third, 'the world will be quiet. Then new earth will rise up from the sea, and it will be lush and green.

'The sun will be gone, but the sun's daughter, just as bright and lovely as her mother, will shimmer in the sky. Crops will spring from the ground. In this way, the world will be born anew.

'There will be some who survive the flood and fire. Odin's sons, Vidar and Vali, will meet with Thor's sons, Modi and Magni. Baldur and Hod will arrive from Hel. Then in the glistening grass they will discover, one by one, the golden chess pieces that once belonged to the Aesir.'

Thor pounds away at the Midgard Serpent at Ragnarok:
from an eighteenth-century Icelandic manuscript

THE MYTHIC TALES from the *Prose Edda* would be told and retold for centuries after Snorri's death, and carried all over the world. They would inspire several other heavy drinkers of the Poets' Mead: Richard Wagner, William Morris and J.R.R. Tolkien. As a young teacher at Oxford University, Tolkien persistently argued that all students of English should read the works of Snorri Sturluson, which he said were of far greater importance than Shakespeare's.

In the 1960s, Stan Lee and Jack Kirby transformed Thor into a superhero, and placed him, along with the rest of the Aesir, within the Marvel Comics universe. I grew up reading those comics, and watching the crude animation series 'The Mighty Thor' on TV. It opened with a rousing chorus:

Across the rainbow bridge of Asgard!
Where the booming heavens roar!

You'll behold in breathless wonder,
The god of thunder,
Miiiighty Thor!

Snorri's determination to conserve the old Norse myths might have seemed a forlorn hope at the time, when romantic, courtly literature from the continent was coming into vogue. Yet today, the influence of his *Prose Edda* percolates right through popular culture, from *The Lord of the Rings* to the *Avengers* movies – all of them based on myths compiled and composed by a lawyer in an Icelandic farmhouse, nearly eight centuries ago.

KÁRI HAS RETURNED from his walk. He's in the kitchen, frying some pieces of haddock Icelandic style, with plenty of butter and some local herbs whose names I can't pronounce. He's whistling through his teeth, sounding like an old kettle.

I put the book down for a moment.

'I've been meaning to ask you something. Let's say Íslendingabók tells us that you do have this ancestral connection to Snorri. Would that really mean anything? After all, there are nearly 800 years between you and him.'

'Well,' he says, 'Snorri is not an obscure medieval figure for Icelanders. He's a father figure of art and culture, on an island that really values those things.'

He pushes the fish around the pan a little more.

'And I value them too,' he says emphatically. 'And so I am curious. And I *do* want to know if I have this connection to a person who wrote these works that I treasure.'

'But is it a meaningful connection if it goes back so far?'

'I don't know if it is,' he admits. 'Because between me and Snorri there are no doubt farmers and thieves and fishermen and decent folk who did nothing much in particular. And they naturally form me as much as any other ancestor does.'

I turn the question around the other way: 'Well, if we go back to Íslendingabók, and they find you're *not* his descendent, what would you lose?'

'Well … logically speaking, I don't think I would lose anything. But I would still have an attachment to Snorri through his work. I think what would be missing is that intimate connection – the connection implied by family and blood. There is something so seductive about that possibility. And maybe because I live so far away … it becomes even more alluring …'

Abandoned shepherd's hut, south coast

CHAPTER TEN
(Kári)

Silver Birch Trees

Our Esja

WE RETURN TO REYKJAVÍK for a day before we hit the road again. The morning after our drive back from the cabin, Richard and I walk the downtown streets towards the northern shore of the Reykjavík peninsula. It's still quiet; the shops are closed, and I can hear the steps and conversations of those around us. We find a coffee shop, and afterwards follow a bike path that runs along the sea wall. The path begins at Harpa, a new concert hall that looks like an assembly of dark blue cubes, answering the ocean light with glass and geometric waves.

Further along, a steel sculpture, shaped like the wooden frame of a Viking ship, commemorates the arrival of the Norse. It's popular with visitors, who come down to take pictures of the sculpture with Esja framing it majestically across the bay.

Richard asks about the mountain's name, whether it's mentioned in the sagas. I haven't given it any thought. I know it only as *Esja okkar*, our Esja, a term of deep affection. 'But it must be a woman's name,' I say. 'It ends with an "*a*", the ending for a feminine noun. Maybe a goddess, a mythical figure.'

'*Our* Esja. People love it that much?'

'Yes, like a guardian spirit. Or a friend.'

When we go back to the apartment, I look it up. Sure enough, there exists a short saga about the settlement of the land under the mountain, giving an explanation of the place names in the area. The saga is only about twenty pages long, and so I read it quickly while we're getting our things ready for the next morning, when we'll had head back on the road and into the countryside again.

THE ROAD NORTH out of town falls under the shadow of Esja, and edges past the modest farms and home fields at the mountain's feet. I'm doing the driving. Richard opens his laptop and begins to work.

'I don't know how you do that,' I say. 'I'd feel sick straight away.'

'When I was in the comedy group, we'd spend hours and hours driving – you know, during tours out to country towns. Endless road trips that sent me a little bit mad, to be honest. I read. That's when I realised I could read just about anywhere.'

'Novels?'

'No. Mainly history. Well, some novels. I read *War and Peace* on the road. I remember how I was completely thrown over by it.'

There's a pause, and Richard returns to his work. I want to disturb him. 'Was *War and Peace* as good as *The Avengers*?' In the past, he's teased me about not keeping up with popular culture.

'Yep.'

'Wow. That good.'

'You haven't read it?'

'Yes, I've read *War and Peace*.'

Another pause. Richard is tapping away, writing then deleting. In my mind, I invent my own kenning for it: 'word-rain'.

'I looked up Esja, by the way. You got me wondering about it.'

'Mmm?' he questions.

'The saga says it was named after a rich Irish widow. She settled here – somewhere called Esjuberg, near the base of the mountain. She was a Christian, but also liked some of the old heathen ways. The potential for magic.'

Richard looks up, interested. 'Is it a good story?'

'Not exactly.'

'Right. Well, thanks anyway.' He goes back to his work.

'The thing is, there's something lacking: that dark tension or feeling of deep strangeness that you get in the other sagas.'

'The feeling that you've missed something. Or that the whole thing's about to get tipped on its head.'

'Yes. That's lacking in this saga.'

'Well, you can spare me the rubbish ones.'

I decide he's not getting off quite that easily.

'But Esja's a really appealing character,' I say. 'She's very fond of her foster-son, a boy called Búi. He's bullied and gets the nickname "Búi the Dog". Eventually Búi gets into a fight. But he does so on his own, without even telling his friends. He's outnumbered and overpowered, but manages to escape. Later, when he tells Esja what happened, she chides him for not asking for help. He's a bit indignant and tells her that he didn't need it.'

'Maybe that's why the saga doesn't work,' says Richard. 'I mean, the sagas are about obligations, aren't they? How friends and family need each other, even drag each other into trouble.'

'But after he says that to her, Esja answers with her own comment: "But you haven't been on your own either, have you?"'

'She means her magic?'

'Something like that, I think. Anyway, Búi finally realises that his foster-mother has been keeping an eye on him all along. "I suppose I haven't been alone," he says. From then on, he lets her help him.'

It occurs to me that this might be a good moment to thank Richard for being here with me on this trip, and the help *he*'s offering. But I let the moment pass, and my gratitude slips under the mountain, much like the memory of Esja and the way she presses Búi into accepting help.

I understand Búi's reticence, though – how it can be difficult to ask for help, or admit that you don't want to do it on your own. Even now, as a married man with children, there's a part of me that wants to pull up at the side of the road, and politely invite Richard to make his own way through Iceland, perhaps just get on a plane back to Australia. Then I could take my own time about all this, and maybe even do nothing.

But, then, travelling has a way of calming these feelings. The road takes you to a new place, you have to find your way, and your thoughts have some time to sort themselves out.

Back at the apartment, I was happy enough to accept the saga's account of how the mountain got its name. But for some reason, I continued looking online, and eventually came across another explanation, a modern one that seeks to correct the saga author. *Esja*, it says, has a cognate in Norwegian (*esje*, meaning 'slate') and Swedish (*ässja*, or 'forge'). During the Viking age, there was even another mountain with the same name, far away in the Hebrides.

On this linguistic evidence, it would seem that the name was carried to Iceland by the Norwegian settlers, the Vikings, and was a geographical term that they brought with them.

Now, as we drive on, I find myself having an internal argument about this modern reckoning and how it sits with the saga's version. I tell Richard about it, how there's something about the linguistic account that grates with me.

'What's the problem?' he asks. 'I mean, do we really have to choose? Can't we have both versions at the same time?'

'I guess so,' I say.

A moment passes, but this time Richard doesn't look back down at his laptop, but rather stares at the last cliffs of Esja.

'Don't you miss those days?' I ask him. 'On the road with the comedy group? It must have been pretty exciting. Travelling, parties, groupies.'

'Oh, family life beats all that. Really easily, actually. Anyway, are you kidding me? I'm in Iceland! I'm on the edge of the Arctic Circle!'

'And heading further north every minute.'

Richard smiles. Then he says, 'Now, shut up and let me work.'

WE CORNER INTO A LONG, flat valley. Further to the north, shadows run the length of ridges like strokes of musical notation. Clumps of brilliantly lush grass grow around them. Above, the sky turns from a morning dankness to pale, cloud-flecked blue, and we reach the side of a steep, barren hillside of scree.

On our left, silver birch trees retain a hold in clumpy fields that run down to the sea. The local word for them is *björk*, which the world knows as the name of Iceland's most famous singer. Björk has something of the tree's character, too. The silver birch is small and very strong, and survives in even the most windblown, exposed countryside. Just like a girl in an Icelandic punk band.

An hour after leaving Reykjavík, we cross the land bridge into Borgarnes, the 'peninsula of rocks' – a small town built within a low fortress of boulders and cliffs. Then, half an hour later, the ridges that have followed us along the roadside begin to taper, like sheets of folded cardboard, into the ground. The road winds, at first into valleys of thick grass and streams that fall over grey stones in diamond steps, and then to the village of Búdardalur, long since the harbour entrance to Dalir, 'the dales'.

This area is famous for having first been settled by a woman, unusual for the time. Her name was Aud the Deep-Minded, a strong and independent widow who, like Esja, made her own decision to come to Iceland, then took charge of a large number of followers and a vast area of land that would ensure that she and her supporters controlled the mid-west, an area that also looked like the country's most promising farmland.

Unfortunately, we know very little of the rest of Aud's life, of what came after she'd settled and become a local leader here. But we do know that she lived and farmed at Hvamm, just nearby, where 300 years later Snorri Sturluson would be born – a son of the dales, and their prosperity.

The Mute Princess

ONE OF Aud the Deep-Minded's descendants was a chieftain named Höskuld,* one of the most important men in the Dalir. But Höskuld owned only a very modest house, and he suffered from it. For a long while, he was anxious to build a better one, something befitting his stature.

The Viking settlers had long since cleared most of the woodlands in Iceland. So, one summer, Höskuld made plans to travel to the mainland, to buy timber for his house.

He made the week-long sea voyage, and from Norway travelled south to a large market that was held each year in Sweden.

It was crowded, and the Icelandic chieftain rather lost his way. Walking through the market, he saw a female slave, a beautiful

---

* This Höskuld is not to be confused with the other Höskuld, Njál's foster-son. But I feel I should say that he was in fact the father of Hallgerd, Gunnar's wife. But please return to the main text and try to forget about that for now.

young woman dressed in rags but with a dignified bearing. Höskuld fell for the girl badly.

He asked the slave trader who owned her whether he would sell him the girl.

'Even though she's poorly dressed, she is my finest possession,' said the slaver. 'But I am willing to part with her. And yet I must tell you that she has one fault: she's mute. I want you to know that before you outlay anything.'

Höskuld said he didn't mind about that. And so he spent all of his money – that is, all the money that he had set aside for timber for his new house – to buy her instead.

The girl's name was Melkorka.

WHEN HE RETURNED to Iceland, Höskuld introduced Melkorka to his wife, Jórun. But Jórun didn't give Melkorka a warm welcome. She told her husband that she would put up with his foreign slave, and even allow her to live in their small house with them. But he wasn't to sleep with her.

Höskuld promised her that. He would sleep faithfully with his wife. But then, these were very small houses, and Jórun probably left the two of them alone from time to time. The slave girl fell pregnant and gave birth to a beautiful boy.

Höskuld loved their son, just as he loved the boy's mother. The fair-haired boy was given the name Ólaf, and Höskuld spent time with him whenever he could.

Sometimes, Melkorka would take Ólaf down to play beside a nearby stream. On one occasion, as Höskuld walked along its banks, he heard voices.

He followed the sounds, and to his surprise discovered that it was Melkorka, who sat in the grass speaking Gaelic to her son. She wasn't mute at all, but rather had chosen silence. From the day of her enslavement, she'd spoken to no one but Ólaf.

When the true nature of her silence was revealed, Melkorka was finally able to tell Höskuld about the true nature of her identity too. She said she was the daughter of an Irish king, Myrkjartan. She'd been kidnapped from Ireland as a girl, and eventually sold on to the slave trader in Sweden.

Höskuld, it now seemed, had fathered a prince.

He told his wife Jórun, but she replied that there was no way of knowing whether any of this was true or not. In any case, she added, she had no fondness for Irish women with mysterious pasts.

Not long after Melkorka began to speak again, the two women had a terrible fight. Jórun began beating the girl, until Melkorka retaliated and punched Jórun on the nose.

Höskuld separated the women, and for the time being there was peace in the house. But he knew that he needed to do something. Jórun had tolerated a silent princess, but would not put up with a speaking one.

The next day, Höskuld finally began the construction of a second house. It lay further up the valley, some distance from his old house, and his first family. This house would be for Melkorka, and from then on Höskuld would go there to visit his son, the boy who would eventually travel to Ireland to meet his grandfather, King Myrkjartan.

Melkorka, though, chose never to return to her homeland, even though she was by then free to leave. It seems that Iceland had become her home, and she felt it was too late to go back.

But one day Ólaf would father a child of his own, a very eloquently spoken boy who would be named Kjartan in honour of his royal Irish grandfather.

Not-So-Long Houses

RICHARD AND I STOP for lunch in a renovated merchant building at Búdardalur village. Richard orders fish soup, a staple of village restaurants. I have lamb, which like the fish is almost always cooked perfectly in Iceland. We have a local ale, and I'm a little drowsy when we finish. But when we go outside the wind is up, and it's only about six degrees. I'm suddenly quite awake again.

Our destination is Laugar, a farm and not-quite-village another twenty minutes or so to the north. But we have time for another stop on the way. We follow the signs to Haukadalur valley, where the foundations of a Viking longhouse have been found. The sagas claim it as the home of Erik the Red, the first Norse settler in Greenland; Erik's son Leif sailed to Newfoundland and possibly even further south, to become the first European to set foot on the shores of America.

But before they undertook these great explorations, Erik's life, as that of his famous son, was formed by the small, domestic spaces of the longhouse. And because the sagas are stories about families, you find them peppered with everyday exchanges between men and women in such buildings, and the conversations that people have with the ones they love – about the future, where and how to live, and often about children too.

There's no escaping the violence of the sagas, and recent attempts to rescue the Vikings from their reputation as pirates and vicious opportunists can only go so far. But, as strange as it may sound, violence really is just one aspect of the Viking world and the people. The sagas take us through the whole building, and outside to where the Vikings lived as farmers, sailors, and settlers of new countries. Their weapons are stacked in a house filled with many other treasures.

RICHARD AND I ARRIVE at the Haukadalur valley where Erik lived, and pull into an empty car park with a rather desolate air. A hut office at its side looks abandoned. I peer inside for some sign of an occupant, but nothing.

'We're out of luck,' I say.

'It *must* be open,' says Richard. 'It's the high season.'

The excavated stone outline of Erik's farm lies a short walk up the side of the valley, and near it, the replica longhouse I'd hoped to show to Richard. 'We can take a look at the outside, at least,' I say. 'It's such a shame that we can't go in.'

I'VE VISITED ONCE BEFORE, nearly fifteen years ago with my wife, Olanda. It was late winter, around April, and like today the place was pretty abandoned. Back then, there were nothing like the tourist numbers of today. I hadn't thought the house would be open so early in the year.

But we very tentatively pushed against the front door, and to our great surprise we found an old man inside, dressed in a coarse cloth outfit, sitting in front of a small fire burning in the centre of the hall.

We felt like intruders, and apologised, but he stood up as briskly as he could. 'No, no,' he said, 'you must come in.' He was just waiting for a tour group to arrive. That was why he was dressed like this, he told us. We should look around the house, seeing as we were here. He introduced himself; Atli was his name. He sometimes took care of the place.

Half an hour later, the tour group still hadn't arrived, and we were still talking to the old fellow about the wooden supports, the turf roof, and the stone flooring of the longhouse. He was animated and full of knowledge, but he preferred to speak Icelandic. I translated for Olanda, who didn't speak the language, so that each part of his lecture was given twice.

For all that, I don't remember much of what he said; I never seem to remember much of what I'm told by guides. But I do remember how much he wanted to make us understand the very close, even claustrophobic life of the first Icelanders that he was helping to reconstruct; I think he must have been rehearsing the words in his mind when we first walked in.

It taught me something about the sagas that I'd never properly realised before. The characters' obsession with family was surely a result of never being able to get away from them; these were essentially single-room lives. As much as this is a literature of violence and conflict, it's also one of almost unbearable closeness.

AS I TELL RICHARD about that encounter, I joke that I wouldn't be surprised to find the old guide here now, fifteen years on, still waiting for the tour group. 'He didn't want us to leave, that's for sure.'

'Maybe there *was* no group,' suggests Richard.

As I was then, I'm a little shocked by just how small the house is, at least from the outside. But longhouse ruins found in Iceland have all been small, typically only about sixteen metres long, and six wide. The sagas paint a rather different picture. We read of dining halls that could house feasts for a hundred guests, and, in one work, of a hall 180 metres long – about ten times the size of the largest longhouse ruins that have been found.

Still. The true dimensions are not in figures, but in the stories that were told inside, and the fires that burnt at their centre. The firelight reached 180 metres, even if the outer walls never did.

Richard and I decide to give it a go, as I did with Olanda, and turn the iron handle on the front door. It opens, and we step inside.

'Hello?' I say.

'Hello,' comes a reply.

In front of the fire sits a young woman with long blonde hair. She's dressed in coarse cloth, her eyes lit by the light of the flames. She stands up and says hello again. 'Come in.'

'Is that okay?' I ask. 'We haven't organised to visit.'

'Yes, yes, it's fine. I'm just waiting for a tour group to arrive. You might as well have a look around.'

I decide that the old man has been turned into a young maiden, even if in her own mind she is her own person. Her name is Sólveig. Like her former incarnation, she begins to tell us about the house. But then she does something that I don't think Atli would have done. She directs us to the side of the house and produces two costumes: one for a Viking warrior, the other a jester's. She says we should definitely try them on, to help us with our research.

'Which one would you like?' Sólveig asks. But before I answer, she adds, 'Well, you are the Icelander. You must have the Viking outfit.'

'I hope that's all right with you,' I say to Richard. 'It means you have to dress up as a jester.'

'Just give me the outfit,' he replies.

We put on our new clothes over the top of the old. Our costumes are very different, and yet we look equally ridiculous. My Viking helmet doesn't fit over my ears, and the wolf fur on my shoulders does, at least on me, have a touch of the IKEA homeware about it.

Sólveig, I notice, is doing her best not to laugh. Perhaps that's because she has succeeded in dressing us up as her dolls.

No matter. We have our photograph taken, so that we can prove to others that we took our research for this book seriously.

'I think we've retained our dignity,' I say to Richard.

'No, we haven't,' he replies.

The authors as Viking and jester.

We look around the house, and walk slowly, talking, to the end, where there's a tiny kitchen and smithy. Sólveig tells us that she's only here for the length of the summer, to earn some money during the university holidays. But I notice that she has all the old guide's fondness for the house, and how intimately it must have functioned.

On either side of the central fireplace are wooden booths lined with furs and skins, which doubled as seats and beds. The house isn't big enough for private rooms, but some privacy is created with wooden dividers. On the walls are weapons and shields, tapestries, skins, and a beautifully crafted loom weighted with grey stones.

In the firelight, the room is, above all else, comforting and warm. But again I feel the overwhelming closeness of it. There is nowhere to be on your own, to speak privately or to think in silence. The house, like a family, offers protection and belonging. But for a sense of yourself, or a stolen moment with the one you loved, you would surely have had to escape outside – to the privacy of a stream, a copse, the sheltering muteness of the wind.

Ultima Thule

Of the beautiful regions of the earth
that my flesh and its shadow have tired out
you are the most remote and intimate,
Ultima Thule, Iceland of the vessels
of the stubborn plough and of the constant oar
of the shy sea nets
of the curious light of the motionless afternoon
that effuses the idle heavens from dawn
and of the wind that seeks the lost
sails of the Vikings …

I have chosen
your language, this Latin of the North
that covered the flatlands and the seas
of a hemisphere and resounded in Byzantium
and in the virgin peripheries of America.

—'To Iceland', Jorge Luis Borges

A S THE YEAR 1000 AD approached, the passing of the first Christian millennium was anticipated in Europe with mounting dread and fascination. The clock of history, rolling over from 997 to 998 to 999, seemed to demand a dramatic cosmological climax: the second coming of Christ, as prophesied in the scriptures.

'Truly, our life lasts a thousand years', wrote one French monk. 'And now here we are, arrived at the last day of the very span of time itself.'

Many Christians had come to accept as a matter of course that the world was slowly winding down from its high point in classical antiquity. People living among the rubble and weeds of once-teeming Roman cities presumed that the world was becoming ever smaller, meaner and more barren, shuttering up in preparation for its final crisis. For the poor and hungry, belief in the looming apocalypse was founded on the hope of release from the miseries of this world with the return of Christ in glory. Planning for the future was pointless when the end of history was at hand; best to get one's affairs in order, hunker down, and await the tribulations of the final days.

In Iceland, however, the borders of the world were not shrinking at this time, but widening to a breathtaking extent, stretching out to the furthermost reaches of land and sea, east and west, all the way from the Holy Land to the Americas.

The decades around the first millennium mark a high point of Icelandic endeavour. At home, Icelanders were creating a poetry that would form the basis of the sagas. Other restless souls journeyed to far-flung places, experiencing the thrill and terror of exploration and combat in strange lands, of adventures that would become the stuff of future sagas.

Young Icelandic warriors were lured towards the great metropolis of Constantinople, on the threshold of Asia, to serve in the Roman Emperor's elite Varangian Guard.* The Varangians were prized by

---

* 'Varangian' originates in the Norse compound word *væringi* – pledged companion. Constantinople was the capital of the Eastern Roman Empire, which endured long after the fall of the empire in the West. After its fall in 1453, historians rebadged this civilisation as 'Byzantium'.

the emperors for their fighting prowess and their sworn loyalty to the occupant of the throne. Their drunken revelry on the streets of Constantinople earned them the nickname 'The Emperor's Winebags'. Varangians were housed in special barracks within the grounds of the Great Palace of the Caesars, where an Icelander could befriend other Viking warriors from Norway, Russia and England. Today, Viking graffiti can be seen in the upstairs gallery of the Hagia Sophia, where a bored Varangian carved 'HALFDAN WROTE THIS' in Nordic runes into the marble balustrade.

From Constantinople, a Varangian might be deployed to do battle in Syria or Armenia. If he survived, he would return to his farm in Iceland with silks and gold, and fantastic tales of Constantinople, which they called Miklagard, the Big City.

Meanwhile, other Icelanders, bolder still, ventured into unknown waters, pushing their longboats out of Breidafjördur towards mysterious lands in the west, whose existence was, for them, little more than a rumour.

Their adventures in the new world are recorded in two Icelandic works: *The Saga of Erik the Red* and *The Saga of the Greenlanders*. Both were written in Snorri's time, more than two centuries after the events they describe. The two sagas overlap and contradict each other in places, but much of their information aligns with the archaeological record, and with what we know of the culture and technology of the indigenous peoples of northeast America.

Erik the Red's farm is as good a place as any to begin the story of the Icelanders in Greenland and America.

Re-creation of Erik the Red's longhouse, Eiríksstadir

ERIK THE RED settled here on Iceland's west coast sometime around the year 970. He married a woman named Thorhild, and they had a daughter and three sons.

Erik earned his nickname for his big, russet-coloured beard and his volatile temper. He became embroiled in several nasty feuds with his neighbours, and he killed one of their kinsmen, a man known as Eyjólf the Foul. Erik was consequently declared an outlaw, and compelled to leave Iceland for three years. Deciding to make the best of his forced absence, he purchased a strong ship and told his friends he planned to go looking for a mysterious land rumoured to exist to the west of Iceland.

In 981, Erik set out into the waters of Breidafjördur, sailing past the great cone of the Snaefellsjökull volcano, and then into the dark waters of the Atlantic, towards an unknown shore.

AFTER FOUR DAYS at sea, an immense glacial land came into view. Erik followed its ice-barricaded coastline down to a small offshore island, which he named Eriksey, and he wintered there.

In the summer he set out once more, sailing around the southern cape of this land and continuing up its west coast. The land here was fertile in many places and easily accessible. Fish and game were plentiful.

When his three years of exile were concluded, Erik sailed back to Iceland with many tales of this land, which he named Greenland. He thought such a name would be more tempting for settlers than Iceland, even though the new place was certainly less green and had a great deal more ice. And so when Erik proposed to build a settlement there, he found there were many folk willing to risk a voyage in hope of claiming new land for farming and grazing.

IN THE SUMMER of 986 AD, Erik led a flotilla of twenty-five ships away from the west coast of Iceland. The crossing was harsh, and only fourteen ships reached the shores of Greenland; the rest were driven back or lost at sea.

Erik and his Icelanders sailed past the glacial east coast of Greenland, looped around the southern cape and found good land close to the southwest tip of the island. They established two colonies: the Eastern Settlement (Eystribyggd) and a smaller Western Settlement (Vestribyggd),* and brought ashore their sheep, horses, cattle and goats. Erik and his wife built a farm in the Eastern Settlement, on good land nestled in the fold of a fjord, where they raised their daughter and three sons. They called their farm Brattahlíd, which means 'The Steep Slope'.

The two settlements grew, and eventually 5000 Icelanders came to live in Greenland. They were pleased to discover an abundance of game – deer, foxes, seals and walrus. In the summer, hunting parties trekked north for walrus and stranded whales. The whale hide was strong and leathery, and could be twined into ropes; the whale

---

* Close to Nuuk, the present-day capital of Greenland.

blubber fuelled their lamps. Most precious of all was the harvest of walrus ivory, a luxury good that could be carved into combs, religious figurines and chess pieces.

In this new land, Erik the Red grew out of his youthful brashness and became a wealthy chieftain, respected for his good judgement. All his sons were seen as up-and-coming young men, but none was so promising as Leif Eriksson.

Illustration of Erik the Red (who almost certainly looked nothing like this), from Arngrímur Jónsson, Gronlandia, *1688*

Vínland

LEIF ERIKSSON had been born in Iceland, but had spent much of his youth in Greenland, on the family farm at Brattahlíd. He had grown into a fine, strong young man, and was known to be intelligent and careful in the way he went about things.

In the year 999, Leif decided it was time to visit Norway, to meet King Ólaf Tryggvason. He set out in his longship from Greenland, but strong winds blew him off course to the Hebrides, the chain of islands to the west of Scotland. He and his men spent some months there, waiting for favourable winds.

At the end of the summer, Leif and his men sailed out again, and this time they reached Norway successfully. Leif was welcomed into the court of King Ólaf, who had done much to spread the Christian religion among the Norse peoples. When Iceland agreed to accept the faith at the Althing of the following year, it was in accordance with his wishes – which at times seemed more like demands.

Arriving in Trondheim, Leif entered the king's service and joined his personal bodyguard. Ólaf was impressed with his new recruit and entranced by Leif's stories of Greenland.

One day, he took Leif aside and asked if he was planning to sail back to Greenland in the summer.

'Yes I am,' he replied. 'If that is your wish.'

'Then I think it would be a very good idea,' said the king, 'if you would return to Greenland as my envoy, and preach the gospel of Christianity to the people there.'

Leif told him this would be a difficult command to carry out in Greenland.

'And I can think of no one more suitable for such a difficult task than you,' said the king, clapping his hands onto Leif's shoulders. 'I believe your good luck will see you through.'

LEIF ERIKSSON SAILED out of Norway with King Ólaf's blessing, and had every intention of returning to Greenland. But his ship ran into bad weather and was blown far off course.

Many anxious days passed at sea before he and his crew spied land in a place where they were not expecting it to be found. They sailed past mountainous icebergs and went ashore, but the land had no grass, just a plain of flat granite stones from the sea to the mountains.*

Leif and his men returned to their ship and continued south along the coast, until they came to a land with white-sanded beaches and broad-trunked trees.†

It was still very cold, so they sailed further south, where they discovered a much milder land, with vine trees, maple trees and fields of wild rice. There was plenty of salmon in the streams and high grass for cattle. They named it 'Vínland', which means 'Land of Vines'.‡ Leif and his crew touched the dew of the grass with their fingers and put the moisture to their lips; they thought they'd never tasted anything so sweet.

Further along the coast, they found two Norsemen who had been shipwrecked. Leif gave them food and offered to bring them back to Greenland with him. From that day he was known as Leif Heppni – Leif the Lucky.

LEIF AND HIS CREW left the shores of Vínland and sailed back east to the settlements in Greenland. Leif's safe return to Brattahlíd was greeted with joy and relief by his mother and father.

Keeping his promise to King Ólaf, Leif began to preach the word of Christ to the Greenlanders. His father Erik did not want to abandon the old gods, but his mother Thorhild accepted the faith enthusiastically. After she converted, she refused to sleep with her husband or have anything to do with him, which saddened Erik greatly.

---

*   The description matches the stark granite cliffs on the northeast coast of Baffin Island in Canada.

†   Probably the densely forested coast of Labrador.

‡   Equally, it could mean 'Land of Meadows', bedevilling the efforts of archaeologists to locate the latitude of Vínland on the North American east coast.

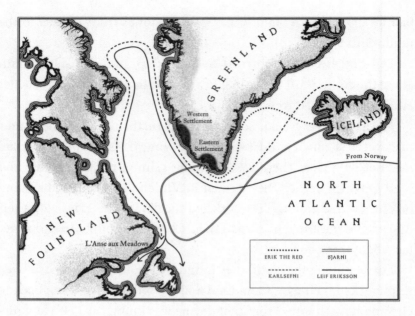

The Norse exploration of Greenland and North America.

There was a guest staying at Brattahlíd at this time, an Icelandic sea trader named Karlsefni, who was held in high regard by many people. Karlsefni approached Erik and asked his permission to seek the hand of a woman at the Eastern Settlement named Gudríd. Erik gave his approval, and Gudríd, well known as a serious and dignified woman, accepted Karlsefni's proposal. And so the Yule feast that year in Greenland was a wedding feast as well. The winter season passed joyously, with entertainment, saga-telling and chess-playing.

There was much discussion that winter of the promising new lands to the west that Leif the Lucky had discovered by accident. Soon there was talk of a voyage, to be led by Karlsefni and another Icelander named Bjarni who also had a ship.

In all, 160 people agreed to join the voyage aboard three ships. They brought livestock with them, in case the land they found was suitable for settlement. Erik the Red's fierce daughter Freydís said she would join the expedition, along with her husband. Erik's younger son Thorvald said he would go too. Neither Freydis nor Thorvald would ever return.

Also among the group was a man named Thórhall the Hunter. Thórhall was known as a sullen, difficult man, who was nonetheless included for his strength and his experience in travelling to uninhabited regions. This man was a heathen, not a Christian.

IN THE SPRING, the three ships sailed up the west coast of Greenland to the Bear Isles.* From there they sailed west for several days.

The first land they came to was covered with great slabs of broken stone, where Arctic foxes hopped from rock to rock. They called this place Helluland – Slab Land.†

After another two days' sailing they reached a heavily forested region with many animals. They named this place Markland – Forest Land.‡

Another two days' sail took them to a stretch of long beaches and small inlets. The area looked promising, so Karlsefni called to him a Scottish man and woman known as Haki and Hekja. These two had been a gift from King Ólaf of Norway to Leif Eriksson; the king had told him to use the couple if he ever needed someone with speed, for Haki and Hekja could run faster than a deer. Leif, in turn, had given them to Karlsefni for the voyage. They wore a special sleeveless garment with a hood at the top, fastened between the legs with a button and a loop.

---

*   Probably Disco Island, off western Greenland.
†   Possibly the Torngat Mountains of northern Labrador, Canada.
‡   Possibly Newfoundland.

Karlsefni put the two runners ashore and told them to go southwards to inspect the land's resources. After three days the couple returned – one carrying grapes, the other wild rice. They affirmed that the land was excellent. So the expedition sailed a little further on until they came to an inlet they called Straumsfjördur – the Bay of Streams.* At the mouth of the inlet was an island, with streams coursing around it. This island was inhabited by so many birds it was near-impossible to put a foot down without crushing an egg.

Deeper within the inlet they found a suitable anchorage and went ashore with their livestock. The land was very beautiful, and the grass was tall and fine.

But the winter that came was very cold indeed. They searched for game and for stranded whales, but there were none to be found. The Christians prayed to God to give them something to eat.

Then Thórhall the Hunter disappeared. A search party looked for him for three days. Karlsefni and Bjarni found him sitting at the top of a crag, staring up at the sky, open-mouthed and dazed. They asked him what he was doing and he said it was none of their business what he did, but he agreed to return with them.

Sometime later the men found a beached whale. Not one of them could identify what kind of whale it was. They cut its meat off and boiled it at once, but the meat made them all sick.

Thórhall the Hunter scoffed at them. 'Do you see?' he said. 'My prayers to the thunder god have delivered food, where your Christian god has failed. Thor has seldom failed me.'

On hearing this, the Christians among them threw the whale meat from the rocks into the sea and begged for God's mercy. Soon

---

*   Possibly L'Anse aux Meadows, on the northernmost tip of Newfoundland. Some have placed Straumsfjördur as far south as the Hudson River, identifying Manhattan as the island in the stream.

after this, the weather became fine enough to go fishing and their hunger was at an end.

In this time, a son was born to Karlsefni and Gudríd, whom they named Snorri – the first Norse child to be born in this new land.

NOW THERE WAS A DIVISION within the expedition. Karlsefni wanted to keep exploring south in search of better land. But Thórhall the Hunter wanted to take one of the ships and go north again towards home.

Meanwhile Karlsefni and his people sailed further south and moored their ships in a fine estuary, with plenty of fish and game. They enjoyed two weeks of peace and pleasure in this sweet land, which they called Hóp (Lagoon).* This land seemed to offer good prospects for settlement.

Then one morning they awoke to see nine skin boats in the estuary.

The men aboard the boats were small, with coarse hair, large eyes and broad cheekbones. In their hands they waved rattle sticks around like flails. Karlsefni and his men hoped it was a sign of peace, so in return they raised their own peace signal, a white shield.

The strange, small men paddled ashore. They wandered around the Norsemen's camp in amazement. Then they stepped back into their canoes, sculled around the headland and disappeared.

The winter set in, and no more was seen of these people they called the Skraelings.† This year the winter was mild, and there was no snow.

---

*   The location for Hóp has been placed anywhere between Newfoundland and New Jersey (Parker, p. 219).

†   Literally 'little men', a Norse word used for the peoples of North America and, later, for the Inuit of Greenland.

Then, early one morning in the spring, the Norsemen awoke to see a great multitude of skin canoes in the estuary, more than they could count, with Skraelings waving rattle sticks on every boat, creating a roaring din. Karlsefni's men signalled peace with their shields again, and the Skraelings stepped ashore and began to trade.

The Skraelings were most eager to purchase swords, spears and red cloth. The Norsemen were not prepared to sell their weapons, but were happy to trade strips of red cloth for animal pelts. The Skraelings happily tied the red strips around their heads.

Trade continued until one of Karlsefni's bulls broke free from its pen and charged into the clearing, snorting and bellowing, startling the Skraelings. They ran to their skin boats, and there was no sign of them for some time.

Three weeks later, the Norsemen saw another great multitude of skin boats streaming towards the settlement. This time the Skraelings were waving their rattle sticks in the opposite direction and howling in a frightening chorus. Karlsefni and his men raised their red shields and moved towards them to do battle.

The Skraelings were armed with war slings, which they used to fling a hail of rocks and stones at the heads of the Norsemen. Then the Skraelings hoisted a heavy black ball into a skin bag attached to the pole of a catapult. They launched the stone, which whistled through the air, over their heads, and crashed into the ground with a thud.* Karlsefni and his men panicked and fled, retreating until they ran into the face of a cliff.

Freydís, Erik the Red's daughter, caught up with the panicked men and confronted them.

---

* Some traditional accounts of the Algonquin people of Ontario and western Québec mention their use of a ballista, similar to the one described here, as a weapon of war (Davis, p. 72).

'Why do you run?' she shouted. 'You should be able to slaughter these wretches like cattle! If *I* had a sword, I'm sure I could fight better than you!'

The men paid her no attention, and turned to flee into the woods. Freydís had trouble keeping up because she was heavily pregnant. The Skraelings were closing in on her.

Freydís ran into a clearing, where she saw the body of a dead man, Thorbrand Snorrason, lying on the forest floor with a flintstone axe buried in his head. She picked up Thorbrand's sword, pulled out one of her breasts and slapped the flat of the sword upon it. This seemed to confuse and alarm the Skraelings. They returned to their skin boats and paddled away. Karlsefni and his men returned to Freydís and praised her courage.

Back at the camp, they discussed what they would do next. Four Skraelings had been killed, but two of their own men were dead. The shaken Norsemen agreed that even though the land was fine and good, they could never be safe and free from fear in such a place. They made preparations to leave and return to Greenland.

ON THE JOURNEY HOME, Karlsefni and Bjarni's ships were separated. Bjarni's ship was carried into the Greenland Sea, where the waters were infested with ship-worms. Soon the vessel's timbers were riddled with holes and it began to sink.

There was a small ship's boat in tow, sealed with tar made from seal-fat, which protected it from the worms. But there was only enough space to take half the crew. Bjarni insisted they all draw lots to see who would board the boat. One of the lots was drawn by Bjarni and he climbed aboard.

As he did so, one young Icelander called down to him from the ship's deck: 'Are you going to leave me here, Bjarni?'

'That's just how it goes,' he said.

'That's not what you promised me when I left my father's farm in Iceland to follow you, Bjarni.'

'Well, what would you have me do?' he replied.

'I suggest we exchange places. You come up here, and I'll go down there.'

'Very well,' said Bjarni. 'I can see you're frightened of death and you want to cling to your life.'

Bjarni returned to the deck of his ship, and he and everyone else who remained on board drowned in the worm-infested sea. Those in the ship's boat sailed to safety.

Meanwhile, Karlsefni's ship sailed north, following the coastline. The crew came upon five Skraelings sleeping near the beach and killed all of them. Among their possessions was a container filled with a food made from bone marrow mixed with blood.*

Further north, they came to a region of dark forests. One morning, Thorvald, son of Erik the Red, was sitting at the ship's helm when an arrow shot him in the groin. Thorvald yanked out the arrow and said, 'This is a rich country we have found. There is plenty of fat around my stomach.' Thorvald died soon after.

They came back to their first settlement, at Straumsfjördur, where they spent the winter. There was much quarrelling at this time, as the men who were wifeless kept bothering the women of the married men.

In the spring they sailed to Markland, where they found five Skraelings – a bearded man, two women and two boys. They stole the children, taught them their language and had them baptised. Then they left the new land for good.†

---

*   A foodstuff closely resembling pemmican, a staple of the Algonquin diet (Davis, p. 72).

†   It's not recorded whether they brought the Skraeling children back with them to Greenland.

After many days at sea, Karlsefni's ship returned to the Eastern Settlement at Greenland, and they spent the winter with Erik the Red. From there Karlsefni travelled to Norway, where he sold the cargo of pelts purchased from the Skraelings.

He was now a wealthy man, and settled his family back in Iceland. His wife Gudríd later made a pilgrimage to Rome, where it's said she met the pope and told him of her adventures in Greenland and Vínland. She then returned to Iceland, where she acquired the name of Gudríd the Far Travelled.

THE NORSE COLONY in Greenland flourished and then slowly declined. Erik the Red had led his settlers there in an unusually warm era, but in the fourteenth century, the northern hemisphere entered a cooler period known as the Little Ice Age. The colder temperatures made life there far more tenuous: the growing season became briefer; hay fell into short supply; the growing sea ice made trade with Norway far more difficult.

Then a new threat emerged: the Icelandic annals of 1379 record an attack on the settlement by Skraelings, in this case the Inuit, who had migrated into Greenland from North America. Adept at hunting, harpooning and dog sledding, they were better suited to the realities of life in the new Greenland than the pastoral Norse people.

The Inuit would later tell their own sagas of their encounters with the Vikings of Greenland, a people they called the Kavdunlait.

One Inuit folk tale mentions a competition between one of their men and the Kavdunlait, in which one of the Norsemen stretched a skin over a frame, and set it up on a little island. The Norseman challenged the Inuit man to see who could fire an arrow closest to the centre of the target. The loser, he said, was to be hurled off a cliff.

The Norseman took his shot and his arrow pierced the target close to the middle.

Then the Inuit man fired and hit the target dead in the centre. The Norseman, by his own rules, now had to die, but would his friends retaliate?

The Inuit archer had no need to worry, because the other Norsemen insisted their countryman keep his word and hurl himself off the cliff. They promised they would take no revenge for this; they said their friend was a fool to wager his life over such a small thing, and that he deserved what was coming to him.

ON 14 SEPTEMBER 1408, a wedding was held in the little stone church of Hvalsey, in the Eastern Settlement of Greenland. Soon afterwards, the couple migrated to Iceland.

It was the last written record of the Norse Greenlanders. The land could no longer sustain them. Within a few decades every one of them was gone, and the colony was still and quiet.

The ruins of the church at Hvalsey, Greenland

KARLSEFNI AND GUDRÍD were not the last of the Norse to visit North America. In subsequent decades, others came to trade with the Inuit people for pelts or to harvest timber from America's forests. But their numbers were too few to sustain a settlement, and the Little Ice Age eventually made sea travel in this region too treacherous.

IN THE NINETEENTH CENTURY, the sagas of Erik the Red and the Greenlanders inspired a quest to find evidence of Viking settlements in North America. Taking the sagas as their guide, archaeologists began their search along the coast of New England in the United States, which they thought best suited the description of 'Vínland'.

In 1961, a Norwegian husband and wife team – archaeologist Anne-Stine Ingstad, and explorer Helge Ingstad – were excited to discover the site of a Viking settlement at L'Anse aux Meadows, on the northernmost tip of Newfoundland. Eight complete timber and turf buildings were excavated, which were dated to the year 1000. The houses included a forge with remnants of slag and bog-iron, and a carpentry workshop for boat repairs. Everyday Norse items were also excavated – iron rivets, a whetstone, an oil lamp, a fastening pin, as well as a spindle and a needle, suggesting that both sexes had inhabited the colony.

This conclusive proof of a Viking presence in the Americas demanded a rewrite of the legend of Christopher Columbus, who could no longer be properly regarded as the first European to step ashore in the New World. Americans who had been brought up on the simple mnemonic 'In 1492, Columbus sailed the ocean blue' had to reckon with the truth that Leif Eriksson and his Icelanders had set foot in the western hemisphere five centuries before the Italian explorer and his men.

Iceland and Norway have quibbled for years over which nation can rightfully claim Leif Eriksson as a native son. The United States seemed to settle the argument (in the minds of Icelanders, at least) when they good-heartedly sent a massive statue of Leif the Lucky to Reykjavík as a gift, to commemorate the 1000th anniversary of the Althing. Today, the statue stands directly in front of the Hallgrímskirkja cathedral, at the highest point in Reykjavík. Leif strikes a heroic pose; the plinth dramatically sweeps up to his feet like the prow of a longboat. He looks like he's claiming Iceland for Iceland. The back of the statue bears the inscription:

LEIFR EIRICSSON.
SON OF ICELAND.
DISCOVERER OF VÍNLAND.
THE UNITED STATES OF AMERICA
TO THE PEOPLE OF ICELAND
ON THE ONE THOUSANDTH ANNIVERSARY
OF THE ALTHING
A. D. 1930.

Leif Eriksson US postage stamp, 1968

ERIK THE RED has to settle for a commemorative longhouse in Breidafjördur. It's somewhat less grand than the heroic statue of his son, but like the saga named for him, the re-creation of his longhouse imparts a deeper sense of what it felt like to live here a thousand years ago, to sit in such a farmhouse and dream of finding a new land in the west.

Salmon River

HALF AN HOUR'S drive north of Erik's longhouse, the landscape changes: the flat, windswept plains give over to rolling hills and valleys. Iceland's hard grandeur is softened and sweetened. The soil is rich, the grass is lush and the sheep are fat. The streams sparkle and the sky is a million miles above our heads.

In the tiny hamlet of Laugar, Kári and I check into a local high school that serves as a hotel in the summer months. The modest building is surrounded by open farmlands. There's a playground for children adjacent to the car park, and a copse of trees on the nearby hillside that Kári calls a 'forest'.

'The sun is shining,' I note, pulling on a jacket, 'but the air is not warm.'

Kári pauses for a moment to recollect a scrap of Icelandic verse, and comes out with:

The sun was beside me,
*Like a thin girl in yellow shoes.**

'That's how the sun feels in Iceland,' he says. 'Just a light presence of warmth.'

---

* The line – '*Sólin var hjá mér eins og grannvaxin kona, á gulum skóm*' – is taken from Steinn Steinarr's poem *Time and Water*.

We go our separate ways after check-in. I read in my room for a while and then resolve to go for a walk into the countryside. I climb over a few farm gates and hike to the top of the hill to take in the view of the patchwork spread of farmlands. There's no one working the fields. The whole country, it seems, is taking its afternoon nap.

As I come back down the hill I hear a voice call out to me. I turn to see Kári reclining against a log, basking in the summer sun. He looks a little stricken, like he's homesick for Iceland while in Iceland. In nine days' time he and I will go back to Australia, and Kári will have to resume his exile from this island that keeps calling to him from the far side of the world.

THE HOTEL'S RESTAURANT has the usual Icelandic staples of simple, well-cooked fish and lamb. It's a little pricey, so Kári and I agree to stick to the cheaper end of the menu. On the drinks page I spot an exotic item. 'What is Imperial Russian Stout?' I ask the waitress.

'Oh, it's very good,' she says reassuringly. 'You should try it.'

Two small bottles arrive promptly and are poured into the glasses, and the stout neatly separates into a pristine white disc, floating atop a velvety black body. The taste is smooth and rich.

'This might be the best stout I've ever had, Kári.'

'It makes the food taste better too,' he says, glancing admiringly at the bottle.

I see a ghostly film of alcohol on the rim of the glass. A quick inspection of the label reveals that this unusually delicious beverage has an alcohol content of twelve and a half per cent, close to triple the standard dose.

'Well, Richard,' Kári says, raising his eyebrows, 'that is quite a lot, but I think we'd better have another round anyway.' The waitress also thinks this is a capital idea, and another two bottles are brought to the table.

Then I order another two.

When the plates are taken away, Kári says that, notwithstanding our earlier resolution to go easy tonight, perhaps we'd better have some cheese, and, while we're at it, we might as well get in another round.

WHEN THE BILL arrives at the table, we're a little shocked. It seems I misread the prices, and our adventure in Russian stout has cost us a small fortune, the equivalent of two bottles of Dom Perignon. (Did we have six bottles or eight? Ten?) But we're in too much of a good mood to make a fuss in front of the good folk of the Salmon River district.

This area is the country of *Laxdaela Saga*, the story of the people of Salmon River, which is why we've come here. *Laxdaela Saga* is essentially the tale of a love triangle, and at its apex is Gudrún Ósvífsdóttir, the most famous woman of medieval Iceland. Manning the other two points on the triangle are the foster-brothers Kjartan and Bolli.

'Like most of the sagas,' Kári says, 'we don't know who the author is. It was written in Snorri's time, but not by him. We know the author probably came from this district, because it's written with such an intimate familiarity with the countryside. And there are many people who believe the author had to be female, that only a woman could write so knowledgeably and sympathetically of Gudrún's dilemma.'

The cheese plate has been cleared and I have an idea.

'Hey. Let's go out and record Gudrún's story tonight. The night air and the Russian stout should bring out something interesting in the telling.'

OUTSIDE THE HOTEL, it's close to midnight, and the Arctic sun has finally taken its leave of us. The blue-grey night sky is clear and cold. I hope no one is observing us; I'm aware of how odd we look: two grown men creeping off into the woods at midnight with sound equipment. The stout has brought out a kind of boyish enthusiasm in both of us.

We talk until we reach the edge of the small, dark forest. It's very still, and smells of wet earth. We each settle on a damp log. Kári looks me in the eye and says, 'I want to tell you the story of Gudrún. And even though she did a terrible thing, I want you to love her, like *I* love her.

CHAPTER TWELVE
(Kári)

The Saga of Gudrún

GUDRÚN
a young woman living at the farm of Laugar, in the Dalir district in Iceland's mid-west

KJARTAN
a young man living nearby at a farm at Laxá River

BOLLI
Kjartan's best friend and foster-brother

GEST
a prescient man and friend of Gudrún's family

HREFNA
a young woman who knows Gudrún, Kjartan and Bolli

THIS IS THE STORY of a woman I love. She lost everything, and her answer to that loss was terrible. She wanted to bring everyone else down with her. But I love her all the same.

Gudrún was a very pretty girl, and was thought the loveliest woman in Iceland. She had beautiful manners, and she cared about them. But she began to have troubling dreams.

In one, she was wearing a lovely bonnet, but it didn't suit her. She didn't like it, so she tossed it off and threw it into the water.

In the next dream, Gudrún was wearing a silver ring that she liked very much. But it slipped off and fell into a lake.

In the third dream, she was wearing a gold ring. She thought it must have been even more valuable than the silver ring, and yet it turned out not to be so. When she hit the ring against a stone, it split and spilt blood.

In the last dream, she was wearing a large helmet. It was covered in jewels and was too heavy for her. It toppled off and fell into the sea.

These dreams troubled her. She wanted to know what they meant.

Gest, a friend of her father's, was visiting the farm. He was known for being able to read such dreams and make prophecies. Gudrún confided in him and asked him to tell her the truth.

Gest said, 'Gudrún, your first dream was about your first husband, whom you won't like and whom you'll divorce. Your second dream, the silver ring, was about your second husband. You will love him, but you will lose him to drowning. The third dream, the gold ring, is about your third husband, who won't seem as fine as that metal is precious. When it split open and spilt blood, that was a sign that he will be murdered. And your last dream was about a great chieftain, the heavy helmet. You will love him but you will also lose him, when he drowns in the sea.

'Gudrún, you have seen your four marriages.'

She flushed red, but thanked him for the reading. Soon afterwards, Gest rode on his way.

Just as he had said, Gudrún's first husband turned out to be a man she didn't like and divorced, and her second husband was a man she did adore but lost through drowning.

Time passed. Gudrún had no choice but to wait for the arrival of her third husband.

NOT FAR FROM GUDRÚN'S FARM is a river called Laxá, or Salmon River, and another farm as prosperous and famous as

Gudrún's. It was owned by a local chieftain, Höskuld, but it was equally well known for the two handsome young men who grew up there: Kjartan, the chieftain's grandson, and his foster-brother and best friend Bolli.

They loved swimming in the river. One day, Gest, the man who'd interpreted Gudrún's dreams, was riding along the river when he saw the two boys coming out of the water. They were drying themselves and getting changed.

Gest was travelling with his own son, who looked at his father and noticed that he was crying as he watched the boys down by the river. He asked his father what was wrong. Why was he crying?

Gest replied, 'I shouldn't say anything. But it pains me to see such fine young men and to know that one day one will kill the other, and in so doing will bring about his own death.' He rode on without saying anything else.

The foster-brothers loved going to Laugar. Gudrún lived there, after all, and it was probably worth the trip up to the coastline to see Gudrún swimming in the hot streams that lie near the farm. Kjartan and Gudrún spent more and more time together, and Bolli was always there too.

A bathing pool at Laugar

Eventually, Gudrún and Kjartan fell completely in love. It was obvious to everyone in the district that they were perfectly suited: both beautiful in appearance, and so refined in their manners. But Kjartan wanted to travel before he settled down and got married. He wasn't ready to become a farmer yet. He told Gudrún that he wanted to go abroad with his foster-brother Bolli.

'Can't I come?' Gudrún asked.

Kjartan replied, 'No. But wait for me. I'll only be gone for three years. Wait for me to come back.'

'You can't ask me to wait,' said Gudrún.

They left things at that.

Kjartan and Bolli went to Norway, and straight away Kjartan was successful at the royal court. He attracted the attention of a princess – the king's sister, no less. But still he was determined to return to Iceland at the end of three years.

KJARTAN, THOUGH, DIDN'T keep his promise to Gudrún. He was held back in Norway.

His foster-brother Bolli did get away in time, and returned to Iceland within three years. He rode straight to Laugar to visit Gudrún. He told her that Kjartan was doing extremely well at court, enjoying enormous success there.

'That's to be expected,' said Gudrún.

Bolli added that he didn't think it very likely that Kjartan would ever come back to Iceland. He lied and told her that Kjartan had fallen in love with the king's sister. But she retained her composure and pretended to be pleased for Kjartan.

Bolli then offered his own hand in marriage to Gudrún.

'I'll never marry another man as long as Kjartan's alive,' she said.

In the months that followed, Bolli kept pressing. He insisted that Kjartan would never return, and eventually Gudrún gave in and married Bolli. They settled at Laugar, and Bolli became part of Gudrún's family.

People said there wasn't much love on Gudrún's side of that marriage. As predicted, the gold ring, her third union, wasn't as precious as she'd thought it might be.

Kjartan didn't know any of this; he was still in Norway. But he did still mean to get away, and eventually he was able to. On the day he left, the king's sister walked with him down to his ship. She took out a present. But she added that it was for Gudrún alone, the woman she knew must be drawing him back. She handed Kjartan a beautiful headdress and said, 'Give this to the woman who's waiting for you in Iceland.'

Kjartan left Norway and sailed to the west coast of Iceland, where he moored his ship. Lots of people came down to the dock to welcome him home. He asked them the news, and they replied that it wasn't good. His best friend Bolli had married Gudrún. He was too late.

A young woman called Hrefna visited Kjartan on his ship. She began looking through the different goods and treasures that he'd had brought back with him. Kjartan watched her handle his belongings. Then he saw her try on the headdress that had been given to him by the king's sister, for Gudrún.

He stepped up to Hrefna and said, 'The headdress suits you. I want it back, and also the girl who's wearing it.'

SO KJARTAN MARRIED Hrefna, and over time was able to fall in love with the girl who'd tried on the headdress. But there was still something strong between him and Gudrún.

Because the two couples lived close by, they began to visit each other. Once, when Gudrún went to Kjartan's farm, she approached his wife Hrefna and asked if she could see the headdress that Kjartan had brought back from Norway. Hrefna agreed to show it to Gudrún. When Gudrún saw it, she said to Hrefna that she thought it was 'the most valuable treasure ever to come to Iceland'.

Later, when Gudrún was walking past Kjartan's room, she stopped for a moment to watch him. He was getting dressed, and was in the middle of a conversation with someone in another room, who yelled out a question about the seating arrangements for dinner. The high seats were reserved for the most honourable people in the room. The man asked, 'Do you want Gudrún to have the high seat, as normal?'

'No,' he replied. 'From now on, Hrefna my wife is always to have that high seat in this house.'

Some time later, it was time for Kjartan and his wife to make a visit to Gudrún's farm. Hrefna decided that she would bring the headdress with her. Once again, Gudrún asked to see it. She looked at it, and then it was put away in a storeroom where the women's belongings were kept.

The next day, when Hrefna went to fetch her headdress, it was gone.

Kjartan was furious. He demanded to know who the thief was.

Gudrún replied, 'Whoever stole that headdress *deserves* to own it.'

THE VISIT WAS wound up. But not long afterwards, Kjartan returned to Gudrún's farm with a group of men, and from the outside he locked all the doors, trapping Gudrún, Bolli, the family and the servants inside for three days. He humiliated her, and made her and the others stew in their own filth.

When Kjartan returned home, he spoke to Hrefna about what he'd done. She had heard some reports already. She said, 'I hear you had a long conversation with Gudrún. Did you get a chance to see her wearing the headdress?'

'No,' snapped Kjartan. 'But you can be sure of this: if she'd been wearing it, there would have been no woman in Iceland more beautiful than her.'

MEANWHILE, GUDRÚN DEMANDED action. She told Bolli that she wanted Kjartan dead. But he didn't respond. He didn't want to fight his closest friend, even if they had become enemies.

One day, she and the household at Laugar heard that Kjartan was riding by. She said to Bolli, 'It seems that Kjartan can ride wherever he wants, because nobody here dares to stand up to him, no matter how much he insults us.'

With that, Bolli and Gudrún's kinsmen set out to ambush Kjartan. They rode to the next valley, Svínadalur – Pig Valley. Bolli and his men approached it from the north, and met Kjartan coming in the other direction.

Bolli's men began to attack, and Kjartan defended himself with a spear. Then he took out a sword. It wasn't a good one; it kept bending, and he had to keep stopping to straighten it with his foot. But still he managed to keep them back.

Kjartan saw Bolli standing nearby, watching. He called out to him, 'What's wrong, Bolli? Why won't you attack?'

His foster-brother ignored him. But then Bolli's companions joined in. 'How can you stand there and watch us getting beaten by Kjartan? Why did you come out if you weren't going to attack him?'

Finally Bolli drew his sword; it was called Leg-Biter. He stepped forward.

As soon as Kjartan saw the sword in his foster-brother's hand, he dropped to his knees. He said, 'What you're about to do is a terrible thing. But I would rather be killed than put up a defence against you.'

Bolli stabbed him, and Kjartan fell. Bolli caught him and held him in his arms. Kjartan was dead.

BOLLI WENT BACK to the farm at Laugar and told Gudrún what he'd done. She said she was pleased at the news.

But Bolli had signed his own death warrant, and not long after the killing, Kjartan's kinsmen came after him.

The attackers killed Bolli, then found Gudrún at a nearby stream. One of them, a man called Helgi, stepped up to Gudrún and told her what they'd done. She was pregnant with Bolli's child by now, and wore a long blue and white sash over her tummy. Helgi took out his sword, still covered in Bolli's blood, and smeared the blood across Gudrún's sash.

One of Helgi's companions said, 'That's an awful, disgusting thing to do.'

'Don't worry,' said Helgi, 'one day the boy in Gudrún's belly will find me and be my killer.'

She did give birth to a boy, whom she named Bolli after his father. That boy would grow up to be the man who killed Helgi.

GUDRÚN MARRIED a fourth time, to a man she came to love, a chieftain. But, as foretold by Gest, he too died, drowned in the sea nearby. He was the heavy helmet that she'd seen in the fourth dream, the one that had toppled into the sea.

After that, Gudrún lived on her own in some sorrow and grief. She became Iceland's first nun at a monastery at Helgafell in Iceland's mid-west. But her son Bolli visited often, and towards the end of her life he asked her a question. 'Mother, which of your four husbands did you love the most?'

She answered, '*Þeim var ég verst er ég unni mest.*' It means 'I was worst to the one I loved the most.'

Wild cotton near Laugar

CHAPTER THIRTEEN

(Richard)

The Sand Winter

A CLOUD NOW SHROUDS the stars and moon. Kári and I can hardly see each other in the forest. Gudrún's enigmatic words linger in the night air: 'I was worst to the one I loved the most.'

'She means Kjartan, doesn't she?'

'Or Bolli,' says Kári.

'How can that be Bolli?'

'You know, *I* think it's Kjartan. I think she *did* love him the most. But was she the worst to him? She manipulated Bolli into murdering his foster-brother, which made his own death inevitable. Even today, there is plenty of disagreement here as to which brother Gudrún is talking about.'

'It's a sad thing to confess in your old age.'

'Yes. It's heartbreaking,' says Kári. 'And this is why I still love Gudrún. It's for that tender moment when we see the crack in all that anger, and underneath it, the wound of love.'

WE PACK UP our recording gear as best we can in the not-quite-dark, and feel our way back down the hill.

'We seem to be talking a lot about the women in the sagas – Gudrún, Hallgerd, Melkorka. So many of these stories seem to turn on what a woman says.'

'The women have to come at things without swords,' Kári answers. '*Words* are their weapons. And if you rely on words to make things change, there's a good chance you'll say something interesting.'

Later, in my room, I think of the bleak coda to Gudrún's saga, and I fall asleep thinking of a line from an Irish playwright: 'It was a long time before I realised that love turned upside down is love for all that.'*

GUDRÚN, LIKE MOST Icelandic women, found her voice was just one among many when it came to the business of finding a suitable husband. In medieval Iceland, as in the rest of Europe, the wishes of daughters were often trumped by the dynastic plans of their fathers and brothers. But while a woman had no legal right to reject a suitor, she could initiate a divorce and retain some of her assets. Some women, like Snorri Sturluson's daughter Thórdís, were able to extricate themselves entirely from their families and live on their own terms.

Saga scholar Carol Clover argues that the standard model of the rights and roles of men and women doesn't really apply to Iceland during the saga era. Iceland at this time, she says, is better understood as a society composed of two classes: a primary group consisting of able-bodied men and outstanding women, and a bigger, broader class made up of everyone else – other women, children, slaves, the old and the infirm. It amounts to a distinction between the admirable and the pitiable, the strong and the weak, the powerful and the disempowered, and either sex might belong to either class. A man might have slipped out of the first category as he became older

---

*   From Hugh Leonard's play *Da*.

and less able to physically defend himself, whereas a widow might only have become more powerful with her advancing age. She could not technically become a chieftain, but she could own a chieftaincy and wield great power through it.

The respected matron was a concept embedded in Icelanders from childhood. Iceland was a maritime society, and while men were away at sea, women would take on the roles of manager, builder, hunter and farmer on top of their traditional duties. With their father absent, children would look to their resourceful mother for wisdom and advice. Viking gravesites also suggest a blurring of male–female roles: while most women were buried with traditional female grave goods, there are other sites where women are laid to rest with weapons, carpentry tools and hunting gear.

In pagan times, the primary purpose of marriage was to manage the passing on of property from one generation to the next, or from one family to another. Extra-marital relations, for men at least, were seen as normal, although a wife would enjoy more power and autonomy than a concubine.

The arrival of Christian marriage brought with it the expectation that sexual activity would be confined to the marital bed for the purpose of procreation, but this idea took hold very slowly in Iceland. In the thirteenth century it was still common for men like Snorri to have several concubines. And, as in pagan times, the property rights of children born within marriage still took precedence over those born outside of it.

Truce-Biter

1231: BY THE WINTER of that year, both of Snorri's legitimate children, his daughter Hallbera and his presumptive heir Jón Little Trout, were dead. His second daughter Thórdís wanted nothing more to do with him, and his youngest, Ingibjörg, was estranged from the husband Snorri had chosen for her. Snorri did have one other son, Oraekja, who was now twenty-six years old, but he was reckless and unstable.

This was the year known as the Sand Winter, when an offshore volcano erupted and ejected scalding gobs of ash onto farms across Iceland. Snorri's cattle were scorched and his fields were littered with volcanic sand. The disaster was demoralising and seemed an omen of worse times to come.

For the moment, the peace between Snorri and his ruthless nephew Sturla was holding. Sturla was showing greater restraint and maturity: instead of taking his revenge for the attack on Saudafell, he reached a settlement with Thorvald's sons, and he began to exercise greater shrewdness and more self-control in his dealings. This made Sturla a wealthy and admired figure across Iceland.

In December that year, Snorri invited Sturla to his Christmas feast at Reykholt. As the platters were taken away, Snorri put a proposition to his nephew. He wanted to invite the sons of Thorvald to Reykholt, to arrange for them to marry two of his step-daughters, but the brothers would need to ride through Sturla's lands along the way. Snorri, suspecting Sturla still harboured murderous intentions towards them, asked him to give his word that the brothers could pass through his territory unharmed.

Sturla shrugged. He told Snorri he'd patched up his differences with the sons of Thorvald, compensation had been paid, and there was really no need for him to offer assurances of safe passage. Snorri insisted that Sturla be sworn to it anyway.

'Here is my hand on it, if you like,' Sturla said.

Snorri pronounced the formal oath of truce, but after Sturla left the room, Snorri's older brother Thórd said, 'I have to say, I didn't think Sturla had the right expression on his face while making that oath.'

'I'm not worried.' said Snorri. 'Sturla will keep the truce.'

SNORRI NOW WROTE to the sons of Thorvald and invited them to come south to meet his step-daughters. When the brothers rode into the dales, a spy in their entourage slipped away to alert Sturla to their presence.

Sturla received the news outside the doorway of his farmhouse. He summoned his men and they rode down the hill, looking for the brothers. The riders crossed a stream and found the sons of Thorvald in a yard of haystacks, accompanied by their entourage of friends.

The two rival groups shouted taunts at each other. One of Sturla's men, a Norwegian archer, tentatively shot three arrows into the haystack yard, but each one missed its target. Sturla contemptuously slapped the bow from the archer's hand and urged his men on. Moving forward gingerly, they picked up stones and hurled them at the young men.

One of the teenagers threw a rock in retaliation, and struck down one of Sturla's men. 'One down! More to come!' he shouted.

Then another of Sturla's followers, Gudmund the poet, was struck down by a second rock.

'Leave him there!' Sturla said with a laugh. 'He lies down like that in every fight.' Then he turned to his men and ordered them to resume the attack, and they flung a hail of stones at the defenders. One rock hit the older brother, Thórdur, and knocked him down. He got groggily to his feet and then was hit in the head by another one.

Sturla now ordered his men to line up with their shields and advance slowly, jabbing forward with their spears. Thórdur, battered and bleeding, lost all his bravado and shouted an offer of truce. He offered to give up his lands, then he promised he would leave Iceland for Norway.

But Sturla was implacable. Several of his men hesitated: they were farmers, not trained warriors, and they were moved by Thórdur's pleading. Sturla angrily ordered them forward.

More rocks were thrown, but there was still a dread of killing and a fear of death. No one, it seemed, wanted to risk throwing themselves into close combat. Again, several of Sturla's men begged him to be merciful, so he shouted an offer to the defenders: he would offer a truce to everyone in the yard, except for the brothers.

At that, the defenders gave up their weapons and left the two young men to die alone.

One of Sturla's men ran at the younger brother, whose name was Snorri, and struck him in the knee with his axe, which almost sheared his leg off. He felt around the stump with his hand, and said with an eerie smile on his face, 'Where is my foot?'

Then Sturla walked up to Thórdur, the older brother, and ordered him to lie down. As he did so, the young man crossed himself and prepared to die.

The first stroke hit him across the shoulders. The second stroke came at the neck, and with the third stroke the head was cut off entirely.

His younger brother, bleeding heavily, watched in silence, concealing his agony. When the axeman turned to him, he raised his hand and cried out, 'Don't kill me yet! I have something to say!'

Then he too was decapitated before he could say it.

AS STURLA RODE OFF with his men, he joked about Snorri's likely reaction to these murders: 'Will he compose poetry about them?' he sneered.

Sturla was now officially a *griðbítr*, or truce-biter. By Viking custom, a *griðbítr* was to be shunned, driven away from God and good men, and treated as 'an outcast, a wolf in places where Christians pray and where heathen worship'. The truce-biter was to have no rest 'in the places where the fires burn ... where the ship sails, where the sun shines, where the snow lies'.

But public reaction to Sturla's shameful breaking of his oath appears to have been muted. It was a sign of the times.

Despite Sturla's betrayal, Snorri calculated that it would go better for him to swallow his indignation. He was pursuing a lawsuit against his former son-in-law Kolbein for deserting Hallbera, and for that he needed Sturla's support in the Althing. So when Sturla offered to pay him compensation for the murder of Thorvald's sons, he cold-bloodedly accepted.

Typically, Snorri pressed the lawsuit hard in the assembly, and the settlement went very badly for Kolbein: Snorri was to be awarded half of Kolbein's chieftaincies, and to be paid a sum of money. Kolbein also had to pledge to support him in the Althing. Finally, to repair the bad feelings between them, Snorri and Kolbein agreed that Kolbein's sister Arnbjörg could marry Snorri's last remaining son, Oraekja.

Kolbein made the preparations, but Snorri snubbed the bride and groom and refused to come to the wedding, making clear his disdain for Kolbein, and perhaps for Oraekja too. Once again, Snorri's high-handedness had instilled a dangerous resentment in a son, and a son-in-law.

Then Snorri made exactly the same blunder with his younger son as he had with Jón Little Trout. When Oraekja asked for the estate at Stafholt as a bride price, Snorri refused.

But instead of storming off to Norway, Oraekja broke away and became a bandit. He gathered up a gang of followers and began a campaign of terror, plundering the countryside like a Viking raider, stealing horses and provisions.

Oraekja began by launching raids on the very lands his father had already given him. Then, in a far more dangerous move, he led his men south into the lands controlled by Sturla. There he murdered Odd Álason, one of Sturla's closest friends, burning him to death inside his farmhouse.

STURLA WAS UNABLE to take his revenge against Oraekja just at that moment. He was in Norway, where he'd been summoned to resolve a longstanding legal judgement against him by the Archbishop of Trondheim.

Back in 1222, Sturla and his father had sailed with a band of warriors to capture the fanatical bishop of Hólar, Gudmund the Good, who had been hiding with his men on the island of Grímsey. Sturla had wanted revenge against the bishop for the killing of his brother.

The sun was just coming up on the beach at Grímsey when Sturla's ship pulled ashore with 300 men aboard. When Sturla spotted Gudmund's chief defender, a man named Aron, he leapt from his ship in a fury, but then his foot slipped on a heap of seaweed and he fell over. As Sturla flailed about in the slimy mess, Aron moved in with his sword for the kill, but one of Sturla's men stepped in and blocked the blow with his shield. In a moment Sturla was back on his feet. Then his men flung so many spears into Aron that they propped him up from all sides and he could hardly fall down.

Sturla and his father found Bishop Gudmund in the church. Sturla contemplated cutting his tongue out, but then thought better of it, and had two priests castrated instead. Gudmund was seized and sent into exile.

Safe in Norway, the outraged Gudmund appealed to the Archbishop of Trondheim, the overseer of the Icelandic church, who issued a legal summons to Sturla to come to Norway and answer for his sins.

A decade had passed since the attack on Grímsey Island, but Sturla needed to resolve the issue if he was to be on good terms with King Haakon.

In Norway, Sturla readily submitted to the archbishop's judgement. For penance, he was required to make a pilgrimage to Rome. *Sturlunga Saga* records that Sturla submitted himself to a painful ordeal through the streets of the Eternal City:

> *He was led barefoot from one church to another throughout the city and was chastised in front of most of the cathedrals. He bore this manfully, as was to be expected; but throngs of people stood outside and marvelled and lamented that such a handsome man should be so ill-treated, and they could not hold back their tears, neither men nor women.*

Sturla, now cleansed of his sins, made his way back to Norway in 1235, where he was brought before Haakon. The former boy king was now thirty years old and approaching the height of his power, and his plans for Iceland had not changed. He asked Sturla if he thought it would be possible to bring Iceland under Norway's dominion. Sturla assured the king, just as Snorri had two decades earlier, that it would indeed be possible, as long as the king had a popular and powerful Icelandic chieftain acting on his behalf.

Haakon asked him to go to it.

Sturla, not Snorri, was now Haakon's man in Iceland.

Surt's Cave

IN THIS DECADE, the last of Snorri's life, Iceland was afflicted by a pervasive sense of loss, of moral decay.

Sturlunga Saga records a farmer's nightmare from this time. The farmer dreamt he was with a group of friends who had gathered to play a ball game in a yard, when a tall figure clad in grey rags approached them. They asked his name and he replied:

Kar I am called
And I have come here
To shake the world
And the hearts of men,
To shatter strongholds
And bend the bows,
To quicken fires
And awaken hatred.

The dream figure asked the men why they weren't playing, and they answered that they didn't have a ball.

'Here is one,' he said. From his robe he produced a heavy stone and beat one of the men to death with it. Then each man took his turn in picking up the rock and striking one of the others dead.

Iceland at this time seemed stuck in this nightmare of meaningless violence. The feuds of the powerful chieftains had poisoned relations between neighbours and kinsmen. Too often, fathers and sons were summoned from their farms to fight the battles of their leaders, armed mostly with rocks and makeshift spears. Icelanders were coming to the same conclusion as King Haakon: that the Icelandic commonwealth had become a failed state.

SNORRI STURLUSON HAD LOST his elder son in a brawl. Now it seemed he was bound to lose his younger son the same way, as Oraekja ran wild across the Westfjords with his gang of bandits. Snorri could do nothing to stop these outrages.

In 1233 Oraekja rode with eighty of his followers onto his father's lands. Snorri stationed some men on the walls of Reykholt, but a party of Oraekja's men crept in through the secret passage from Snorri's outdoor bath.

Now, with his father at his mercy, Oraekja presented Snorri with a demand to be given the estate at Stafholt. Snorri quickly agreed, and a full-scale attack was averted.

The news spread fast across Iceland: the great and powerful Snorri Sturluson had been put under siege in his own home, by his own son.

Snorri couldn't stop Oraekja, but his nephew Sturla surely would, when he returned from Norway.

AFTER A THREE-YEAR ABSENCE, Sturla sailed back to Iceland in 1235 as King Haakon's new lieutenant. He came ashore and rode to his father's estate, where he learnt of Oraekja's raids on his property, and of the murder of his friend Odd Álason.

All pretence of a truce was now cast aside. Sturla mustered a large force of men and prepared to attack Snorri and to deal with his renegade son.

Sturla and his father led a body of 1200 men towards Reykholt. Snorri, unable to put up a defence, fled with his wife Hallveig for the southwest of the island. And with that, he surrendered Reykholt, his great keep, to his nephew without a fight.

Sturla moved into Reykholt, then took over Snorri's estate at Stafholt as well, and used it to set a trap for Oraekja. He offered his cousin a deal: if Oraekja agreed to remove all his raiders from the

Westfjords, then he could have Stafholt after all. In the meantime, Sturla said, their fathers would hammer out some kind of peace deal.

Oraekja was greatly relieved, and said this arrangement would suit him just fine. He gave up his banditry and lay low for several months at Stafholt, hoping not to attract Sturla's attention.

Then in the summer, Sturla invited him to Reykholt for a friendly conversation. But when Oraekja and his men came to the door, they were stripped of their weapons and clothes, and sent up to the attic, where they were kept under guard.

THE EPISODE THAT FOLLOWS is one of the strangest – and grisliest – in *Sturlunga Saga*. Parts of it cannot possibly be true. Nonetheless, the saga records that Sturla ordered the now helpless Oraekja to be separated from his friends and put onto a horse. Accompanied by Sturla, and his men, Oraekja was led up towards the Langjökull glacier, into the badlands of Iceland's interior.

After several days' ride, they came to Surt's Cave, an infamous lava tunnel that had long served as a hideout for outlaws. It was named after the fire giant with the flaming sword, mentioned in Snorri's *Prose Edda*.

Sturla and his men led Oraekja into the dark cave, rimmed with massive blocks of basalt. A hundred metres in, they entered the place they called the stronghold, beneath an open skylight. Then, according to the saga, Sturla's men seized Oraekja and held him down. Oraekja whimpered in terror and begged for mercy. Ignoring his cousin's pleas, Sturla handed his henchman a knife and ordered him to gouge out Oraekja's eyes with it. Then, on Sturla's instructions, the man 'gelded' Oraekja by cutting away one of his testicles. After this hideous mutilation, a satisfied Sturla rode off, leaving the butchered Oraekja under guard.

Despite the severity of the attack, the saga records that Oraekja was led out of the cave and taken to the church of Skálholt to recover. He was soon 'much restored' and 'still had his sight and was fit' – all of which appears to undermine the account of his torture.

In any case, Oraekja's days as a marauder were finished.

Surt's Cave

IN DESPERATE NEED of allies, Snorri rode to the estate of Gizur Thorvaldsson, his slippery former son-in-law. Gizur was now twenty-eight years old and a powerful chieftain in his own right. The saga describes him as a man of moderate height, with strong arms and piercing blue eyes. Gizur spoke softly, and could conceal his thinking from potential enemies under a guise of affability. Snorri was getting older; his power was being eclipsed by such men.

While staying with Gizur, Snorri plotted to take back Reykholt. He contacted his cousin Thorleif and together they raised a 400-strong troop of men. But word of his plans got to Sturla, who confronted them with a much larger force of more than 700.

Snorri wanted to attack there and then, to strike hard before Sturla could prepare his men for battle, but Thorleif thought such an attack would be too dangerous.

'Then' said Snorri, 'we'd better turn back.'

'We can't do that either,' said Thorleif. 'The enemy will come after us and cut us to pieces as we retreat. It would be better to move our forces to the high ground and sue for peace with Sturla.'

'I don't care what you think,' Snorri retorted, perhaps thinking of the torture Sturla had inflicted on his son. 'I will not risk falling into that man's hands.'

And with that he took off, leaving Thorleif in the lurch. Snorri Sturluson, the great chieftain who had once led 700 followers to the assembly at Thingvellir, now made his exit with just a single kinsman to attend him.

They rode down to the harbour where Snorri boarded a ship bound for Norway: an escape that did nothing to improve his reputation for cowardice. The year was 1237 and he had just four more years to live.

Part

III

Under the Mountains

Ísafjördur

EIGHTY KILOMETRES NORTH of Gudrún's farm at Laugar, Richard and I turn off the bitumen and join the gravel roads that search out the country's fjord lands. It's well into the second week of our travels together in Iceland; we've reached the most northwesterly point in our journey, an area closer to Greenland than it is to Reykjavík.

On the map, the Westfjords peninsula rears up like an animal's head, as wild on the page as it's known to be in real life. At its northernmost reaches, the countryside is virtually uninhabitable. The farms there haven't lasted into the modern age, and the fields and valleys have been abandoned or set aside as nature reserves.

But a little further south, the regional capital Ísafjördur prospers. It does so under the strain of a winter darkness that's famous even in Iceland, and in spite of a distance from Reykjavík that is made worse by poor roads or a heart-stopping flight to get here. Across the mountains, to the southwest and east, are half a dozen fishing villages that still cling to slim bays and narrow foreshores.

Only a few thousand people live in Ísafjördur, but it's by the far the biggest town in the region. We drive into its mountain surroundings and watch the town emerge slowly. It makes only a faint impression on the landscape: a low line of houses that curve along the shore and out onto a wide spit.

Among them are the red and white buildings of the high school. As in Laugar, it opens its dormitories to tourists during the summer holidays. But I know this one much better, for I once taught English here for a year.

After Richard and I check in I look around, half expecting to meet my colleagues. But I haven't told them I'm coming, and everyone's away on holidays. Ten years on, the place is unchanged. It has the slightly hospital-like feeling that I remember from then: heavy doors with bright handles, polished floors, even the faint smell of canteen food.

I call on Richard in his overheated room, and find him opening his windows as far as they'll go. The sun is streaming in.

'I can't seem to get the windows open any further,' he says.

So we decide to head out, and follow the foreshore to the old part of town. It's fresh outside, but not properly cold. The oldest houses are very pretty. They crowd onto the spit of land, which makes a slow bend into the middle of the fjord.

The further along we go, the stronger the wind becomes, and the closer we seem to the town's origins. The streets narrow, and the houses change from concrete to wood, the larger buildings from shops to warehouses and fish plants, with plastic crates of cod stacked near their wide metal doors.

At a pebble beach near the very end of the spit, we find two rowing boats, moored in grey shallows. In the old days, the fishermen went out in these, rowing to the deep waters that lie beyond the protection of the fjord. In summer, with no night and mild weather, they could stay out as long as it took to fill the boat with cod.

It's high summer now, but there's snow on the hills. I feel the first real chill of the afternoon. 'I know it was hot inside, but I need to warm up,' I joke.

'Coffee?' suggests Richard.

'Yes, let's find a coffee in the sun. That would do it.'

But before we go, I put my hands into the water of the fjord, and enjoy the last sting of winter that remains there, no matter the month.

Returning

IN JANUARY 2004, on one of the rocky headlands at the small resort town of Noosa, I was married.

Olanda and I had first met three years before, while I was studying for my doctorate. She was working as a travel agent in the campus travel agency, and I needed a ticket – to Iceland. She hadn't ever sold a ticket to there before, and so our first conversation was about how you got to Reykjavík, and what it was like.

I told her that it took a long time to get dressed before you went outside in the mornings, and she laughed. She told me about some of her own travels – how she'd lived in Canada, and fallen in love with London. And how she was waiting for the moment when she might recommence those adventures abroad.

'I love Europe,' she said. 'I miss it. How long will you be there?'

I told her I was going for research towards my doctorate; I'd be gone for six months, maybe longer.

That would have been that, had it not been for a decision that I made that same year: to change my name by adopting the Icelandic tradition of a patronymic. Doing so would affect all my documents

– my birth certificate, passports, bank accounts, and even the ticket that I had bought to Iceland.

Eventually, I'd have to pop back to see Olanda, and ask about getting a ticket reissued in my new name.

THE SOURCE OF my old surname was something of an accident, but also very much part of my unusual situation in life. Moments after I was born, the hospital staff in Reykjavík asked my mother for the name of my father. She was still tired from the long birth, but knew that she wanted to leave that part of the certificate blank. Yet technically she was still married – to Ed. She told the nurses that her husband's name was Edwin Reid, and so, from a legal point of view, I was deemed to be Ed's son. My name was Kári Reid.

I never thought very much about what all this might mean until I was seventeen, and decided to visit my father – our third meeting, when, during the gap-year visit to Iceland, I made the promise of secrecy my mother had made, then asked him for 100 dollars.

Before I flew to Iceland, while working in Scotland, I wrote to the Icelandic Embassy in London to say that I'd be travelling to Iceland in September, and that I wanted to look for work. I told them that I'd been born Iceland, and naïvely assumed that this would be enough to get me a work permit.

I didn't hear back. But embassies work slowly, I understood that much. So on my way through Europe I visited the embassy in person. They told me that as a child born to a foreign woman in Iceland, I was entirely a foreigner too. I was not Icelandic, and had no particular claim to be either.

Over a decade later, with the secret of my identity over, I decided to adopt my patronymic. In Iceland, these are used instead of surnames; they are formed by adding -*son* or -*dóttir* to the father's given name. So, in my case, *Gísla-son*; the vowel change to –*a* marks the possessive. To others, it must have seemed as though I were trying to claim Gísli as my father. I think he interpreted it this way, for he sent a message though my brother Björn to say it was fine with him.

But in fact that wasn't the reason. It was true that I'd always wanted my father in my life, but when I took my patronymic I did so for other reasons. He seemed beyond reach, but I felt that I could make a small correction to the official records, and lay claim to a name that would in other circumstances have been mine since birth. It was, in a way, an answer to that moment when I was seventeen and turned up at the Icelandic Embassy in London. An answer to the potential tyranny of forms and the power they have. And how silences have a way of living on, of finding new places to reside, even once a secret is over.

After changing all the rest of my documentation, I went back to the travel agency to change the name on my ticket to Iceland. This was not such a terrible thing. I was still thinking about the beautiful girl who'd organised my itinerary the last time I'd been. And she had, after all, shown such an interest in Iceland.

That day, I put my hands on the counter, in between the brochure stand and the back of her computer screen, and asked if she'd like to go see a movie one of these days. She said yes, and then went on with changing my name on the tickets to Iceland.

THREE MONTHS AFTER Olanda and I went on our first date, to a movie at the university theatre, I left for Iceland. And eventually she joined me. I realised that I didn't want to live without her, and late one night, in a phone booth in downtown Reykjavík, I rang to ask if she would come over and help me see out the rest of my time.

She had saved some money, and could afford to spend three months in Reykjavík. She did it for me, I know. But also as a return to something that she'd left behind when she came back to Brisbane after her years in Canada and England. She had felt different during those years, both freer and more at home. Perhaps she would feel like that in Iceland too.

'It's very cold,' I said from the phone booth. 'I can't feel my hands or my feet right now.'

'I love the cold.'

'And the wind?' I could hear it whistling under the folding door of the phone booth.

'I'm sure it'll have settled down by the time I get there.'

It hadn't. She arrived in March, while the winter storms still held on doggedly. I remember the day she arrived very well: it was minus six, blowing a gale, with squalls of wet snow thrashing against us as we walked down to the sea. All the Icelandic weather elements.

But it was also the beginning of her relationship with the country – one that had a lot to do with me, but would also come to run its own course.

In 2004, not long after we were married, I was offered the English-teaching job in Ísafjördur. Even by Icelandic standards, this was going to mean living in a remote and difficult place. In Reykjavík, people talked about how terribly dark it got in Ísafjördur, and how the steep mountains cut you off from the rest of the world.

We arrived in August, late summer, with nothing but a few suitcases. The school had organised an apartment for us, but it was completely empty. We went up to the school office to say hello, with the thought that we might have to sleep at the school dorm for a few nights. The principal, Ólína, welcomed us warmly and took us to meet her deputy, who gave us a tour of the school buildings.

We came across Guðni, the school caretaker. 'Do you need anything?' he asked.

'We haven't brought very much,' I confessed. 'We've got a bit of setting up to do.'

'You have beds?'

'No.'

'A sofa, chairs, a TV?'

'None of those things either.'

'I see.' Guðni took out his phone and made a call. 'The way I see it,' he said as he hung up, 'you might as well have a little bit of everything.'

Half an hour later, Guðni had filled his trailer with two beds, four chairs, a small table and a rug. He'd also packed us bed covers, towels, crockery and cutlery.

'I can ring around for a TV, if you want,' he said.

'No, really, it's fine. We'll survive for a couple of days without one.'

The deputy principal returned. 'Everything okay?' he asked.

'Yes, Guðni's been very generous. I feel like we're taking half the dorm with us.'

'Nonsense,' he replied. 'You might as well settle in if you can.'

THE DEPUTY PRINCIPAL'S name was Guðbjartur, and in the months to come I'd rely greatly on him and the other teachers for company and conversation. Most people in Ísafjördur were either under twenty or over sixty. In the in-between years, people left to work in Reykjavík or abroad. And so the school and the hospital were among the few employers of people our age.

Guðbjartur had been working here for three years. He and his wife and their two young children had moved here from Selfoss, a town of about the same size as Ísafjördur, but in the south, 'pancake country' as it was called by people in the Westfjords.

As we were leaving the school that first day, he told us to be sure to come along to the town square for a festival that Saturday night. Everyone would be there.

'What's happening?' I asked.

'It's 100 years since Icelanders got our first prime minister, Hannes Hafstein. When the Danes finally let us rule our own lives. Hannes started his political career in Ísafjördur.'

We promised to come, then jumped into Guðni's car, our borrowed furniture bumping along behind us in his trailer. Our apartment was a little way out of town. After we'd unloaded, Guðni drove us to the shops. The afternoon was getting on and we imagined they were about to close. But maybe we'd have time to look for a television and fridge.

Again, Guðni took out his phone. I didn't want to listen in, but I noticed that he was talking about us. When he was finished, he turned to Olanda and said, 'They'll stay open a bit later today. You'll have time to do your shopping.'

We bought a fridge, and then a TV. The man who sold them to us said we must come along to the festival, then drove us home. Within four hours of arriving in Ísafjördur, we had an apartment filled with furniture.

SUCH WAS MY REINTRODUCTION to living in Iceland. I'd last lived here as a boy of ten, before Mum and I moved first to England, and four years later to Australia.

I was a little overwhelmed by the landscape too. It wasn't the Iceland I knew, for I'd grown up entirely in Reykjavík. But neither was it as intimidating as we'd expected – at least not yet, in late

August. The fjord, though more closed in than the landscapes of the south, was also very intimate and sheltered. It seemed to offer an invitation of sorts – to rediscover my birthplace, not through the brief joys of visits, but through the slower patterns of everyday life.

THE NEXT DAY, we found that the first of the autumn berries had begun to grow in the valleys at the end of the fjord. We bought bikes, and rode in search of them, finding small woodlands and streams. We cooled our beers in the water, which came down off the hills freezing cold.

Olanda collecting berries

Then, a couple of nights after we arrived, we joined just about everyone else in Ísafjördur as they milled around the town square waiting for the festival to begin. Guðbjartur and his family were there; they smiled and said hello, but he seemed shy outside work. We exchanged a few remarks about how it was a nice, bright evening, then stood almost beside each other, but not quite. The man who'd sold us our television and fridge took up the space between us and Guðbjartur, and asked if our appliances were all working okay.

'Yes, thank you,' I said. 'I think it's a good fridge.'

I looked around, and noticed that the reserved feeling between us and Guðbjartur was present elsewhere too, as though we were all on our best behaviour that night. Ólína, the school principal, was MC. Her voice seemed to drift high up from the stage, over the harbour, and then back towards us, somehow travelling out to sea first. There was music as well – performances by local choirs and ensembles. But throughout the festivities the evening remained quiet, even solemn. I wondered whether 'festival' was really the right word for what was happening, or whether I'd become too Australian to see it. I'd expected people to be having fun.

At the end, the President of Iceland, Ólafur Ragnar Grímsson, stepped up onto the stage and delivered a speech about the political contributions of the Westfjords, and the great figures who'd come from the area. I'd heard that he, too, had been born in Ísafjördur, and mentioned this to the electrical salesman.

He smiled. 'He's the barber's son.'

THE HEAD OF LANGUAGES at the school was Ingibjörg, an attractive woman in her forties with a busy, distracted manner, but also gregarious and warm. She liked to walk through the school corridors singing Beatles songs, drawing attention to herself and lifting the atmosphere.

The following Monday, the first day of term, she drew me aside and handed me my class lists.

'And reading materials …what do you use?' I asked. I still didn't really know what I'd be teaching.

'Well, there are texts set down from last year, but it's up to you.'

I looked at last year's English syllabus. *The Great Gatsby* was there, *Gulliver's Travels*. And *Hamlet*.

'How do they manage reading Shakespeare?' I asked. 'Even English-speakers find that hard.'

'I think they'll love it,' answered Ingibjörg. 'You'll do fine.'

I wasn't as confident. My first class was a group in their final year, aged nineteen. They were friendly but quiet; a little shocked, I think, to be taught by an Australian-Icelander who knew much less about their school system than they did. But one student, Amy, was the daughter of an Australian woman who taught at the primary school in town, and straight away I recognised a different kind of openness in her.

We worked around the class introducing ourselves. I asked Amy what she was planning to do when she finished school.

'I'm going to Australia,' she said.

'And you?' I said, looking at her friend at the same table.

'I'm going to Australia with her.'

Most of the students had plans to get away. They didn't want to work in fishing.

'We're all connected to the fishing,' said Rögnvaldur, a young man with a handsome face and light brown hair. But that wasn't the future.

One student, an absent-looking boy with thick glasses and a black heavy-metal T-shirt, said he was going to 'walk the world, man, be a free spirit'.

His friends laughed, but nodded as well.

I was worrying about the Shakespeare on the reading list. 'Do you really cover *Hamlet* in this class?' I asked.

Yes. They'd all read some Shakespeare already. They were happy to take on more.

'Do you use abridged versions? Simplified text?'

At this, even the free spirit who was going to walk the world one day bristled with injured pride. 'Of course not. We read the whole thing in the full original.'

SOME OF MY STUDENTS were already working on front desks in the tourism industry, in restaurants. One day, as a class exercise, I asked them to find descriptions of the Westfjords from English-language travel articles and guidebooks. One descriptor for the landscape around us came up rather often: 'inhospitable'.

'We're not inhospitable,' they said.

'No,' I explained, 'here it refers to the landscape. That it's hard to live here.'

They didn't quite believe me. For a while, I thought they weren't getting it, the difference between unwelcoming people and an inhospitable landscape. But then I began to feel that in fact they didn't like to separate the two things out.

That was also how I felt about Iceland: the landscape was intense, and it could be difficult. But it brought you home as well. 'Let's write our own guide, then,' I suggested. 'You tell me what it should say.'

They had trouble taking the exercise all that seriously. It's hard to write about your own town. But I kept their pretend entries for a guide book, even the silly ones:

The Westfjords is the oldest part of Iceland, consisting of fifty deep fjords. It was settled by Norwegian traders who were too lazy to keep going to Greenland.

The flower garden used to be a popular place for kids to play gun fights.

*The nearby village of Bolungarvík has a population of 900.
The kids in Bolungarvík and Ísafjördur have been fighting over
nothing much for as long as anyone can remember. Bolungarvík's
restaurant is called Finnabaer.*

*Because of a bad avalanche in 1995 that killed an elderly man
and wiped out many summerhouses, a massive protective
wall has been constructed in Tungudalur, just near town.
The story of the name 'Tungudalur': there was once an old
priest called Dag Raudfaxi, or Dag the Red Haired. He fought
with a terrible ogre called Solvi Marhnutur, that is, Solvi the
Extremely Ugly, and won the day by cutting out the ogre's
tongue.*

The farmers in Hrafnseyri are very helpful.

*Hannes Hafstein, the first prime minister of Iceland, lived in the
same house as Jóhannes now lives in.*

*The nearby village of Thingeyri boasts an excellent pool. People
from outside Thingeyri claim that family connections there
are too close. This suggestion is hotly denied by people from
Thingeyri, who say that Ísafjördur people are jealous of the
Thingeyri swimming pool.*

*A paintball field is being made in Seljalandsdalur and will be
ready in a few months.*

*The farmer at Aedey and his brothers are said to have been
famous for their childhood pranks.*

Every summer the famous Ögur dance is held. Suitably enough,
it is named after the Ögur farm where it is held. Traditional
rhubarb porridge is served.

There is a famous minister at Vatnsfjördur – he is a local legend.
One funny story about him concerns a pig.

IT WAS STUNNING country, and over time my students and I got used to each other. We did read *Hamlet* and other classics, and while I helped with their English they helped me to better remember the country of my birth. The Icelandic reserve was only a first step, and underneath it there lay curiosity and humour.

But at the same time I worried about what Olanda would do. She couldn't sit looking at mountains all day. I was busy teaching, but there didn't seem to be anything for her. She asked around about work, but everywhere got the same answer: she needed to learn Icelandic.

'Well, that's not too bad, then,' she joked. 'It's only the most difficult language in the world.'

She enrolled in evening classes, but her days were still empty. To feel more a part of things, we moved out of the apartment that the school had organised and into a flat near the centre of town.

One day, after the first snows of October, we walked up the steep mountain sides behind us to look at the town from higher ground. Across the water, the mountains opposite stood in deep silence, but it was a generous reserve, and not oppressive; there were columns of rock, but filled with a wild poetry.

There were two hollows in the side of one of these mountains. My students said that they marked the places where trolls had once sat down to rest. From where we stood, we could make out the snow drifting upwards from their base, as though the trolls had only just stood up again.

I WAS UNSURE about what would happen next – whether we should plan for a long stay in the Westfjords, or look to move to Reykjavík, where Olanda would have a better chance of work. My siblings lived there too. I'd only known them for five years, and I wanted to spend time with them.

In emails and phone calls, they told me that they were giving my father Gísli updates on our life in Ísafjördur. I was never tempted to contact him. But once I asked my oldest sister Fríða if she thought he would sign a declaration of paternity. I was a dual British–Australian citizen; when I was five, Mum had chosen British citizenship for me, to be the same as hers. Iceland's more recent part-membership of the EU meant that I no longer needed to worry about work permits. But having the right to work in Iceland wasn't quite the same thing as having the records set right. For that to happen, I would at some point have to get my father's name added.

Fríða replied that she would try to bring it up with him, and for a moment it looked like he would sign the declaration. But in that hazy, sometimes drifting way of family life, the matter seemed to be dropped, and I decided not to push. It really didn't matter any more. I was back in Iceland, and busy enough with that return.

I ASKED OLANDA NOT TO TRY for work at the fish factories. It wasn't fair of me to tell her what to do, but it didn't seem right to bring her all this way just for her to end up gutting fish.

'Except you didn't bring me,' she said. 'We decided together to come and try this.'

'I know. But ...'

Language remained the main problem. One day, on an errand to collect a book waiting for us at the post office, she tried to speak Icelandic. The woman at the counter more or less refused to understand what she was saying, and would only reply in her own broken English.

'No one will even try to speak to me in Icelandic,' said Olanda when she got back.

'Your Icelandic teacher does.'

'She yells at us.'

'I think that's just Icelandic,' I said. 'It sounds like yelling, but really she's probably being very friendly.'

'How am I ever going to get a job if I can't even collect a parcel in Icelandic?'

She handed the parcel to me.

'Who served you, anyway?' I asked.

'Oh, you know, the frowny one.' We called her this because she wouldn't answer our hello when we saw her delivering letters to our place.

'There you go,' I said. 'She's miserable. I wouldn't take it personally.' But I also knew it wouldn't change, not in the first few years. Not until her Icelandic was better.

'I'm going to have to ask at the fish factory,' she said.

'I'm not sure you need to.'

'I can't go for walks all day,' she said.

'You'll smell of fish,' I said.

She waited for a moment, then added, 'Apparently the gear they give you is really good. You don't come home smelling of fish.'

'Who told you that?'

'My Icelandic teacher. And she reckons the conditions at the sushi-making factory are excellent. Much better than the regular fish factory.'

'Don't listen to anything she says. She yells at you, remember.'

EARLY THAT WINTER, Ísafjördur had its heaviest snowfalls in ten years – since 1995, when the last bad avalanches had come, and claimed dozens of lives in the Westfjords. One morning, we woke to find the streets around our house had disappeared under hills of snow.

For days, there was no traffic in town, as there was too much snow to be cleared. Ísafjördur would just have to wait for a warm change, when enough snow would melt and the roads could open again.

But we were safe. The snow was packing solidly, and probably wasn't going to slide down the face of the hills. So we walked and walked. We loved the town while it was like this, quiet and shaped by new street patterns that formed out of the cleared snow lanes. We even rode our bikes, zigzagging through it as if it were soft sand.

One day, we explored the hilly streets behind our flat. These were in the highest part of town, supposedly the most prosperous too. My students joked that the people who lived there were the 'fine folk', and sometimes called them the 'quota millionaires': a reference to the old fishing families who'd sold their fish quotas to big companies.

'So people here were that rich?' asked Olanda.

'In that boom-bust way of fishing towns,' I replied. 'At least they were after the Cod Wars.'

'The Cold War?'

'No, *Cod*,' I said. We laughed. 'Iceland's great military moment. Three wars against the British for control of the fishing grounds.'

Mainly, it had been patrol boats and trawlers thumping into each other. Three wars over the extent of fishing rights, all of which Iceland won, until it had established an exclusive fishing zone that extended 200 miles out to sea.

The spoils of that conflict, and Iceland's control of its fisheries, were around us on the high streets of Ísafjördur: large, cement houses that looked down on the older ones. They were grand houses but also a little boring, at least compared with the cramped, odd-shaped homes on the spit. The new buildings had none of the awkward, uneven charm of a port village. But then, neither did they have the stink of fish that seemed to hang close to shore.

'Which would you rather live in?' I asked Olanda as we trudged up the hill.

'The old houses, of course.'

'Too close to the avalanche zone up here?'

'It's not that. I'm not scared of getting buried by snow. It's because those old buildings have a story. You can feel it when you walk past them.'

'You don't mind the smell of fish?'

'It's the smell of money, right? Isn't that the expression?'

'You're not working in a fish factory,' I said.

'Who said anything about that?'

THE FOLLOWING WEEK, the first gales of winter arrived with their full, uncompromising violence. It grew darker and darker, until at last the sun disappeared behind the mountains. It wouldn't reappear for months.

We still hadn't bought a car; I didn't get a driver's licence until I was older, and Olanda didn't really want to drive. So we kept walking or bicycling everywhere, even when the wind made it hard to stand upright. We learnt to lean into it. But one day, we were suddenly caught off guard by the gusts and forced into a standing huddle on the footpath. We just couldn't move. Car after car drove past us, and I cursed them for not stopping – rather that than my own stupidity in having us out walking in this weather.

Then I heard the voice of the school principal, Ólína.

At school, I often found her voice a little harsh. In a blizzard, I felt there could be no sweeter sound. 'Kári and Olanda. Get in! What are you doing out in this?' We rushed in, while she laughed. 'I saw two people and wondered, Who could be walking in this weather? And then I realised it could only be you two!'

I think Ólína was talking about our Australianness, and what seemed to the locals to be our slightly insane willingness to ignore the obvious and keep going on as normal. The fjord was closing in, and the world here was going indoors. I knew it would be that way for the next few months, but I wasn't quite ready to accept it.

Actually, I think Olanda understood it all better than I did. I was *back* in Iceland, and in love with that. But in many ways she was better at adapting to our new home. So, despite my protests, Olanda did begin asking for work at the fish factories down on the spit. And that Christmas, while we were on a short holiday in Reykjavík, the phone rang and suddenly she had a job. It was at the sushi-making factory.

I felt bad about it, and even mentioned to my students that I was worried about her working there. They told me not to be. Everyone had had a turn working with the fish, one way or another – on the trawlers, in the factories, or delivering the fish for export.

'None of us would be here if it wasn't for cod,' said one.

Her daily shift would begin at six each morning, several hours before first light. On the first day, I asked if I could walk her to work.

Not because she needed a guide; there was no way of getting lost in Ísafjördur, and no danger, apart from blizzards and patches of ice.

But the darkness here was different, magnified by the knowledge that it would be dark from now until spring, when the sun would finally climb back over the mountains.

'What are we going to do?' I asked, as we followed the foreshore to the old part of town. For some reason, living here didn't feel certain, even now that she had a job and I was established in mine.

'Kári, this a wonderful place.'

There was sea ice pressed up against the ocean wall. It crunched slowly backwards and forwards, as though it were deciding on whether to be still or find a way back out.

CHAPTER FIFTEEN
(Richard)

Darkness and Light

IN THE MORNING, I walk outside the double doors of the school dormitory and reel at the spectacle – at cliffs so sheer, and so tall they attract clumps of cloud at their crests. Ísafjördur's landscape has a thrilling, nightmarish quality to it, like the dream of the wave that rises up before you, doubles in size, then doubles again.

Kári warns me that if I refer to Ísafjördur as a 'village', the locals will politely correct me and assert that it is, in fact, a 'town'. I ask him how he amused himself while living in such a small and remote 'town'. He tells me he was very happy here, and the distant, fond expression on his face tells me this is true. He takes me to a bakery and buys a *vínarbrauð*, a rolled pastry laced with custard and jam that he used to enjoy as a boy. This Icelandic treat, with a name that means 'Vienna bread', is in fact a kind of Danish. It's another import like the Icelandic hot dog; Icelanders have taken a distinctive dish from elsewhere, improved it, and claimed it as indigenous to the island.

Our second day in Ísafjördur we spend walking all over the town, and by evening we're powerfully hungry. Ísafjördur, like just about every small town in Iceland, is blessed with a modest tin and timber café–restaurant, which offers a short menu of simple dishes. Again I'm drawn to the *fiskisúpa*, the Icelandic fish soup. It arrives in a small stainless-steel tureen with a dob of cream and a sprig of Arctic thyme.

THAT NIGHT, I call Khym in Australia. I mention the fish soup.

She groans in frustration: she gets annoyed when I enjoy good food without her. Khym knows more about the world's cuisines than anyone else I've ever met. After we got married we moved into an apartment with a kitchen no bigger than a closet, and so she published a cookbook of easy recipes for young couples like us, living in constrained circumstances. I still use her cookbook today. Khym's family are Singaporean, and she grew up amidst the food traditions of the Straits-born Chinese, a happy blend of Malay, Chinese, Portuguese, Indian and English cooking. She's never been to Iceland, so I describe the fish soup and ask her if it sounds like an adaptation of a French dish, given that it combines fish with dairy.

'Oh, no,' she says. 'There's a long tradition of using milk with fish on the Atlantic coast. It comes from the salt cod they used to eat. Salt cod was a kind of poor man's protein before refrigeration came along. There was plenty of cod around and it could be preserved by drying and salting it. The Vikings chewed it on their ocean voyages. The Portuguese ate it too as they sailed around the world. They call it *bacalhau*.'

When she's answering a question about food, Khym will often half-close her eyes and use expressive hand gestures, as if she were holding the ingredient in front of her. I know she's clasping an imaginary salted fish right now on the other end of the line.

'So how does milk come into it?'

'Ah!' she says. 'Salt cod had to be reconstituted by soaking it in milk overnight to extract the saltiness. The Portuguese mashed it up and mixed it with onions and potato to make those fishcakes. I love those fishcakes.'

Fiskisúpa, Ísafjördur

THIS IS HOW YOU MAKE *fiskisúpa*, or Icelandic fish soup:

Chop up a good-sized onion and a leek, and sauté them in a large pot with some butter. Add a dash of sherry and let it reduce a little. Pour in several litres of water mixed with chicken or vegetable stock. Throw in a dash of red wine vinegar and let the concoction simmer for around fifteen minutes.

Then add chunks of haddock or cod or Arctic char (if you happen to be in that part of the world), and a finely chopped tomato. Let it all simmer for five minutes, then pour in half a litre of cream, and let it simmer for another five minutes, taking care not to let the soup come to a boil, otherwise the cream might curdle. Ladle it into a bowl, place a tablespoon of thickened cream in the centre, and sprinkle with chopped chives. Served with fresh bread and beer, this soup will warm your winter bones very nicely after a long day's hiking around the fjords.

Khym signs off, and I work into the night: looking at my books and prodding various scholastic databases for stories from Ísafjördur's past. After a few hours, I've managed to dig up some odd little tales and a startling new saga, one I'm sure Kári has never heard of, written four centuries after Snorri's death. The common thread I find running through all these stories from the Westfjords is the persistence of the old Icelandic folk magic.

ÍSAFJÖRDUR SIMPLY MEANS 'ice fjord', but for much of its life the settlement here was named Eyri, which means 'sand spit'. The area was founded in the ninth century by a Viking named Helgi Hrólfsson, who came here with his son, Thorstein Ill-Luck. The fishing was mostly good, but the farmlands were meagre, confined to a narrow strip of land along the water's edge. If the fish stayed clear of the fjord, the people would starve. In such times, a witch-wife would sometimes be asked to bring back the food with magical rites. The *Book of Settlements* records the presence of a sorceress in the northwest known as Thuríd the Sound-Filler, so called because during a famine, she used a form of Norse witchcraft called *seiður* to fill up the waters of the sound with fish.

Seiður was primarily women's magic, to be practiced by a *völva* – a sorceress. A *völva* would use drumming and chanting to fall into a trance, enabling her to travel through the Nine Worlds nested in the branches of Yggdrasil, the world-tree. Having grasped the alternative futures on offer, the *völva* could then use magical rites to veer the course of time towards the best of all possible worlds.

The *Galdrabók*, an Icelandic grimoire from the seventeenth century, contains forty-seven spells and stave-runes to be used by desperate Icelanders hoping to draw a lover close or hold starvation at bay. These spells would typically be activated by a *völva*, who would chant its words, then engrave a stave-rune to fix it in place. Depending on the spell, the stave-rune would be carved into a tree, or the hide of a red dog, or above the door of a farm. Icelanders used these stave-runes to summon fish into the harbour, to see a ghost, or to kill the livestock of an enemy. There were stave-runes that forced a man to fall in love with a woman, and others to make a woman fart in church, thereby disgracing her. These heathen practices would never be entirely expunged from Iceland.

*Ægishjálmur, the helm of awe: a stave-rune used in Icelandic
magic to induce fear and protect against abuse of power*

WHEN ICELAND OFFICIALLY accepted Christianity in the year 1000, the religion of the Christians soon displaced public worship of the Norse gods, but the old magical practices associated with it were never entirely eradicated. A subterranean river of pagan thought and expression still coursed its way through the lives of the Icelandic people.

When the commonwealth failed in 1262 and Iceland became a colony of Norway, the island entered a new era of terrible hardship, becoming one of the poorest countries in Europe. At the same time, the wealth and power of the Catholic bishops in Iceland swelled, thanks to a tithe they imposed on their parishioners. They used this pool of wealth to acquire more land from the chieftains.

In 1380, control of Iceland passed into the hands of the Danish crown. But the power and status of the Catholic bishops remained unchanged until 1540, when King Christian III of Denmark commanded his Icelandic subjects to renounce the church of Rome in favour of the Lutheran church. The nine monasteries and convents of Iceland were dissolved and their wealth was confiscated by the Danish crown.

In 1550, the last Catholic bishop of Iceland, Jón Arason, tried to lead a revolt against the Lutherans, along with his two sons.* All three were captured and condemned to death without a trial. After his sons were beheaded, Jón Arason was offered a reprieve: his life would be spared if he renounced his allegiance to the pope. He refused and said he only wanted to join his sons.

As Jón's neck was placed on the chopping block, a priest named Sveinn came to console him.

'There is a life after this one,' he said.

'*Veit ég það, Sveinki,*' Jón Arason replied. 'That I know, little Sveinn.'

Either the executioner's blade was blunt or his strike was faulty; it took seven chops of the axe to end the life of Jón Arason.

---

* Iceland was a very long way from Rome, and the Vatican's rules of clerical celibacy were often overlooked.

But Jón Arason had a daughter named Thórunn, who wanted to avenge her father's death. One night, she received word that the representative of the Danish king and his entourage would be staying at a farmhouse at Kirkjuból, near Ísafjördur. Thórunn's kinsmen broke in through the roof of the house and murdered every one of the Danish visitors.

Afterwards, there were reports from local farms that the ghosts of the Danes had taken to haunting the Westfjords. So the bodies of the Danes were dug up, and their heads removed then stitched onto their arses to prevent them from rising from their graves. There were fewer reports of ghastly visitations after this, but the Lutheran church would soon set itself against macabre practices such as the ritualistic violation of the dead.

IN ICELAND'S FIRST Christian centuries, magical practice was seen as a kind of mischief, to be frowned upon but not persecuted. A distinction was made between harmful 'black' magic and benevolent 'white' magic, which was used to undo diabolical spells and expel harmful ghosts.

The publication in Germany in 1486 of *Malleus Maleficarum*, *The Hammer of Witches* brought an end to official tolerance of magic across Europe. The book, written as a kind of manual for inquisitors, was a damning treatise on witchcraft. It became a phenomenal bestseller, rivalled in popularity only by the Bible. The authors of *Malleus Maleficarum* condemned sorcery as heresy, and recommended torture to extract confessions. Those found guilty, they reasoned, should be condemned to death as a matter of public safety.

As the seventeenth century began, the crusade against witchcraft intensified. In 1617 the King of Denmark declared a crackdown. He decreed that in his realm there was to be no distinguishing between white and black magic: all sorcery was deemed to be wicked and was to be forcibly suppressed.

Yet within the scattered farmhouses of Iceland, still these old folk practices refused to die, and were held in silence like a guilty secret. There was a comparative restraint in persecuting pagan magic: an aversion to torture, a reluctance to create mayhem among close-knit communities on the say-so of a vengeful farmer or a delusional fisherman.

But an accusation of witchcraft coming from the mouth of a charismatic priest was another matter altogether.

The Saga of Pastor Jón

IN 1644, the parish of Eyri in the Westfjords welcomed a new Lutheran pastor named Jón Magnússon. Upon his arrival, Pastor Jón moved with his family into the farmhouse next to the church, at the end of the sand spit at Eyri.

The new pastor was articulate and energetic, although somewhat highly strung. Seeing that the church had become badly dilapidated, he ordered repairs to its timber walls and its broken wooden pews. A beautiful new altarpiece was commissioned and the cracked windows were replaced. With the church restored, Jón could direct his attention to his parishioners, whose souls, he believed, had similarly fallen into serious disrepair.

The pastor did not believe in half-measures when it came to holy worship. His prayers were emotional, often accompanied by moaning and tears, and he distrusted those among his flock whose prayers were not as passionate as his own, accusing them of 'sinful hard-heartedness'. To his mind, the world was full of peril; the devil was not a distant king of hell, but an ever-present menace. He could feel the devil's hot breath on his collar, even here, in this tiny settlement at the edge of the world.

Pastor Jón's fanatical determination to purge the district of its pagan ways would plunge the little community into a convulsive crisis, culminating in a witchcraft trial. These events are chronicled in an extraordinary document, the *Píslarsaga*, *The Saga of My Sufferings*, published in 1659 and written by Pastor Jón himself. The events in the *Píslarsaga* took place a full decade before the Salem witch trials of Massachusetts.

ONE EVENING, IN the month of October 1655, Pastor Jón Magnússon and his household sat down at their table in the parish house in Eyri. As they did so, a girl with the power of clear-sight said the ghost of a dog had entered the room. She saw the demon-dog come up to the window, then trot out the door, down the trail that led towards Kirkjuból.

The path chosen by the demon aroused the pastor's suspicions. Within the settlement at Kirkjuból lived two farmers, a father and son, both named Jón Jónsson.

The pastor didn't much care for either man. He had rebuked the younger Jón Jónsson in church for having punched his own servant girl Asta in the head. The father had called the girl a liar, and would not be reconciled with the servant girl, nor the pastor.

The younger Jón Jónsson was a fine-looking man, with curly golden hair and fair skin, but the pastor believed these appealing qualities could not redeem the coarseness of his soul. So when the younger Jón Jónsson had called on him to ask permission to marry his foster-daughter Rannveig, the pastor had withheld his assent.

After this refusal, the pastor understood that the father and the son had both come to hate him. This was troubling, because it was rumoured among the people of Eyri that the two men were well versed in the old sorcery. Now, after this ghastly visitation from a dog-spirit in his own home, the pastor suspected foul play: that the two men's lust for revenge against him had put them in league with the devil.

A WEEK LATER, the pastor travelled to Kirkjuból to preach there. A local farmer, Snaebjörn Pálsson, ferried him across the fjord and accompanied him on horseback to the settlement.

There were only three properties at Kirkjuból, and a little half-church, attached to one of the stone and turf farmhouses. The pastor lodged with Snaebjörn, not far from the Jón Jónssons.

After midnight, he was wakened in his bed by a foul presence. He felt it gnaw at his feet, like a rat. The thing tormented him and would not allow him to sleep.

The next morning at the half-church, the groggy pastor said he wanted to address the unhappy state of affairs between the families at Kirkjuból. He urged the small congregation to cease their petty bickering. But Jón Jónsson the elder stood up and angrily repudiated him. Jón Jónsson the younger was not even in church; he was at the Danish store buying liquor and getting drunk.*

The pastor rode back to Eyri. The next day, at midday, he was overcome by an oppressive need for sleep, and could hardly wake up until evening. Then, at dinner, he felt an invisible cat rubbing against his legs, causing an unnatural, nauseous sensation in his stomach.

---

* In seventeenth-century Iceland, imported goods such as timber, sugar, coffee and tobacco could only be lawfully purchased at one of twenty authorised trading posts, protected as a monopoly by the Danish crown.

All that night in bed, he was assailed by weird and evil thoughts. When he began to pray, he felt something akin to a large dog jumping on his body, clawing his neck with red-hot needles.

These demonic visitations were repeated every night that week.

On Sunday, the pastor told the congregation of the attacks. He did not name anyone, but he did say he was astonished that someone from his own parish should practise sorcery against him. As he spoke, he noticed the queer expressions on the faces of both Jón Jónssons, and took this as evidence of their guilt in this matter.

At the conclusion of the service, the younger Jón Jónsson shook the pastor's hand, and as he did so, the pastor felt a burning sensation in his palm. He rubbed his hand against the altarpiece and the burning subsided. (Later, at the inquiry, Jón Jónsson would confess that he had inscribed a magic stave-rune on his palm that day.)

THE TORMENTS INCREASED in nature and number. On the following Sunday, the pastor observed Jón Jónsson from a distance. The pastor saw the older man walk slowly up to the parish house, whereupon he stopped and stared malevolently at the window of the upstairs bedroom, the *baðstofa*. Surely, the pastor reasoned later, the man must have been muttering an incantation under his breath, because from that moment on, he could barely bring himself to take his usual seat next to that window.

Later, the old man was observed staring in the same baleful manner at an alcove within the church. When the pastor went there to lay down and pray, he felt a trampling of feet, fists and knees upon his back. Then the devil blew into his right ear, creating such a terrible hiss that it was impossible to gather his thoughts for prayer.

NOW THE DEMONS multiplied in form and number in the pastor's house. Those with clear-sight spotted them in every corner of the hall and in the *baðstofa*. Then two ghastly apparitions were observed inside the house that bore a close resemblance to the Jón Jónssons. Conclusive proof, if more was needed, that the two men had allied themselves with the devil to destroy him.

One night as the pastor lay on the *pallur*, the wooden bench at the side of the *baðstofa*, he felt a disturbance under the boards. As an experiment, he asked a servant to fire a rudimentary gun at the place where he knew that a spirit was crouching. The gun roared and the pastor instantly felt the demon lunge onto him and pound at him. Then it attacked the servant. From this, the pastor understood the demon to be a *draugur*, a lowly spirit commanded by incantations, and vulnerable to fire.

The pastor's home was in an uproar. Everyone now believed they could sense demonic activity. Someone would shout, 'Look! It's here!' Another would cry: 'It's got my foot! My head!' These torments were followed by bouts of intense itching or numbness among the family. Some complained of a burning sensation in the chest and of a lump in the throat. At night all the beds quivered and shook. Frightening cracking noises were heard under the boards.

By now it was late November, and the settlement of Eyri was in near-constant winter darkness.

LISTENING TO THE GROANS of anguish among his household, the pastor now understood that the life of every member of his family was at risk. Despite his soreness and exhaustion, he travelled across the fjord to see Magnús Magnússon, the local sheriff. The pastor insisted he arrest the Jón Jónssons at once for sorcery.

To the pastor's amazement, the sheriff seemed uneasy, and tried to shy away from taking action. The pastor snapped that he would take the matter up with the sheriff's superiors.

He rode back to Eyri and took himself straight into the church to say his prayers. But when he prostrated himself, he again felt a blast of wind in his right ear, which sounded like it came directly from the maw of some hellish dog. He was filled with such dread and nausea he could not finish.

Then the devil's torments humiliated him before his own congregation. When he rose to speak, he became overwhelmed by *æðigaldur*, madness magic, and lost his wits entirely. He ran to the church doors, but when he pushed them open, he was too terrified to look at the sky. He flung himself to the floor, but his heart was cold and there was no devotion in it to God. He could only wail, emitting a sound that distressed the people present.

THE PASTOR WOULD BROOK no more delay from the authorities, and at his insistence, the sheriff agreed to convene a court at Eyri to investigate the charge of witchcraft against Jón Jónsson, father and son.

The court sent a deputy to Kirkjuból, to look for incriminating evidence within the farmhouses. In the house of old Snaebjörn Pálsson, the deputy found pages of calfskin parchment containing runes and letters. Snaebjörn Pálsson was very unwilling to part with them; he clutched the pages to his chest and refused to hand them over. Several of these parchment leaves were pulled from his grasp and brought before the court, and there were some who said they were certainly pages of magic.

In court, Jón Jónsson the elder now hung his head in sullen silence. The pastor saw this as evidence that the man was suffering the condemnation of his own conscience. Someone spoke in favour of fettering the accused in iron shackles. At this, Jón Jónsson the younger stood up and cried damnation upon himself and all good things, both in this world and the next. The courtroom reeled in shock when Jón Jónsson the elder repeated his son's words.

To the pastor's frustration, this shocking outburst had no effect on the court's deliberations, and the Jón Jónssons were given an opportunity to prove their innocence. The court invoked an old Icelandic legal principle known as *tylftareiður*, the judgement of twelve. If the Jón Jónssons could find twelve people to swear to their innocence, the charges would be dropped.

The pastor was incensed. He thought this precaution was stupid beyond belief. It was almost as though they were trying to prolong his agony. Everyone in the district knew Jón Jónsson the elder had been practising magic for a good thirty years. Why then was the trial moving so slowly? He wondered why the judges cared so little about the pain and terror that were still being inflicted upon his household, but he was too exhausted to voice his dissent, and simply lay upon a pew in the choir stall.

Meanwhile, Jón Jónsson the elder was begging local people in the courtroom to testify on behalf of him and his son, but the villagers recoiled from him, like sheep before a wolf. The pastor thought their readiness to debase themselves in such a frantic manner further betrayed their guilt: if they were innocent, surely they would act with serene confidence that God would vindicate them. What was wrong with the court? Why could they not see this as clearly as him?

The unbecoming behaviour of the father and son had made them repugnant in the eyes of many, and they failed to gather the twelve sworn testimonies that would have acquitted them. The magistrates now said they would need to consult the Althing and be guided by its decision before they could take further steps. Some sympathy was expressed to the pastor for his sufferings, but they claimed they could do no more for the moment.

The two Jón Jónssons left the courtroom to make their way home. Those in the courtroom blessed with the power of clear-sight said they could see a company of invisible demons following them to the shore. As the father and son boarded their boat, the waters of the fjord appeared to be churning unnaturally, as if affected by an underground disturbance.

THE AWFUL YEAR came to a close. The pastor was now too infirm to carry out his priestly duties and was confined to his bed. The cruel torments gave him no respite; he said he felt like his body was being squashed like soft cheese, and stung by the points of a thousand tiny needles.

After Christmas, he insisted the sheriff open a new investigation, to consider evidence that had been disregarded by the first inquiry. This failed to eventuate.

Meanwhile, there were reports that the devil's torments had spread throughout the community. Those who had refused to give sworn testimony on behalf of the Jón Jónssons now claimed they too were suffering diabolical torments. It was said that a Pastor Tomas of Snaefjöll had tried to pray for Pastor Jón, but a strange insect had flown into his face and disrupted him.

Worse still than all these physical ordeals was the spiritual crisis that confronted the pastor. 'My heart,' he said, 'has become desiccated and drained of all the dew of God's grace.' He was terrified by the thought that the devil might be drawing him to the point of worshipping him. In his distress, he asked his servants to tie him to two boards shaped like a cross, in the hope that God would see him fastened in this manner and take pity on him.

One night, he saw a figure over his bed, leaning toward him and praying over him. The figure was clothed in pristine white linen and appeared as diaphanous as a white cloud in the sky. The figure whispered to the pastor, 'May God help us all by the protection of His holy angels.' Then he disappeared.

IN APRIL 1656, a new inquiry into the goings-on at Eyri was convened at the courtroom. The pastor had gone over the head of sheriff Magnús Magnússon and appealed to another magistrate of the northwest, a man named Thorleif Kortsson, and here the pastor had at last found an ally.

Thorleif Kortsson was short in stature, and spoke with a mild voice that understated his determination to expunge sorcery from Iceland. Two years earlier, he had successfully prosecuted three young warlocks in the Westfjords for using magic to induce hysteria among women in a church. The men had been burnt at the stake.

Thanks to Thorleif Kortsson, the new inquiry at Eyri was to show far more zeal than the previous one. The court soon established that the Jón Jónssons had failed to gather twelve sworn statements attesting to their innocence. Men were sent to arrest them and put them in irons.

The sheriff's men arrived at the Jónssons' farmhouse in a tense mood; they anticipated fierce resistance. Yet the two accused appeared resigned to their fate. The father declared he had no desire to live any longer, but the younger Jón admitted he was still very much afraid of death.

The pastor, too weak to leave his house at Eyri, was kept apprised of news from the courtroom. But now, just as it seemed certain the two men would be condemned for their diabolism, someone came to the pastor with astonishing news: the accused had repented and undergone a sincere change of heart.

The father and son were brought to the pastor's house, and he staggered to the door to receive them. Too weak to stand alone, he had to be supported by two servants. The pastor stretched out his arms to greet them. Jón Jónsson the elder accepted the embrace and asked humbly for the pastor's forgiveness, and then was taken away.

Then the younger Jón Jónsson was brought to the door, where he bent down to pray. The pastor was shocked by how greatly the young man's appearance had altered. His ruddy complexion was now darkened and swollen, his golden hair now the colour of ash.

But as the pastor looked down upon his prostrate form, he felt a wave of nausea ride over him. As he urged Jón Jónsson to repent, the young man reached up and punched the pastor with his fist. Jón Jónsson then walked away, saying, 'May God grant us all a good night!'

The pastor could not see a flicker of repentance in his face.

THE TWO MEN were brought before the court, fettered in irons. The local people in the courtroom were asked by the magistrates to raise their hands if they knew the elder Jón Jónsson to be a longstanding practitioner of magic. Most of the people did so, and said they could not deny it.

The elder Jón admitted that he did own an old calfskin book, and that he had once practised magic on a cow and a fox. When pressed, he confessed he had indeed caused the pastor's illnesses by means of witchcraft.

For his part, Jón Jónsson the younger confessed that he had tried sorcery on a small dog, but had only succeeded in confusing the creature. He said he had given two magic stave-runes to his friend

Markús. One was to be placed in the bed of a girl he wanted to marry; the other was to prevent drowning at sea. He also admitted he had carved a stave-rune into a whalebone and cast it to the winds with a curse, and had uttered the following heathen words:

> *I bring you beer,*
> *Fine fellow,*
> *Mightily compounded*
> *By potent magic –*
> *The magic that Odin,*
> *Lord of the Aesir,*
> *And evil Gyda*
> *Have made as potent as can be.*

WITH GUILT NOW clearly established, the court could find no reason for leniency. Indeed, they agreed that to show mercy would be to endanger everyone in the district. The court concluded that in placing themselves in league with the devil and causing immense suffering to the pastor and his flock, the father and son had forfeited their lives. This death sentence was pronounced on 11 May 1656.

Men were sent by the court to gather up every piece of firewood, charcoal and brushwood they could find. They brought the wood to the place of execution,* and doused it in tar and fish oil. The father and son were strapped to a stake in the middle of the heap and it was put to the torch.

It was a drawn-out business. Twice the fire refused to take hold of the younger Jón Jónsson. When the flames at last began to scorch him, he was said to have screamed out every name he knew for the devil.

---

*   The site of present-day Ísafjördur Airport.

The two men were dead, but the pastor's sufferings still did not abate. So the deputies searched through the charred ruins and discovered a portion of the young man's face, still unburnt, as well as fragments of the brains of the father and son. The remnants were carefully collected and burnt again, this time to ashes. Only then did the visions and hauntings that had plagued the district cease. For the moment.

There was still the matter of compensation to be dealt with. The pastor was acknowledged as the principal victim of the Jón Jónssons. The court noted sympathetically that he was now completely bedridden. 'God alone knows,' the magistrates said, 'how long he will survive, or what his end will be.' Therefore, the court ruled, he should receive a substantial apportionment of wealth from the sale of Jón Jónsson the elder's property in compensation for his injuries. Jón Jónsson's daughter Thuríd asked only that she be given her father's fur-lined silk cap, which she wore the following Saturday.

For the pastor, the verdict was a vindication and an official rebuke to sheriff Magnús Magnússon, who had been so reluctant to prosecute the Jón Jónssons. 'Why was there no prior action, Magnús?' the pastor later wrote. 'I wonder whether trousers full of fear might be the cause!'

JÓN JÓNSSON and his son had been utterly annihilated. But incredibly, the pastor was still besieged at night by demonic torments, by invisible fists and knees. Again, there was that terrible spiritual malaise, the shameful coldness and alienation from God.

The pastor could only conclude that someone else in the parish must be using witchcraft against him. When he pondered the matter, he recalled a moment when Jón Jónsson's nineteen-year-old daughter Thuríd had passed by his house. She had been walking alongside a cow that had belonged to her father, and she had stroked it in a manner that struck the pastor as sinister.

Pastor Jón rode out again to Kirkjuból. When he arrived, he led Thuríd Jónsdóttir into the half-church to speak with her. He stared hard at the girl. He believed he could detect a dark, smudgy circle around her head, throbbing like a malignant black halo.

The pastor commanded her to pray, but as she did so, he saw there were no tears in her eyes, and her prayers struck him as barren and cold. He told Thuríd her prayers would most likely not be heard or accepted by God. Then he spat in her face.

Still the demons lingered in his house at Eyri. One morning he stepped outside and there, beside the gable of the *baðstofa*, he saw for a moment the apparition of a young woman in the shape of Thuríd. She wore a broad-brimmed hat, and a wide black coat with skirts that fluttered in the wind. The pastor moved towards the apparition but it disappeared.

The pastor knew that Thuríd had been taught her letters by her father. There was no doubt in his mind now that Jón Jónsson had also schooled her in the arts of heathen magic, and that she wanted revenge for the deaths of her father and brother.

Again the pastor wrote to Thorleif Kortsson, asking him to begin legal proceedings against the daughter. Hearing of this, Thuríd fled to the neighbouring district of Holt, where she took refuge with the dean of the church. Pastor Jón had to tread carefully here, as the dean was his immediate superior. Nonetheless, he wrote a letter to the dean, accusing Thuríd of witchcraft. A synod of five priests met at Holt to consider the matter, and concluded that the pastor's charges were without any merit.

Pastor Jón then tried to press the case at Thingvellir. Twice more he brought forward charges of witchcraft, but Thuríd spoke well at the Althing, and unlike her father, was able to gather twelve people to attest to her innocence. She was later acquitted in a local court.

In his rage and bitterness, the thwarted pastor took up his pen and recorded an account of his torments, and the dilatory response of the authorities, in the *Píslarsaga – The Saga of My Sufferings.*

THE *PÍSLARSAGA* BURNS with the pastor's agony and self-righteousness. To read it today is to be struck by how unwittingly its author incriminates himself. We can only speculate across the distance of three and half centuries as to the underlying neurological or psychological disorders suffered by this man. One scholar attributes the physical disorders – the shaking and exhaustion, the pins and needles, the congestion in the throat and the chest, the feverish visions, the painful hissing in the ear – to an outbreak of the flu in the pastor's household.

The winter sunlessness of Ísafjördur is never mentioned in the saga of the pastor's sorrows, but I wonder how hard it was for an anxious Christian soul to watch the sun dip below those massive cliff walls in December, plunging the little settlement into primitive darkness. Who knows what he imagined he saw flitting in the shadows beyond his feeble orb of candlelight.

UNLIKE HER FATHER AND BROTHER, Thuríd Jónsdóttir would survive the attack on her family by Pastor Jón Magnússon. Having won her case at the Althing, she brought a countersuit against the priest, accusing him of persecuting her, but a church synod held at Holt failed to resolve the matter.

The witchcraft hysteria subsided, and the pastor returned to his duties. His son Snorri was ordained as his assistant, but was expelled from the clergy after fathering a child out of wedlock.

In 1689 the pastor retired and moved to Kirkjuból, to live with Snorri and his family. He died in 1696.

The first census of Iceland records that Thuríd Jónsdóttir grew old and resided with her son's family on a croft in Dýrafjördur, until she expired in 1703 at the advanced age of sixty-five.

AFTER A STRANGE NIGHT immersed in the saga of Pastor Jón Magnússon and his attendant demons, I wake up to a bright and clear morning. Cold air is streaming through the narrow opening of my dormitory window.

There's some radio work to do, so, galvanised with three cups of understrength filter coffee, I pick up the sound gear and bring Kári with me down to the pebbly beach of the fjord. I want to record what's known in radio jargon as 'atmos' – atmospheric background audio – of water lapping onto the shore. The wind is blowing noisily into the fjord. I try to imagine what this place would have been like in the seventeenth century, with only a church, the pastor's farmhouse, and a few wooden boats leaning on the shore.

The landscape here is so dramatic and liminal it feels like an illusion cast by the Aesir. I tell Kári, 'Perhaps if they lifted the spell, all we'd see is a hardscrabble little fishing village at the edge of the world.'

'It's not the edge of the world for the people who live here,' Kári points out. 'It's the very centre of the universe. Icelanders are no different from Australians in this. They boast that they live in the most special place on the planet, and they worry that because they're so far away, they're beneath the world's notice.'

Next to us on the beach is the Westfjords Heritage Museum:

a grand old timber warehouse with low walls and a high pitched roof. The museum's exhibits include some old boats, nautical paraphernalia and a collection of 190 accordions. On some days, the staff make a show of putting out salt cod to dry on the big pebbles, for the benefit of cruise-ship tourists.

Arctic idolators worshipping the sun and moon: illustration from Olaus Magnus, History of the Northern Peoples, *1555.*

'I have a theory, Kári, and I don't know if you'll like it much. My theory is that the manner in which a new settlement is consecrated somehow stamps its character forever. The first night the convicts were brought ashore at Sydney Cove there was an orgy, and Sydney's been a hyper-sexualised city ever since. Maybe Iceland is the same. Doesn't *The Book of Settlements* tell us the first thing the Vikings did when they founded a new settlement was to consecrate the land to the gods, or build a temple to Thor?'

'Yes. They wanted to plant their gods into the soil of Iceland straight away.'

'Well, the Christians might have overturned that soil to sow a new crop, but they never did eradicate the old weed that was planted here in the first place.'

Hawk Valley

IT'S TIME for us to head out further into these fjords, to find our way to the key locations of the saga of Gísli the fugitive, also known as Gísli the Outlaw: the doomed warrior, the man of unbending honour whose name was given to Kári's father. It is among the grimmest of the sagas, and it begins with a magical rite of blood-brotherhood that goes badly wrong.

Guðrún Nordal had smiled and shaken her head when I'd mentioned the saga to her at the Árni Magnússon Institute. 'Oh, Gísli's Saga ...' she'd said. 'When you read the saga, you think the landscape must have these big open spaces. But then you go to the valley where it happens in the northwest, and it's so frustratingly small. And you see this "river" they talk about is really just a little brook. All you have to do is jump over it, and you can be in someone else's bedroom in two minutes.'

Most scholars tend to stress the internal struggle of Gísli in this saga. Guðrún had a different take on it, which I liked very much.

'This is a saga about a *family*,' she said firmly. 'It's like your Christmas party. You have to meet these same people every year, every birthday, all the time. You're all related. And you can't get away from it. These relationships are so complicated. It's like they're doomed in their intricacies.'

THE NEXT DAY, we drive south to a farm in the Westfjords called Haukadalur – Hawk Valley. We pull up on the side of the dirt road, next to an open field. I see a couple of farmhouses in the distance. We slide down a grassy slope to the edge of the little brook that Gudrún mentioned. It's another one of those days when although the sun is shining as hard as it can, there's not much warmth to be had from it.

Kári tells me it was Gísli who built the very first farm here in the tenth century. According to the saga, his brother Thorkel wasn't much help, so the brothers fell out. Then, just a little further up this stream, a second farm was built by a powerful chieftain called Thorgrím. He was married to Gísli and Thorkel's sister, Thórdís, so Thorkel moved in with them.

'Does everyone's name in this saga begin with "Thor"?' I ask.

'Don't focus on the names too much. The point is that the families were too tightly intertwined in this place, and the farms were too close together.'

The Saga of Gísli

GÍSLI
a settler in the Westfjords

THORKEL
Gísli's brother

THÓRDÍS
Gísli's sister

AUD
Gísli's wife

VÉSTEIN
Gísli's closest friend

THORGRÍM
Thórdís's first husband

BÖRK
Thórdís's second husband

ÁSGERD
Thorkel's wife

FOUR FRIENDS. Gísli, his brother Thorkel, Thorgrím his brother-in-law, and his best friend Véstein.

But this is also the story of the women in their lives: Gísli's sister Thórdís, who married Thorgrím, and Gísli's wife Aud, who was Véstein's sister.

What Gísli wanted most was to hold them all together, and to keep them whole as a family.

ONE DAY, Gísli came to the local assembly. He was accompanied by his brother Thorkel and his two friends Thorgrím and Véstein. The four men were making a show of themselves. Other people began to notice them. Someone even said, 'I wonder how long those four will be friends.'

Gest Oddleifsson, a man known for his prophecies, gave an answer. 'Those four men won't be as close in three years as they are now.'

Gísli later heard about the prophecy, and decided to do something about it. He'd keep his group of four together through a pact of blood-brotherhood.

They began a ceremony. They cut out a long strip of turf, and used a piece of wood to pitch the turf up high enough for them to walk underneath it. They then cut themselves, and let their blood run down their arms and into the soil, where they mixed it with their hands. They were now ready to swear allegiance to one another.

But at that crucial moment, one of the men, Thorgrím, stepped back. Something was stopping him from becoming part of this group. He looked around at the men he was standing with, and for a moment stared at Véstein, Gísli's best friend.

'What's the matter?' asked Gísli. 'It's time for us to swear the oath.'

Thorgrím answered, 'I feel myself to be bound enough if I swear allegiance to you and your brother, without being bound to this other man here. I won't give Véstein my oath.'

When Gísli heard this, he too recoiled. He said, 'I can't bind myself to you, Thorgrím, if you won't swear blood-brotherhood with Véstein.'

With that, the whole thing fell apart.

There was a problem beneath the surface. None of them would say what it was, but afterwards nothing was ever quite the same again between the four friends.

Soon enough, what had been a band of four split into two bands of two: Gísli and his best friend Véstein; and Thorkel and his best friend Thorgrím.

They weren't enemies. Not yet.

Haukadalur

FOR A WHILE AFTERWARDS, Gísli and his brother Thorkel continued to live and farm together in the valley of Haukadalur. Their wives would spend the days working inside, and to pass the time they talked as they worked.

Gísli was a diligent man, who toiled hard as a farmer. His brother, though, wasn't. He was lazy, he didn't help much around the farm, and he didn't share Gísli's outlook on family life.

In fact, Thorkel spent most of his time inside, moping around. One day, he walked along the hall inside the farmhouse, and there he heard his wife, Ásgerd, talking to Gísli's wife, Aud. The women were doing their day's work, cutting out shirts for the men. They were talking about things from the past, before they were married.

Thorkel overheard his wife say to Aud, 'Would you cut out a shirt for Thorkel for me?'

Aud replied, 'You wouldn't be asking me to do that if it was a shirt for my brother Véstein. You'd want to cut *his* shirt yourself.'

Ásgerd said, 'Well, I heard you spent a lot of time with Thorgrím before you married Gísli.'

Thorkel listened, and when the women had finished their conversation, he turned away and said, 'There's blood in those words.'

IN A SENSE, Thorkel had heard nothing more serious than two women talking about something that happened long ago, attachments that they'd had before they married. But he'd also just heard his wife confess that she once loved another man, and that his brother's wife had as well.

Suddenly, everything was a mess. These were not two couples. This was the beginning of a feud, and everyone was implicated.

Thorkel couldn't bear what he now knew. That night, he told his wife Ásgerd that he wasn't going to sleep with her any more. He said she could sleep on her own, for some time at least.

Ásgerd put her arms around Thorkel's neck and replied, 'You either take me back into this bed right now, or I'm going to divorce you and take all my property with me.'

He backed down, and they slept together as normal. Thorkel's venom would no longer be directed at her. It had to find a new home, a new victim: her former lover Véstein. His brother's closest friend.

After that, Thorkel became restless, and began talking about leaving the farm that he shared with Gísli. He thought it would be better to move further up the valley to where his sister and her husband lived, and join them at their farm instead of living with his brother. Thorkel said he wouldn't mind if Gísli kept the land, as long as Thorkel could take his share of the other possessions.

Thorkel was hoping to put some distance between him and Gísli. But Haukadalur is a narrow valley, and the farms were very close. If Gísli's best friend ever came to visit Haukadalur from his home in the next valley, he wouldn't be far out of reach of his new enemy.

TIME PASSED. Véstein and Gísli travelled abroad together, as did Thorkel and Thorgrím.

After they all returned to Iceland, Gísli held an autumn feast, a tradition in those times. His wife Aud invited her brother, Gísli's best friend Véstein, to attend.

During the feast, a bad storm came through the fjord. It brought very heavy rain, and in the middle of the night all the men had to go outside to cover the hay that lay exposed in the fields.

Véstein wanted to join in and help. But Gísli told him to stay inside. He worried that Véstein would be vulnerable to attack. He understood his brother's temperament and the hatred he harboured, and thought Véstein would be much safer indoors.

The rain began to get through the cracks in the roof, and eventually Véstein had to run his bed longways along the hall, in order to stay dry. Just before morning, while the others were still outside working to cover the hay, someone came into the house and walked up to Véstein's bed. The intruder then lifted the covers, and drove a spear through him. Véstein was dead.

A servant was the first to see what had happened. He ran up to the body, but refused to take the spear out. Whoever did so would be honour-bound to avenge Véstein's death.

When Gísli came back inside and saw his friend's body, he pulled the spear out and placed it inside a chest. He would now have to be the one to avenge the murder of his best friend.

But who was the murderer? Was it Thorkel, his brother? Had he acted out of jealousy for his wife's old affection for Véstein, all on the basis of a conversation that he'd once overheard?

A BURIAL WAS HELD in the valley for Véstein. During the ceremony, shoes were tied around his feet. These were called *helskór*, Hel-shoes, and were meant to ease a fallen warrior's way into Valhalla.

Thorgrím, Gísli's brother-in-law and his brother's best friend, was present at the burial. During the ceremony, he walked up to the corpse, and in front of all those who'd come to farewell Véstein, fastened the laces on the shoes. Then he turned to everyone and said, 'I don't know how to tie Hel-shoes if these come undone.'

Véstein was dead, and Thorgrím meant him to stay that way.

Gísli began to wonder who the murderer was. Up until then, he must have thought it was his brother. But here was Thorgrím boasting over the dead body, rubbing it in.

After the funeral, Thorkel approached Gísli and said, 'Brother, I want things to go back to the way they once were between us. I want us to be close again.'

Gísli replied, 'That's well said. But promise me one thing: that if you ever feel the pain that I feel now, you will be as good to me as I'm being to you.'

Thorkel promised him that.

GÍSLI FELT BLEAKNESS and deep grief. Yet Thorgrím kept on needling him with insults towards his dead friend.

Gísli's grief hardened into hate.

One night, Gísli took the spear out of the chest. He walked along the stream that runs through the valley, between his farm and Thorgrím's. He broke into the back of the farmhouse, through the barns and past the farm animals that were being kept in out of the cold. Then into the hall.

There were still some lights burning. He put them out, and in the darkness worked his way to Thorgrím's bedroom.

Thorgrím lay asleep with his wife Thórdís, Gísli's sister.

Gísli walked into the bedroom and placed his hand under the covers. He put his hand on his sister's breast. She woke and said, 'Why is your hand so cold, Thorgrím?'

Thorgrím replied, 'Do you want me to roll over?'

Gísli waited while they made love. When the couple fell asleep again, Gísli lifted the covers, and drove his spear so deep into Thorgrím that it fastened itself to the planks at the base of the bed.

Now Thorgrím was dead too, killed with the same spear as Véstein.

Thórdís woke, and screamed. The attacker was gone. She yelled out that Thorgrím had been killed.

Gísli had run through the house and outside, and made his escape back along the frozen stream.

Straight away, others ran out of Thorgrím's farm to see what Gísli was doing, whether he'd been out that night. They couldn't be sure it was him, but then who else would have avenged Véstein's killing in this way?

Thorkel entered Gísli's farm and approached Gísli's bedroom. He saw Gísli's shoes on the floor. They were covered in snow.

Thorkel pushed the shoes under the bed.

GÍSLI SAID HIS HOUSEHOLD would organise the burial mound for Thorgrím. The body was placed in a boat; in this version of the funeral ritual, it wasn't pushed out into the fjord but rather a turf mound was raised over it. The mound was to be sealed. But Gísli had one thing he wanted to do first.

He walked down to the shore, and picked up a massive boulder. He carried it back and dropped it onto the mound. The planks of wood gave way and cracked.

He said, 'If the weather moves this mound, then I don't know how to fasten a boat.'

NO ONE BUT THORKEL KNEW who'd killed Thorgrím. But one day, when Gísli and the others from the valley were playing a ball game on the frozen ponds at the mouth of the valley, Gísli lost his temper and, facing Thorgrím's burial mound, uttered a verse that he should have kept to himself:

I saw the shoots reach up
through the thawed earth
on the grim giant-Thor's mound
I saw that Gaut of battle-gleam,
Thrott's helmet
has silenced the spear-rattler,
given one, greedy for land,
*a plot of his own, forever.**

HIS SISTER THÓRDÍS heard the verse. At first, she didn't understand its meaning. But all the same she memorised it, just in case she could decode it later.

IT NOW FELL to Thorgrím's brother, a powerful man called Börk the Stout, to follow up the case for the killing. He visited Thórdís at

---

*   'Gaut of battle-gleam' and 'Thrott's helmet' are both metaphors for 'warrior' and refer to Gísli himself. The 'grim giant-Thor' is Thorgrím. Poem translated by Martin S. Regal.

her farm and stayed with her. Eventually he moved there too, and married his brother's widow.

But Börk didn't know that Gísli had killed Thorgrím.

To begin his pursuit of the unknown killer, he had a curse performed by a sorcerer. It proclaimed that whoever had killed Thorgrím would never benefit from the help of others in Iceland.

Meanwhile, Thórdís worked away at deciphering the poem, until finally she realised that Gísli's poem had been a confession. He'd killed her husband in their marital bed, while she lay next to him, after they had made love.

For a while, she kept it to herself. But it weighed on her, and one day, as she rode past the burial mound of her dead husband, she told her new husband Börk that Gísli was the killer.

A legal action was brought against Gísli, and a judgement of outlawry passed down. Gísli would have to leave Iceland, or his enemies were legally entitled to kill him. He didn't want to go abroad; he had no other choice but to flee into hiding – deeper into the Westfjords.

Gísli approached his brother Thorkel for help. But now, just when Thorkel was needed most, he hesitated. Thorkel replied that he was willing to warn Gísli if he knew that there was about to be an attempt on his life. But he could do no more than that.

Thorkel had once promised Gísli that he would act honourably, even if he lost someone as dear to him as Véstein had been to his brother. Gísli turned on Thorkel and said, 'I would not have given you that reply if you'd come to *me* for help.'

In many ways, Thorkel's promise was a good one, and he would always keep to it, and warn Gísli whenever he could. But Gísli felt it as pure betrayal. His sister had already married his pursuer, and now his brother was failing him too.

GÍSLI SOLD THE FARM at Haukadalur and began a new life as an exile. He left his wife Aud, and a foster-daughter, Gudríd, behind and travelled in the company of a single slave, Thórd the Coward. He didn't think much of the conditional promise that his brother had given, and he started to become desperate. He would have to rely as much on trickery as on bravery and strength.

Börk the Stout and his men soon came in pursuit. When Gísli saw them, he told Thórd the Coward to swap cloaks with him. He handed Thórd his fine, black cloak. 'This is a gift,' he said, counting on Thórd's stupidity. 'For your loyalty to me. Put it on now.'

They swapped clothes; Gísli dressed as the slave. Then he added, 'If you hear men calling out, don't answer them. Just keep riding.'

Thórd, they say, was as stupid as he was cowardly, and accepted Gísli's instructions without demur. When Börk and his men approached, Thórd and Gísli separated. Thórd made for some nearby woods, but the ground was heavy and he was slow. Börk's men saw his fine black cloak, and thought – as Gísli knew they would – that he was the man they wanted. One threw his spear at Thórd, catching him between the shoulder blades.

Thórd fell down, dead.

Gísli got away. He rode back to the farm at Haukadalur and collected what possessions he could, then left the valley for the last time. But now he also asked his wife Aud and Gudríd to join him. They took a boat down to the water and sailed out past the headlands, heading south along the fjords.

They landed at Geirthjófsfjördur, a narrow, abandoned fjord where Gísli could build a small farm so they could at least spend the winters in safety. His enemies would struggle to attack them here.

He still hoped to escape his legal troubles. He sent messages asking for help from Véstein's kinsmen; he wanted them to offer a settlement for the killing of Thorgrím. But they made a mess of the legal proceedings, and Gísli remained an outlaw.

Geirthjófsfjördur, where Gísli went into exile

GÍSLI BEGAN TO HAVE vivid dreams, and slept badly. One night Aud woke him to ask what he was dreaming.

'There are two women in my dreams. One is good to me, the other is cruel and prophesies only evil things. Tonight I dreamt I was walking towards a hall. When I went inside, I saw my kinsmen there, waiting for me beside seven fires. The good dream woman walked into the hall behind me. She said I had seven years left to live. She then told me to stop following the heathen ways, and to use the time I have left to be good to the poor and helpless.'

Aud listened to his dreams, and tried to soothe him. But he began to worry that he would be trapped if he stayed in the fjord, and took to travelling around the country on his own. He tried again to get help from his brother, but Thorkel wouldn't put himself in any danger. He gave Gísli homespun cloth and silver, but no more support than that.

Gísli took shelter where he could, but by the spring he missed Aud, and couldn't stay away any longer. He returned to the fjord.

As winter came on, his dreams intensified. Now the bad dream woman was coming more and more often. She said she was going to bathe him in blood and pour bile over him. He felt his death chasing him in the wilderness.

WHEREVER HE TRAVELLED on the mainland, Gísli was unable to persuade his friends and kinsmen to give him help. But the curse that had once been placed on Thorgrím's killer had not made any mention of the many small islands off the coast. Gísli's cousin Ingjald lived on one of these: Hergilsey, off the south coast of the Westfjords.

The next autumn, Gísli sought to escape the dreams that came on in winter, by taking refuge with Ingjald. First he visited his brother once more, but this time Thorkel wouldn't even come outside to talk.

Gísli picked up a piece of wood and carved runes onto it, a message for his brother. He threw the timber through a window into Thorkel's house.

Thorkel picked up the wood and finally came outside.

'I can't help you,' he told Gísli. 'Take horses. Take one of my boats. But that's all I can do.'

'Let this be our last meeting, then,' said Gísli. He had tired of trying to get his brother's full support.

He took one of his brother's boats and rowed to Hergilsey Island. He unloaded his belongings, capsized the vessel and sent it drifting back to the mainland to make it look as though he'd drowned.

Ingjald welcomed him warmly, and invited him to stay.

Ingjald had a son called Helgi, an enormous, dim-witted fellow whom Ingjald would tether by the neck to a large stone. His nickname was Ingjald's Fool, and they say he looked more like a troll than a human being.

Gísli travelled widely in these years, sometimes retreating into the heaths and mountains, sometimes returning to the farm and to Aud and Gudríd. He began to spend his winters with Ingjald, and kept himself busy with building work. People started to suspect that Ingjald was hiding Gísli, for no one else at the farm, least of all Ingjald's son, was capable of the craftsmanship that was starting to appear: beautifully made boats that were as finely constructed as his poetry and rune craft.

When Börk heard that Gísli might be on the island, he sailed across with fourteen men. Gísli and Ingjald were out fishing, and saw Börk approach. Gísli rowed Ingjald back to the island, then asked a slave woman to get into the boat and row him towards Börk and his men.

'When they talk to you, tell them I'm Ingjald's Fool. I'll sit at the bow and act like him.'

As Börk neared them, he questioned the slave woman. He called out across the water, 'Have you seen Gísli?'

She said didn't know, but she could say that there was a brave-looking man on the island.

Börk listened, but not his men. They told Börk they were having too much fun watching the fool. Gísli had wrapped himself in the fishing nets and was floundering about.

Börk said to the slave woman, 'It must be awful to have to look after such an idiot.'

Once again, Gísli got away.

GÍSLI MADE MANY such escapes, outwitting Börk and his men and humiliating them year after year. But he knew that he had only so much time left to live: he trusted the prophecy in the dream that had given him seven years. He began to spend more time with Aud.

The following spring, two scruffy young men appeared at the local assembly. No one knew who they were, but they were very noticeable. They walked around asking who was attending the assembly. They particularly wanted to know how to find the booth belonging to Thorkel, Gísli's brother.

Someone pointed Thorkel out. He was dressed very finely in a Russian hat and a grey fur cloak pinned with a gold clasp. He held a sword at his side.

The young men stepped towards him. Seeking to flatter Thorkel with a courtly mode of address, the older asked, 'Who is this handsome, noble-looking man?'

'That's well said,' replied Thorkel, and introduced himself.

'You have an excellent weapon in your hand. May I see it?'

'An unusual request,' said Thorkel. 'But yes, I'll let you.' He handed the sword over, still in its sheath.

The young man unfastened the sheath and held up the sword.

'I didn't say you could draw it,' said Thorkel.

'I didn't ask.' The young man stepped forward and cut at Thorkel's neck. His head came clean off.

There was chaos in the booth. The young men were pinned down to the ground. People were shouting at each other.

As they lay on the ground, one of the boys asked the other, 'What are they arguing about?'

'I think they're trying to remember whether our father Véstein had sons or daughters.'

The sons had come back.

LATER, THE TWO YOUNG MEN escaped their captors at the assembly, and made their way to Geirthjófsfjördur to seek protection and shelter from Aud, their father's sister, and Gísli's wife. They would have to put their lives into the hands of their victim's brother.

After five nights in the open, they arrived at the farm. Gísli happened to be there at the time. Aud answered the door, while Gísli went into hiding in an underground room.

The brothers told Aud that they had killed Thorkel in vengeance for Véstein's death.

Aud said, 'I'm going to send you to a kinsman's farm. You must go there, and not stay with us. I'll give you food before you go, and tokens, so that they believe who you are.'

The young men sat down to eat, but were overcome with tiredness. They fell asleep on the benches where they sat.

Aud tried to wake them, but couldn't. She went to Gísli's room, and said to him, 'I'm going to ask you to do something for me now, and to honour me more than I deserve.'

'Thorkel is dead, isn't he?' Gísli asked.

'Yes, and the boys who killed him are here. My brother's sons. Your friend's sons. They need our help.'

Gísli drew his sword. He was honour-bound to avenge Thorkel, his brother, even though the two had fallen out. 'I can't help them,' he said.

'Stop,' said Aud. 'Let them leave. You don't need to do anything.'

She went back upstairs and eventually woke her nephews. The young men stepped back out into the night, protected, as Gísli was, by Aud's generosity and love.

BÖRK THE STOUT had failed thus far to kill Gísli. In desperation, he hired a killer called Eyjólf to hunt Gísli down. There was disgrace in this, but it would be worse to allow his brother's killer to live.

Eyjólf arrived at the farm. He found Aud and her foster-daughter on their own.

He sat down. 'We can make a deal,' he said. 'I have 300 pieces of silver that I will give you if you tell me where Gísli is hiding. I promise that you won't have to see him killed. After he's dead, I'll arrange a better marriage for you.'

'Maybe you're right,' Aud replied. 'Money helps grieving.'

Eyjólf tipped the silver pieces into her lap.

Aud began to count the silver, placing each coin into a large purse. While she was counting, she asked if she could do whatever she wanted with it.

'Of course,' he said. 'It's yours.'

So she stood up and swung the purse into his face, smashing him on the nose. 'Now,' she said, 'you can tell everyone the fine story of when you were hit by a woman.'

ONE NIGHT, the bad dream woman came to Gísli and told him that she was now going to undo everything that the good dream woman had promised him. She took hold of him and began to wash his hair in blood. She showed him his attackers coming for him. He woke feeling their blades cutting into his face.

It got harder to fall asleep in the farmhouse; his dreams seemed worse there. He asked Aud and Gudríd to come with him to a hideout further up the valley, on one of the high ridges above the fjord.

It was early winter, there was frost on the ground, and they left a trail behind with their coats. Shavings fell from a piece of wood that Gísli was using to carve runes.

That was how the attackers found them. They followed the trail until they came to the hideout.

Gísli said he was ready to fight.

A Viking sword.

He killed one of the attackers. Then Eyjólf appeared from another side and stood in front of Aud.

She picked up a club and hit him on the arm.

Gísli said, 'I always knew I was well married, but now I see just *how* well.'

The attackers pushed Aud and Gudríd away. Gísli ran further up the side of the valley, to a high crag called Einhamar. His enemies came at him from two sides. Finally, they could reach him.

This was where he made his last stand. He jumped off the ridge, aiming his sword at his killers. They raised their spears, and Gísli, making a final lunge at his enemies, fell onto them.

Outlaws

Abandoned house, Westfjords

THE BLUFF ABOVE Geirthjófsfjördur is covered in broken yellow rocks, embedded in the hard soil. It feels like we're standing on the shoulder of some huge muscular creature, a frost giant. A fierce wind blows in from the Atlantic, cold enough to sting the ears, but nothing in the landscape moves, other than little tufts of weeds that shiver and shake. Everything is fastened to the barren rock.

Neither of us was quite prepared for the solemn bleakness of this place. Was it just as desolate a thousand years ago, in Gísli's time?

Kári points down to the water's edge far below, where I see a narrow carpet of pale green between the bluff and the sea. 'I suppose,' Kári says, 'that's where Aud kept her farm.'

'That little farm,' I say, 'would become your whole world. That, and the fishing. There's nothing else here at all.'

THE RETURN DRIVE to Ísafjördur takes us back along the looping roads that skirt the fingers of the Westfjords.

I observe to Kári that Gísli's Saga is another story in which everything turns on the words of a woman, or in this case, two women: the banter between Ásgerd and Aud. All the elements were in place, but they needed the words of women to catalyse them, like a chemical reaction: 'There's blood in those words.'

When I'd talked about this moment with Guðrún Nordal at the Árni Magnússon Institute, she'd said she thought this was a classic case of male over-reaction. 'These women think they're having a private conversation,' Guðrún had said. 'One of them asks, "Did you love him?" When you're a woman, this is a very innocent question. Why not answer it? Why not chitchat about it? It has no bearing on what's happening now, you're all married anyway.'

WE PULL OVER to stretch our legs on the edge of another fjord. An abandoned stone house overlooks the pebbly beach, surrounded by patches of grass, sand and purple heather. Kári crouches on the shore and trails his fingers through the water.

I'm still thinking about that astonishing moment when Gísli puts his cold hand on his sister's breast in the darkened bedroom, and she thinks it's her husband, Thorgrím. Maybe this is what drives Gísli all along. The whole man-of-honour thing is just a mask for a man secretly possessed by an incestuous jealousy he doesn't fully understand.

When I try to picture Gísli in his final years – haggard, worn down by constant vigilance – I think of the rook of the Lewis Chessmen, a famous set of bug-eyed and battle-haunted Norse chess pieces held by the British Museum, exquisitely carved from walrus ivory and whale tooth. The rook is the standout, fashioned as a berserker warrior so eager to get into battle he chomps down on the edge of his shield.

The rook as beserker warrior: one of the Lewis Chessmen at the British Museum

The pieces were discovered in 1831 on a beach on the Isle of Lewis, in the Outer Hebrides in Scotland. The British Museum, where most of the chessmen are displayed, places their origin in twelfth-century Norway, but there is some dispute over this. Icelandic scholars argue that the pieces are just as likely to have been fashioned in the south of Iceland, by a brilliant craftswoman known as Margret the Adroit.

ICELANDERS HAVE LONG PRIZED the game of chess, or *skák*, as they call it, for much the same reasons as they cherish the sagas: as a rich, immersive experience, full of human drama and conflict. *Skák* is a diversion that sharpens the wits, costs nothing and helps to while away the winter darkness.

In his *Heimskringla*, Snorri Sturluson recounts a famous chess match between King Canute of the Danes and his brother-in-law Earl Ulf that got somewhat out of hand. The two men had fallen out, and Ulf had come to the king's court to patch things up. Ulf tried to charm Canute, but every attempt at conversation fell flat. Exasperated, he proposed a game of chess, and the king agreed.

Canute made a poor move; Ulf took his knight and put it to one side. Undaunted, the king plonked the piece straight back on the board, looked Ulf in the eye, and told him to make another move. Ulf decided he'd had a bellyful of all this bad behaviour: he knocked over the board and the two men threw ugly insults at each other.

Ulf knew he'd gone too far. He fled to a nearby church for sanctuary, but the king sent in his bodyguard, who assassinated Ulf in the choir stall by running a sword through him on Christmas Day 1026.

CHESS WAS INVENTED in India, where it was known as *chaturanga*. It passed into Persia, and then Baghdad and Constantinople, where traders carried the game to the furthest reaches of Christendom, and eventually to Iceland. Along the way, Europeans altered the pieces to more closely resemble the figures of their medieval courts: the vizier became a queen, the elephant a bishop. Everywhere chess was introduced it sparked a craze, even in the most far-flung outposts.

Directly to the north of Iceland is a dot of an island called Grímsey, the northernmost part of Icelandic territory. With a tiny population of eighty-six, the island is sustained almost entirely by fishing, tourism and its centuries-old obsession with chess. In the Middle Ages it was said the people of Grímsey took their chess so seriously that losers were sometimes required to hurl themselves off a cliff.

In 1879, an American scholar named Daniel Willard Fiske visited Iceland and sailed past the little island. When told of the islanders' love of chess, Fiske impulsively donated an expensive marble chess set to every family on Grímsey. Later he bequeathed a sum of money to establish a library, which stands there today and houses a fine collection of books on chess.

Although Fiske never set foot on Grímsey, the islanders revere his memory, and his birthday is celebrated as Grímsey's 'national' holiday, with a cake party. The closeness of Professor Fiske's name to *fisk*, the Icelandic word for fish, can't have hurt his popularity either.

EVEN TODAY, it's common to see Icelanders frowning over a chess set in cafés and public places.

In the latter part of the twentieth century, this love of *skák*, and a lingering fondness for outlaws like Gísli, led the people of Iceland to welcome a rogue genius into their midst. Iceland offered him sanctuary when no one else would take him, even though he'd lost his mind.

The Saga of Bobby Fischer

ON 11 JULY 1972, a smartly dressed Russian man walked onto the platform of Laugardalshöll, an indoor sports arena in Reykjavík, and sat down at a table set for a chess match.

It was late afternoon. The stadium was filled to capacity and the platform was surrounded by cameras, transmitting grainy images of the strangely static scene to a vast international TV audience. Crowds in New York City watched the moment live on a gigantic screen in Times Square. Groups of people gathered around TV sets outside department stores across Europe and America. Iceland, the lonely, forgotten nation at the top of the world, was revelling in its moment at the centre of the world's attention.

The Russian at the chess table was Boris Spassky, a thirty-five-year-old citizen of the Soviet Union and the reigning World Chess Champion. Spassky, with his bouffant hair-do and his sharp three-piece suit, cut a much more stylish figure than the grey and dowdy Soviet leadership. His expression was neutral, calm, betraying nothing of the tension of the moment and the weight of expectation that lay upon him.

SPASSKY HAD BEEN a child prodigy. He played his first game at the age of five on a train, being evacuated from Leningrad while the city was under siege by Nazi Germany. At ten, Spassky beat the Soviet champion. At sixteen he was a grandmaster. In 1969 he defeated fellow Soviet Tigran Petrosian to become World Champion, consolidating the ongoing Soviet dominance of the game.

The Soviet regime loved chess. It was low-tech and cheap, yet gameplay was endlessly sophisticated. They treated the game like an Olympic sport, providing high-performing players like Boris Spassky with an income and coaching support.* Soviet domination of international chess allowed communist leaders to assert their ideology over the decadent West; to them, it was only to be expected that the communist system should churn out so many brilliant grandmasters.

Spassky had come to Reykjavík to defend his title against an American challenger: a lanky twenty-nine-year-old New Yorker named Bobby Fischer. Inevitably, the match between the Russian and the American was billed as a Cold War battle, a struggle between American individualism and the communist hive-mind. Whoever prevailed in Iceland would deliver his side a major propaganda victory.

Reykjavík, located roughly halfway between Washington and Moscow, was the perfect location for such a clash. And now, on day one, the eyes of the world were fixed on the city's Laugardalshöll sports complex. But only one player had shown up. Bobby Fischer's leather chair was empty.

---

*   And yet Spassky took care to distance himself from politics, and declined to join the Communist Party. Later he would claim he had secretly been a traditional Russian monarchist and Orthodox Christian all along.

AT 5PM PRECISELY, the chief arbiter, Lothar Schmid, opened the match by gently tapping the button mounted on the chess clock. After a moment's pause, Boris Spassky moved his queen's pawn two squares forward and tapped the clock again, setting off a countdown. Fischer now had one hour to show up and make his first move, otherwise he would forfeit the game.

The Icelanders in the racked seating were taut with suspense. This was their nation's big moment on the world stage. Would the whole thing collapse into an embarrassing non-event?

TV footage of Spassky waiting for Fischer

BOBBY FISCHER HAD ALSO been a child prodigy. He and his sister were raised in Brooklyn by their mother Regina, a brilliant and erratic woman of Polish-Jewish extraction. Regina spoke eight languages, including Russian, and was sympathetic to Soviet communism and progressive causes. Her political activism brought her to the attention of J. Edgar Hoover's FBI; her file would eventually amount to some 900 pages.

Occasionally the family would be visited by Paul Nemenyi, a Hungarian-Jewish mathematician, who would take Bobby on outings around New York. Regina had led Bobby to believe his father was a German scientist named Hans-Gerhardt Fischer, who had disappeared from the scene when Bobby was a toddler, but it seems that Paul Nemenyi, who made regular child-support payments to Regina and paid for Bobby's schooling, was his real father. The two had had an affair, and Regina had wanted to shield Bobby from the stigma of being born out of wedlock.

Nemenyi was distressed by Regina's poverty and her instability. When he died of a heart attack in 1952, Bobby was still a young boy. Bobby only learnt of his death when he asked his mother why Nemenyi didn't visit any more. Then she added: 'Didn't you know? He was your father.'

Bobby first encountered chess at the age of six, when his sister brought home a plastic set from the candy store next to their walk-up apartment. By seven Bobby was obsessed, reading every chess book or magazine he could get hold of. He would eat his meals next to a little chessboard where he could compute different strategies, or simply play against himself. His mother, worried her son was spending too much time staring at a board game, took him to a psychiatrist, who shrugged and told her there were bigger things in the world to worry about than chess.

At thirteen Fischer was blitzing American grandmasters, who called him 'the Boy Robot'. At fourteen he became the youngest player to win the United States Chess Championship. Regina wrote to the Soviet leader Nikita Khrushchev and wrangled an invitation for her son to visit Moscow, the capital of world chess. The Boy Robot was given a handsome welcome, but he alienated people with his rudeness. In the Moscow Chess Club, he was overheard referring to his hosts as 'Russian pigs'.

At fifteen Bobby became the youngest ever international grandmaster. He made several TV appearances where he was introduced as a boy genius. In 1958 he was invited on a game show called *I've Got a Secret*, looking like the classic all-American kid, with a crew cut and checked shirt. His responses to the host's questions were quick-witted, but his demeanour was dead-eyed and wary; Bobby was already accustomed to patronising adults who hoped to exploit his unlikely fame.

As his chess career soared, his relationship with his mother deteriorated. Unlike Regina, Bobby was no communist sympathiser: he loathed the way the Soviet chess authorities connived to lock outsiders like him from tournaments; he resented Regina's political obsessions, and her inability to pull the family out of their hand-to-mouth existence.

Bobby was taken up by a wealthy and eccentric member of New York's chess community, a man named E. Forry Laucks, who wore a small swastika on his lapel and collected Nazi memorabilia. Despite his political sympathies, Laucks was seemingly unbothered by Bobby's Jewish heritage, and might even have managed to impress his unseemly politics upon his young protégé. Bobby had often complained about his mother's Jewish friends and their 'intellectual' conversation. Now he began to make anti-Semitic remarks and to express an admiration for Adolf Hitler.

At sixteen Bobby dropped out of high school to devote himself to chess full-time, then he ordered his mother to leave the apartment. 'She keeps in my hair,' he told a reporter, 'and I don't like people in my hair, so I had to get rid of her.'

BOBBY FISCHER WALKED OUT of a tournament in Switzerland in 1968, aged twenty-five, and refused to play for another two years. In 1970, when he returned to competitive chess, his gameplay was more lethal than ever. One chess master claimed that the beauty and lucid expressiveness of Bobby's game put him in the company of Brahms, Rembrandt and Shakespeare.

In 1971, Bobby trounced the Soviet grandmaster and concert pianist Mark Taimanov. The match was expected to be close, but Fischer won 6–0. Forced to resign in the final game, Taimanov shrugged and said sadly, 'Well, I still have my music.' Fischer won his next two matches effortlessly, giving him the right to challenge Spassky for the world championship.

BY 1972, BOBBY FISCHER was twenty-nine years old, and tall enough to fill a doorway. He'd become a handsome young man, with a fondness, like Spassky, for sharp suits. His demolition of his Soviet opponents and his brooding, charismatic presence had made him a minor celebrity. The looming confrontation with Spassky catapulted him into international superstardom. Feature articles were published in *Life* magazine and *Sports Illustrated*.

But his genius-level intellect was tethered to an exacting and unstable personality. Bobby's narrow devotion to chess had left him unworldly and naïve; he was humourless, and awkward around women. 'I object to being called a chess genius,' he once said in an interview, 'because I consider myself to be an all-around genius who just happens to play chess.' Those who knew him thought his arrogance was a bluff to conceal an underlying awareness of how ignorant he was of anything outside the sixty-four squares of a chessboard. This anxiety, combined with a growing understanding of how much money the system had screwed from him over the years, contrived to make Bobby Fischer, on the eve of the championship, a supremely difficult and demanding human being.

BOBBY WANTED THE CHAMPIONSHIP match to be held in Belgrade, but Spassky insisted the Yugoslav summer would be intolerable for him. Reykjavík came in with the next highest bid, and so, after some wrangling, the city was named by FIDE, the international chess body,* as host.

Iceland had secured the deal with a $125,000 prize purse: an unprecedented sum for a chess match, which it hoped to recoup through sale of the television rights. Even so, for Fischer the potential winnings weren't enough and he threatened to walk unless *all* income from the match, less expenses, went to the players. The Icelanders sent a curt reply: changes to the financial arrangements were out of the question. Fischer then said he didn't want to play in Iceland anyway; he had visited Reykjavík for a tournament years earlier as a teenager, and said he thought the conditions there were too basic.

This retort must have stung the Icelanders, for it contained a germ of truth. Reykjavík had grown since World War II from a fishing village into a small city, but Icelanders were painfully aware that to the outside world, their capital looked like a shabby, isolated outpost. Reykjavík in 1972 had few modern hotels and a poor telecommunications infrastructure. Television was monopolised by the state broadcaster RUV, which broadcast only six days a week, and went off-air entirely throughout July. Perhaps the Icelanders themselves harboured secret doubts: were they really capable of hosting an international event on this scale?

FIDE hunkered down into a round of painstaking negotiations with Andrew Davis, Fischer's lawyer. Davis was an aggressive New Yorker who revered Fischer's genius, so much so he refused to charge him a fee for his services.

Bobby blew hot and cold: one day he would tell his friends he was definitely going, the next he would say he couldn't possibly go unless every single one of his demands was met. He had walked out

---

* FIDE: Fédération Internationale des Échecs, or World Chess Federation.

of tournaments before, so no one could tell if he was bluffing. In New York, the media kept badgering him: would he go to Reykjavík? Tiring of the scrutiny, he took off upstate.

THE RUSSIANS, MEANWHILE, had little choice but to proceed on the assumption that the match would take place as planned. Boris Spassky arrived at Keflavík Airport on 21 June, two weeks ahead of the scheduled opening game. He was greeted on the tarmac by Guðmundur Thórarinsson, President of the Icelandic Chess Federation. Guðmundur had been the key figure in bringing the match to Reykjavík, and for his trouble he would be caught in an agonising state of uncertainty over the weeks to come. He had brought his two young daughters to the airport, and they gave Spassky a bouquet of flowers, which he graciously accepted.

The champion checked into the Presidential Suite of the Hotel Saga, Iceland's most luxurious hotel. Each afternoon he played tennis on a court especially built for him. He impressed the Icelanders with his dignified bearing and his good manners. After a few days, he travelled out into the countryside to enjoy the wilderness and catch fish, which pleased the locals even more.

THE OPENING MATCH was fast approaching, but Bobby Fischer still wouldn't budge from New York. The press discovered he was hiding out in a resort in the Catskills. Bobby bluntly rejected every compromise position put to him, yet he still behaved like a man who fully expected to go to Iceland. Each day he alternated between rigorous physical exercise and intense study of Spassky's game.

On 28 June he was at last coaxed by his lawyers into a limousine bound for JFK airport. He'd brought with him a bag of oranges that he stipulated were to be squeezed in front of him on the flight, to avoid KGB tampering. Fischer was to be accompanied by his friend Anthony Saidy and lawyer Andrew Davis, who were doing their best to placate him, willing to do anything to get him on the plane.

Just before they climbed into the limousine, Davis called Guðmundur Thórarinsson to hit him with a new, last-minute demand for a bigger slice of the ticket sales.

'I am sorry,' Guðmundur said icily, 'but we have gone as far as we can … We have done everything in our power to satisfy Mr Fischer. But we have begun to wonder if it is possible to satisfy Mr Fischer. We Icelanders are a generous people, Mr Davis, but we are also a proud people. We will be freely generous, but we will not be forced to be generous.'

The lawyer, aware that Bobby was looking for an excuse to walk, put down the phone and told his client they should get in the car anyway; he would call Guðmundur again from the airport. Maybe they would reach a deal after all, if he could persuade Guðmundur this would be his final demand. Trying to arrive at a form of words that would satisfy his skittish client, Davis said he had come up with a deal that would give the players *everything*, and the Icelanders *nothing*. Bobby's eyes lit up and he agreed to get in the car.

THE LIMOUSINE DRIVER, an ex-butcher from the Bronx named Morris Dubinsky, began the journey in high spirits, excited to be ferrying a genius to the airport, but Bobby's petulant behaviour wore him down to a nub in the space of an hour and a half. As he listened to Bobby's petty demands, he concluded the chess master was suffering from a 'hernia in his head'.

Arriving at JFK, Dubinsky took the liberty of checking in the luggage while Bobby went to buy a digital clock. When Bobby came back to the car and realised his bags had already been put through, he lost his temper and shrieked at Dubinsky for acting without his permission.

Dubinsky had had enough. He told Bobby he'd better shut his mouth. 'You may be a genius at chess,' he said, putting his fists up, 'but in everything else you're a big jerk!'

There were sighs of relief when Bobby entered the departure terminal of JFK, but when he caught sight of a crowd of reporters waiting to film his departure, he panicked. He ran back out of the terminal, flagged down a taxi and was gone.

Just after 1 a.m., Saidy and Davis found Bobby in the bar of a motel near the airport. Bobby said he wanted to lie low at Saidy's parents' home in Long Island for a few days. Saidy told Bobby it was a difficult time, because his father was inside on his deathbed, in the last stages of cancer. Bobby replied, 'That's okay! I don't mind!'

The opening match was scheduled to start in just three days.

THE SOVIET TEAM was furious. Spassky felt humiliated by Fischer's antics. A *Washington Post* reporter accused Bobby of playing mind games with his opponent, of trying to discombobulate Spassky by keeping him in a state of outrage and uncertainty. Fischer retorted with, 'I don't believe in psychology. I believe in good moves.'

The Icelanders proceeded with preparations anyway. In Laugardalshöll, the match officials set up a table with a locally made chess set. The exquisite hand-carved pieces were lovingly positioned on a board with dark squares cut from pale green Icelandic rock.

THE FORMAL WELCOMING CEREMONY was set for the evening of 1 July 1972, at the National Theatre of Iceland. It was to be a glittering social event, attended by the US and Soviet Ambassadors, and the President of Iceland. Guðmundur Thórarinsson was scheduled to officially launch the event with a speech at 5pm, but he was stuck in phone negotiations all day with Fischer's lawyers. At 4.50pm, Andrew Davis told him it was clear no agreement was possible and the match would just have to be cancelled.

Guðmundur now had to rush to the opening ceremony still in his work clothes. When he arrived at the National Theatre at 5.15, he was pulled aside by a Foreign Ministry official who dressed him down for being late and inappropriately attired.

Guðmundur walked up to the lectern and looked out at the expectant crowd with no idea of what to tell them. In the front row, Bobby Fischer's seat of honour was conspicuously empty.

Looking up at the dress circle, he saw President Kristján Eldjárn, an older man who he thought could sense his awful predicament. In that moment, Guðmundur decided not to close the door. If the match had to be cancelled, he could announce it later, but not now. Swallowing hard, he improvised his way through a short speech and officially opened the match.

At the party afterwards, he was again criticised for his lateness. Guðmundur couldn't let on about the dire situation without having it become a major international news story, so he simply apologised.

'I'm sorry' he said. 'I shall try to do better. It won't happen again.'

THE NEXT DAY GUÐMUNDUR appealed to Iceland's prime minister, Ólafur Johannesson, for help. Deeply concerned, the prime minister called US Ambassador Theodore Tremblay into his office.

Tremblay was quietly furious with Fischer; he had been forced to sit next to his empty chair at the opening ceremony, in a state of acute embarrassment. Worse still, Fischer's intransigence was threatening to become an issue of national security. Iceland was a member of NATO, the security alliance that bound the United States and Canada with Western Europe into a common defence strategy. Iceland's central role within NATO was to act as a massive, unsinkable aircraft carrier in the North Atlantic. The United States had accordingly constructed a huge airforce base at Keflavík to house its fleet of long-range bombers.

Keflavík had brought much-needed foreign investment into Iceland and jump-started the local economy, but the Americans had never been very popular with Icelanders; they were seen as too brash, too boastful, too rich. Alarmingly, the Icelandic Government had just brought several communist ministers into its cabinet, and was mulling over the base's future. Bobby's antics only reinforced a perception of American arrogance and privilege. Spassky's patience and geniality, on the other hand, had won the admiration of many Icelanders, who felt an affinity with the ideologically non-materialistic Russians, who lived in a similarly cold climate. If Fischer failed to come to Iceland, Ambassador Tremblay knew the Icelanders would hold America responsible for the blow to its finances and to its national pride. Tremblay agreed to help, and he sent an urgent telegram to the US State Department.

THE FOLLOWING DAY in Long Island, Bobby Fischer picked up the phone and heard a distinctive, accented voice rumbling in his ear: 'This is the worst player in the world calling the best player in the world.'

Henry Kissinger, President Nixon's national security advisor, was an avid chess player. He told Fischer that America wanted to see him go to Reykjavík to beat the Russians. It was a matter of national honour. It would be great for democracy, he said, to have an American win the championship.

Fischer's lawyer Andrew Davis was just as keen as the Icelanders to bring his client to Reykjavík. He needed more time to bring Bobby around, and he asked for a postponement on the basis of his client's 'ill-health'. No medical certificates were produced, but the FIDE president agreed to the request. Now it was the turn of the Soviet team to sulk and threaten to walk away.

Appearing before an international press conference, the long-suffering Guðmundur Thórarinsson was asked by a journalist if he was worried. Guðmundur looked up to the heavens momentarily, then smiled sadly and said, 'No.'

'I just wondered,' the journalist went on, 'if you've ever seen Mr Fischer, if you have any proof he exists.'

'That's a good question,' he sighed. 'I think we can agree he exists.'

Then a second intervention came in the form of Jim Slater, a wealthy British businessman and chess fan. Slater had been following the controversy closely, and he offered to double the prize funds. He said, provocatively, that Fischer would have to accept the offer, or be exposed as a coward.

BOBBY FISCHER EMERGED from Icelandic Airways flight 202A at Keflavík well after midnight on 4 July. When he spotted the throng of journalists waiting on the tarmac, he leapt down the ramp and dashed towards the first car in the convoy. Guðmundur Thórarinsson, determined to observe the formalities, stepped in Fischer's path and almost compelled him to shake his hand and accept his official welcome to Iceland. Then Fischer pushed past him to dive into the waiting limousine. A police escort accompanied him, at his request, on the hour-long drive through the lava fields to Reykjavík.

The Russians were still indignant, but now that he was in Iceland, Fischer seemed embarrassed by his previous bad behaviour. He wrote an earnest personal apology to Spassky, which went some way towards smoothing things over with the Soviet team.

Media coverage of the Fischer–Spassky match now completely dominated international headlines and news bulletins. As a two-man competitive spectacle, it would only be equalled that decade by the Muhammad Ali–George Foreman 'Rumble in the Jungle' in Zaire.

LATE ON THE AFTERNOON of 11 July, the crowd filed into the Laugardalshöll leisure centre, while the rest of the world tuned in to the live telecast, hosted by network sportscasters with headsets and matching blazers.

Spassky was alone at the table. After he made his opening move, he tapped the clock and waited.

Five minutes of agonising stillness passed.

Spassky got up from his chair and strolled around listlessly.

Another minute passed.

Then, at the seventh minute, viewers saw Bobby's tall frame loping out from behind the curtain. His arrival was greeted by an explosive ovation from the relieved Icelanders. He said he'd been caught in traffic.

Fischer sat down, studied the board and moved out a knight.

As Spassky contemplated his next move, Fischer swivelled around in his chair and glared at the cameras. Then he got out of his seat and walked over to chief arbiter Lothar Schmid to complain that they were too loud. He returned to the board and the two men settled into a cautious opening and middle game.

By the time they reached endgame, it looked like finishing in a draw.

Then, inexplicably, Fischer made a terrible blunder: he took a 'poison pawn', which allowed Spassky to take his bishop, resulting in a shocking defeat for the American in game one.

AFTERWARDS, BOBBY BLAMED the cameras. He demanded they be removed from the stadium. The Icelanders, dependent on television revenue, refused. Instead they tried to placate him by hiding them behind the walls, with small window openings. Bobby still wasn't happy, and he refused to show up for the second game. This time the hosts called his bluff. A miserable Lothar Schmid declared after an hour that the forfeited game was to be awarded to Boris Spassky.

Later that night, Schmid awoke in bed in tears, 'because,' he later said, 'I thought I had destroyed a genius with my decision'.

The score was now 2–0 in Spassky's favour. The match would go to the player with the best score out of twenty-four games.

FISCHER NOW INSISTED the third game be played in a back room at the stadium, away from the cameras. Spassky, ever the sportsman, agreed. Fischer set everyone's teeth on edge by arriving late again. As he entered the room he spotted a closed-circuit TV camera and flew into a rage. Schmid tried to calm him, but Fischer screamed at Schmid to shut up.

Spassky now lost his composure and demanded they return to the main playing hall and hold the game there. Operating on instinct, Schmid grabbed both men by their collars and pressed them down into their chairs. Spassky made the first move automatically and game three was underway.

Fischer played aggressively, using a risky play known as the Benoni Defence. The name Benoni comes from the book of Genesis, and translates from Hebrew as 'Son of My Sorrow'. Spassky was overpowered and eventually had to resign the game.

The score was now 2–1. Spassky was still ahead, but the Russian was troubled by the darkness he'd witnessed in Bobby that evening. He told Schmid he thought he'd seen something bestial in him. Those who knew Bobby believed he was simply terrified of losing.

THE FOURTH GAME ended in a draw. The fifth went to Fischer. Some commentators thought Spassky looked perturbed, off his game.

Game six is remembered today by chess masters as a game of great unfolding majesty. Bobby's friend Anthony Saidy described it effusively as a 'symphony of placid beauty'. Fischer began with an opening he'd never used before, catching Spassky by surprise. Slowly and relentlessly, Bobby closed in on Spassky, stripping him methodically of his defences. Spassky resigned, then rose to his feet and applauded the victor. Bobby was taken aback by his opponent's generosity. 'Did you see what Spassky did?' he said on the way back to the hotel. 'That's a real sportsman.'

Local hostility towards the brilliant American now began to thaw. Some Icelanders expressed admiration for Bobby's evident determination to live by his own rules. Fans now clustered around him when he appeared in public, eager to collect his autograph.

GAME SEVEN ENDED as a draw. In game eight, Spassky blundered and lost.

Game nine was another uneventful draw, but game ten was another display of relentless strategic brilliance by Fischer. The win put him solidly into the lead.

Spassky kept his nerve, regrouped, and began to fight back. He won game eleven convincingly, and the arena erupted with cheers of 'Boris! Boris!'

Game twelve was a long hard slog that ended in a draw.

Fischer won the thirteenth game with a series of manoeuvres so complex that a baffled Spassky remained fixed at the board afterwards, trying to comprehend what had happened to him.

The next three games were all drawn.

Then creeping paranoia in the Russian camp led to claims of 'non-chess means of influence'. They sourly accused the Americans of coating the surface of Spassky's chair with a chemical to put him off his game. Spassky himself claimed on television that he was being secretly bombarded by radiation from the lighting rigs to 'disrupt his brainwaves'. Icelandic officials inspected the chairs and found nothing. In the lighting fixture they found two dead flies. The New York *Times* went to print with a tongue-in-cheek headline: 'Who Killed Those Two Flies – And Why?'

Games seventeen to twenty were also drawn. Fischer still held the lead, eleven and a half to eight and a half. They were now at match point.*

GAME TWENTY-ONE BEGAN on 21 August. Most observers thought it would end in a draw when it was adjourned for the night, but after exhaustive analysis, the Russian team realised Spassky was stuck.

The next day Fischer arrived at the stadium, but for once it was the Russian's chair that was empty: Spassky had phoned Lothar Schmid earlier to concede the game, and the match.

---

* Once a player gets past twelve and half points, he cannot be beaten in a best of twenty-four match.

Schmid strode up to the microphone and told the crowd it was all over: Bobby Fischer was the new world chess champion.

It was an anti-climactic ending to forty-one days of high drama. Fischer slipped away from the media pack for a celebratory steak and glass of milk. Spassky merely expressed a desire to 'sleep and sleep and sleep'.

The Poison Pawn

BOBBY FISCHER'S VICTORY made him one of the most famous men in the world and ignited an international chess craze. He returned to the US and appeared on several talk shows and in a TV special with Bob Hope. Against all expectations, Bobby was wickedly funny.

Several times he reaffirmed his intention to defend his crown. Commentators predicted he would continue to dominate the game for another decade.

But Bobby's mental health was slowly deteriorating. He told his friends the KGB and the Israeli secret service, the Mossad, were spying on him. He thought his gold fillings might contain tiny electronic listening devices, so he had them all removed.

Bobby was scheduled to defend his title in 1975 against the new Soviet challenger, Anatoly Karpov. He sent FIDE a list of 179 demands. They complied with all but two. Bobby shot back with a note resigning his championship, thereby forfeiting the title to Karpov.

He had held the title for just three years. Chess commentators who knew him said he was simply frightened of losing, afraid of destroying his mystique as a genius.

BOBBY BECAME MORE and more reclusive. Despite his Jewish ancestry, he was drawn to the notorious forgery *The Protocols* *of the Learned Elders of Zion,** and he sank into the fug of anti-Semitism. He entertained a paranoid fear that his inflammatory anti-Semitic statements had made him a target of Israel, and that the Mossad was plotting to assassinate him. In the sixties he'd joined an apocalyptic Christian cult called the Worldwide Church of God, and given them money. In return, the church lavishly rewarded him with gifts, private jet travel and expensive hotels. But he fell out with them in 1977, accusing the church of taking its orders from 'a satanical secret world government'.

In 1981, he was arrested in Pasadena, California, by police who mistook him for a suspect in a bank robbery. Afterwards he insisted he'd been 'set up' and 'framed' by his enemies.

IN 1992, AFTER nearly two decades of obscurity, Bobby announced that he would play an unofficial rematch against Boris Spassky in Belgrade, a competition billed as 'The Revenge Match of the Century'. As always, there was a major hitch: Yugoslavia at the time was subject to a United Nations embargo for the war crimes of its leaders. The US Government accordingly sent Bobby a cease-and-desist letter. He called a press conference and spat on the document, and the match went ahead as planned.

Observers of 'The Revenge Match of the Century' thought it a disappointing spectacle. The two men were past their prime. Fischer beat Spassky again, and collected several million dollars of prize money, but his violation of UN sanctions forced him to become an expatriate.

---

*   A forged document, published in Russia in 1903, purporting to be the minutes of a secret meeting of Jewish elders scheming to dominate the world. The fabrication was copied and disseminated in Germany by the Nazis and in America by Henry Ford.

Bobby took up residence in Hungary, then the Philippines and Japan. In exile, he came to detest the United States as much as Israel. He rejoiced in the attacks of September 11, 2001. In an interview on Philippines radio he bellowed, 'I applaud the act. The US and Israel have been slaughtering the Palestinians, just slaughtering them for years ... Nobody gave a shit. Now it's coming back to the US. Fuck the US. I want to see the US wiped out.' He signed off by shouting, 'Death to America!'

In 2004, Bobby was arrested in Japan for using a revoked US passport. He was still the subject of an outstanding arrest warrant for his violation of the UN sanctions. The Japanese Government rejected his request for asylum and ordered him to be deported, but there was nowhere he could go. He was stuck in detention in Japan for nine months.

AT THIS POINT, a desperate Fischer reached out to the one place that might still take him in: Iceland. Still in detention, he wrote to Reykjavík in January 2005, pleading for citizenship. Iceland's chess community rallied to his cause. The campaign was led by none other than Guðmundur Thórarinsson, who clearly bore no hard feelings for the grief Fischer had given him three decades earlier. Bobby was remembered fondly in Iceland for having put the country 'on the map'. He was proclaimed a *vinur Íslands* – a friend of Iceland, a term bestowed on well-known people who declare their affection for the place.

Lilja Grétarsdóttir, then president of the Icelandic Chess Federation, noted that Icelanders have always had a soft spot for outlaws.

'It goes back to the sagas,' she said.

THE ALTHING, ICELAND'S national parliament, awarded Bobby Fischer residency and then full citizenship. Guðmundur Thórarinsson saw it as a proud moment: 'In the end,' he said with satisfaction, 'we, this small nation of 300,000 people, intervened, and went against the United States and Japan, the two strongest economies in the world, and we got him to Iceland.'

Fischer flew into Keflavík Airport. Hundreds of students, appalled by his outrageous political opinions, were there to give him a parody of a hero's welcome.

Bobby emerged from the plane and walked down the ramp. In the thirty-three years since his last visit, the stylish young man had become a bedraggled figure. Nine months of detention in Japan had left him with a wild beard and hair. He looked like a homeless man.

Again he tried to push past Guðmundur's extended hand, this time successfully, and dived into the waiting car, avoiding the press pack.

Bobby was taken to the same hotel he'd stayed in thirty years earlier, where he showered and trimmed his beard. Appearing at a press conference, he happily consigned his former criticisms of Iceland to the past. 'You've got a wonderful country here.' he said gratefully. 'Fresh air, fine people, excellent food.' But to his Icelandic friends' dismay, he then decided to settle some scores. He singled out an American sports journalist named Jeremy Schaap from the crowd. Schaap's father had mentored Bobby as a boy. 'I knew your father,' Fischer said darkly, his voice rising. 'He rapped me very hard. He said I didn't have a sane bone in my body. I don't forget that.'

Someone tried to distract him from going down this unpleasant path, but he was not to be diverted. His voice became shrill as he pointed a bony finger at Schaap: 'His father many years ago befriended me, took me to Knicks games, acted like a kind of father figure, and then later, like a typical Jewish snake, he had the most vicious things to say about me.'

Schaap, deeply offended, replied, 'Honestly, I don't know that you've done much here today to disprove anything he said.' The room froze into an embarrassed silence as Schaap turned and walked out.

ICELANDERS TRIED TO OVERLOOK Fischer's anti-Semitism, to dismiss it as a vulgar eccentricity from a gifted but unbalanced mind. But the broken-down chess master couldn't restrain himself. He embodied Churchill's definition of a fanatic: a person who can't change his mind and won't change the subject.

Kári Stefánsson, the brilliant neurologist and founder of Decode, sought out his company, hoping to enjoy long conversations with another person with a genius-level intellect. But Bobby found conversation almost impossible, and would harangue anyone who came near him with long, paranoid monologues. Eventually Kári Stefánsson gave up on him. 'The last time I saw him,' he said, 'I turned him away from my table because I'd had enough of him.'

In his final years, Fischer cut a lonely figure in Reykjavík. Kári Gíslason remembers seeing him shuffling along Laugavegur one day in baggy clothes, looking unhappy and distracted. By now he was widely shunned, but to look at footage of Fischer in these years is to see a tormented man clearly in the grip of mental illness.

In 2007, he saw Björk perform at Reykjavík's concert hall. Bobby admired her music and they were introduced after the performance. He told her he loved soul music. Björk said, 'Soul is dead.'

Bobby suffered from a kidney disorder, which he refused to have treated, and he died of renal failure in Reykjavík on 17 January 2008. He was sixty-four years old.

EVEN BOBBY'S FUNERAL was controversial. On his instructions, he was buried in secret, in the early hours of the morning in a church graveyard on the south coast. The ceremony was conducted without the knowledge or permission of the church's pastor. Somehow, a Roman Catholic priest was persuaded to perform funeral rites in a Lutheran cemetery. It was attended by a group of five mourners, including Japanese chess master Miyoko Watai, who might or might not have been Bobby Fischer's wife at the time. Today the gravesite is a tourist attraction.

THE KINDEST OBITUARY for Bobby Fischer was written by talk-show host Dick Cavett, who was deeply saddened by the news of his death. Bobby had appeared as a guest on his show several times, and Cavett had been impressed by his warmth and dry comic wit. Cavett tried to put out of his mind the later image of Fischer as the angry, bearded King Lear of Reykjavík. He wanted to remember him as the funny young genius he met in 1973, who seemed to have a brilliant future in front of him.

Bobby Fischer, 1971

Cavett concluded the obituary with some lines from E.E. Cummings, written decades earlier:

> *Jesus*
> *he was a handsome man*
> *and what I want to know is*
> *how do you like your blue-eyed boy*
> *Mister Death.*

Sun Coffee

I CAN SEE THAT RICHARD has grown very fond of Iceland while we've been travelling together. But by our last day in the Westfjords I notice that he's taking to Ísafjördur even more. He somehow straight away recognises its precariousness, its dependence on the sea. It's a familiarity that has maybe as much to do with his character as with geography or place. I'm learning that Richard likes life's uneven edges, and how they grant a certain freedom. It's easier to express the complexities of life in a place that hasn't ever expected things to go smoothly.

The town has changed in the ten years since Olanda and I lived here: tourism has brought restaurants, good coffee, and a steady hum of activity. There are suddenly lots of jobs that allow young people to stay and live here after school, rather than move south or abroad.

But much is the same, too. Like the feeling that you're in a small port town that has had to scrap its way through history. Tourism hasn't yet straightened out the crooked old buildings, and Ísafjördur still belongs to the sea more than it belongs to the rest of Iceland.

On an island apart from the rest of the world, this town is more separate still.

We spend the day doing our own thing. I read, and walk around town. At dinner, Richard asks me how Olanda eventually got on working at the fish factory. He's impressed that she took the job. 'It was so much the right thing for her to do,' he says. 'For an educated person to throw herself into whatever was on offer. A lot of people wouldn't have dared.'

'I couldn't stop her,' I say. 'Anyway, she loved it. She still talks about it as one of the best jobs she's ever had. Mostly it was other foreign women working there, Thai women who'd married Icelandic men. Also a couple of Germans, and Poles. The way Olanda describes it, they spent most of every shift singing and laughing.'

'I'm not sure I would have left,' Richard says. 'Reykjavík is great, but this place is something else.'

'Olanda would've got a better job eventually. But things weren't good at the school. The principal and my department head Ingibjörg got into an awful row.'

'Over?'

'Ostensibly some marking discrepancies. The principal checked some of Ingibjörg's marking and thought it had been incorrectly done in places. Then there was formal warning of some kind, and the teachers' union got involved.

'To begin with, it felt like one of those weird situations where a minor issue escalates way beyond what anyone expects. But I think there was more to it, some background that was hard to get a clear sense of. Their two families had once been really close. The husbands were related – cousins, I think. Then there was the argument about Ingibjörg's marking. Within a couple of months, the whole thing was in the media – in the papers, on TV. The country got swept up in a very bitter feud in the Westfjords. In the end, it went on for a couple of years, and both of them eventually left the school.'

'And you were drawn into this shitfight?'

'Yes. Ólina, the principal, was on a drive to modernise the school, change standards. I suddenly realised that I'd been brought in as part of that. I ended up getting played a bit by both sides. They were very different women, both with strong personalities. I liked them: Ólina's intelligence and drive, Ingibjörg's exuberance and warmth. But they accused each other of being behind the media reports, and of damaging school life.

'Then, one morning, I got a call from a radio station asking me for an interview about it. I said no, but then a day later I was on the local news anyway. I can't remember what the report said, exactly.'

'A saga feud.'

'That's exactly how it felt. Neutrality wasn't an option, even if that was what you wanted. I tried to stay out of the way, but some mornings you just couldn't. There were shouting matches in the coffee room, tears.'

Flateyri

OLANDA AND I didn't want to leave Ísafjördur, but with things the way they were at the school, I began to keep an eye out for other jobs – even though it was only some six or seven months since we'd arrived. Actually, I think most of the teachers were looking. The fjord offered shelter, but in moments like this it seemed to narrow and amplify everything that was happening. The Northern Lights were more intense here, but so were the storms.

At first, my students saw the whole thing as mystifying, and a little bit funny, but eventually they became as dispirited by it as I was. We threw ourselves into our work – the reading materials and writing tasks. Maybe because the atmosphere at the school was such an unhappy one, my students became more supportive. In the end I felt very close to them.

One of my students, Halldór, had come back to finish his studies after a few years away from them. He was quite a bit older. Early on in the school year, he mentioned that he was from Flateyri, a village in a nearby fjord. He had a rather serious way of talking; when he told me about his background, it sounded like he was presenting his qualifications.

In the years away, Halldór had worked as a chef, but now he seemed dedicated entirely to music. In Iceland, it sometimes feels like everyone's a poet, a writer, a musician. There's even that saying about it that I'd mentioned to Richard: '*Að ganga með bók í maganum.*'

But Halldór's obsession with music was different, and somehow part of those qualifications he'd presented to me in class. 'I am from Flateyri' and 'I am a musician' were joined. The Westfjords had enabled his art in a way that other places couldn't.

In class, his composite self appeared during our group discussions, in the way he switched between post-war Icelandic rock history, a new music festival in Ísafjördur, and the perilous situation of the fishing villages: Flateyri was only barely holding on in the age of factory trawlers and large commercial fish plants in the south.

'What will happen?' I asked once. 'Once the fish factories close, is there anything left for people to do?'

'Flateyri will survive,' he said. 'My brother's starting a studio.'

'In the village?'

'In the fish-oil tank!'

He wasn't joking. Halldór showed me a picture on his phone of a cylindrical two-storey concrete bunker. It had first housed herring oil.

'He's going to put a studio in that?'

'Why not?'

I liked Halldór very much. In the past, I'd also worked as a musician, and we had plenty to talk about. His serious side turned out to be fairly easy to pierce. Underneath, I discovered a kind wit and much warmth. He didn't mind when I teased him that he was even more nostalgic about Iceland than I was.

'Oh, yes,' he answered, laughing. 'I think I'm Flateyri citizen number one.'

'Out of how many?'

'Two hundred.' Then, '*At least* 200.'

ONE DAY, HALLDÓR called out across the classroom and asked how much of the Westfjords I'd actually seen.

'Not a lot,' I confessed. 'We don't have a car. I was here a few years ago with a friend who hired a car, and did get to Haukadalur. That's about it.'

I could see that he was horrified by this, but he laughed it off and said, 'Then you haven't seen the Westfjords.'

I wasn't as sure. How remote did we need to be before we felt like we were experiencing the real thing? Surely Ísafjördur was getting close. But after class, Halldór stayed back and asked me if I wanted to visit Flateyri with him.

'That sounds great,' I said. Later on I asked a colleague whether this would be okay.

'To be friends with a student?' she asked, taken aback.

'Yes.'

'I hope so. Most of the teachers are related to half of them.'

So the following Saturday, Halldór picked me up in a small blue hatchback and we drove out of Ísafjördur, on a proper excursion into the wider territory of the fjords. It was early winter now, and enough snow had settled to leave the area entirely black and white, with shining, opal-like patches of gravel and fallen rocks darkening the fields of snow.

The road climbed into a tunnel connecting Ísafjördur and the next fjords. The walls had been left untreated; you could still see the bore marks in the brown rock, like a pre-historic taint.

'This tunnel saved Flateyri,' explained Halldór. 'And the other villages. Before it was built, we had to drive over the mountain. The road was closed half the year.'

'How did you get to school?'

'Kids had to board.'

A few minutes later, we re-emerged into daylight and swept down a winding road to the isthmus. The tunnel might have connected the villages, but the steep landscape on this side still seemed very separate to me, its own world away from the main town.

'This is incredible,' I said.

'Yes. There it is,' said Halldór. He pointed towards the open sea. 'Flateyri is right at the end.' And a small boast: 'When the sun's out, we see it, no matter what time of year it is. Not like in Ísafjördur.'

'Well, actually I've asked a few students when we'll see the sun make it over the mountains in Ísafjördur. They haven't been very precise about it. They say something about a Sun Coffee, and the corner house of one of the streets downtown.'

'That's about it,' replied Halldór, but didn't seem to want to elaborate either.

I left it for now. Here in Flateyri, the sun was indeed out – not high, but there was enough space between the mountains for it to appear and shine across the wide, bowl-like opening at the head of the fjord. Across the water, pyramid-shaped mountains warmed to the brown of an old hearth. But behind them, the shadows began again.

The waterfront at Flateyri

SOME YEARS BEFORE, in Australia, I'd heard about an avalanche that had hit the Westfjords. It had happened in 1995, when I was still an undergraduate, studying the sagas as part of my literature degree. I generally tried to keep up with news from Iceland, but these avalanches had been news the world over. Not far away from Ísafjördur, at Sudureyri village, fourteen people had been buried under the snow and killed. Another avalanche had hit Halldór's village of Flateyri, killing twenty.

'Those avalanche-breakers went in a year later,' said Halldór, pointing up to behind the village. 'Can you believe we had to fight to have them put in?'

'What was the other option?' I asked.

'Close the village. That's how the politicians think about us. That we'll have to abandon the place one day.'

As we drove down the main street, I wondered whether Halldór's determination to keep the village going wasn't his answer to that night, when the avalanche hit and nearly took it all away. Maybe his music was part of his answer too.

I could see that the village needed him. The shops were closed or boarded up; the only place to buy food was a petrol station that was being kept open through a community cooperative. The last employer, the fish factory, was struggling to stay afloat.

'But how will the village survive when the fish factory goes under?' I asked again.

In class, he hadn't hesitated. Flateyri would survive. But here he seemed prepared to admit it. 'I don't know,' he said.

'And what about you? Won't you have to leave when you finish school?'

'Maybe. Maybe not. *You're* here, aren't you? All the way from Australia!'

The Corner Window

THE WAR BETWEEN the teachers at the school gathered more momentum each week. I began to dread going to work on Mondays, knowing that at some point in the week there would be shouting in the coffee room. Group counsellors were being brought in, the union was even more involved. But the base notes of the fight were much too personal to be fixed by administrators and mediators. It was as though these people didn't know how sagas worked.

Olanda, meanwhile, did her daily shift with the other migrant workers of Ísafjördur. I envied the easy atmosphere at her workplace, although now and then there were rumours of staff cuts, even of closing down the factory. Not even Ísafjördur, the district centre, was safe any more.

Towards the end of January we felt the days begin to lengthen beyond one or two pale hours around noon. Surely, it wouldn't be too much longer before we saw the sun reach over the mountains again. It had been nearly three months since it last did so.

But each time I asked about Sun Coffee, I got the same inconclusive answer about a corner window in one of the old houses. Eventually, I pulled Halldór aside. 'I know you're not from Ísafjördur, but could you please show me this window that everyone keeps talking about?'

'Sure.'

At lunchtime, we walked from the school to the spit. 'It's just a tradition,' said Halldór.

'About a window?'

'Not exactly. The rule is that the town can celebrate the return of the sun into the fjord when it hits the first corner window of the outermost house on the spit.'

As he spoke, we arrived at the magical side street where this tradition took place, and followed it until we reached the other side of the spit, facing open water rather than the inside of the fjord. On the corner was a little house, and on its second floor a window tucked neatly into the shell of the building.

'That's it,' said Halldór. 'When the sun makes it into that room, the owners tell the town and Sun Coffee begins.'

'Which is ... coffee, I imagine?'

'Coffee and sun pancakes.'

'Special pancakes?'

'Well, *pancakes*. Just like other pancakes.'

I wondered why my students had been coy about it. Maybe it was too quaint and low-key. But I loved the idea, and even how the special celebration, when it eventually did come later that week, turned out to be very like any other morning coffee. Our version at the school was a line-up beside a buffet table serving thin pancakes, cream and rhubarb jam. Other homes and workplaces had their own. But we all shared in the brightness in the room at the thought of having stepped out of winter.

Mountain Songs

THE STRENGTHENING SUN marked a change for me and Olanda, too. As the weeks passed, job advertisements began to appear for teaching positions beginning the following year in other towns. I applied for a job in Reykjavík, and got it. We decided that we'd leave Ísafjördur in May, at the end of the term.

Halldór also made that decision. He was going to leave his village so that he could study music in the capital; he now had the school qualification he needed in order to take a place in college.

On his last day at school, he walked with a group of fifty graduates to our apartment. This was another tradition: final-year students wake their teachers very early on the last day of school.

Student farewell (Halldór second from right)

They'd all been out the whole night before, of course; they arrived at five, dressed in blow-up Sumo suits, some rather deflated. They were singing a song they'd made up during the night. It wasn't very good, but I loved it:

Hey Doctor Kári,
Doctor Kári,
Doctor Kári.
Hey Doctor Kári.

That was the whole song, but it went on for some time.

'I'll see you in Reykjavík,' I said to Halldór, when they finished. 'Be sure to look us up.'

IN THE YEARS that have followed, Halldór and I have become good friends. We've even recorded an album together; on one of my visits to Iceland, he and I drove up to Flateyri and co-wrote a dozen songs in his brother's studio, The Tank.

We meet for coffee whenever I'm in Reykjavík. When my sister Fríða remarried in 2010, he and I performed a song at the service.

By then, five years had passed since Halldór had left the village. But he still worried about its future, and how so many of the people from Flateyri were now scattered across Iceland and Scandinavia.

After the wedding service, we sat down and talked. He told me about a male choir he'd started and was directing. It was called Fjallabraeður, Mountain Brothers, and it was made up entirely of people who were originally from Flateyri.

The main aim of the choir was to meet up in Reykjavík and sing, to hold the idea of the village together in songs, even if its original inhabitants lived all around the world. But they'd also recorded an album, and remarkably, it had just gone to number one in the Icelandic charts.

The choir is now onto its third album, and has become one of the most-loved acts in Iceland. It's not known outside the country, perhaps because it is such a local project. In 2014, Halldór travelled across the island to record as many Icelanders as he could for a song that he wrote with the poet Jökull Jörgensen. In the end, 30,000 voices featured in the recording.

The song is called 'Iceland', but maybe it should be 'Flateyri, Iceland', even if that's a bit of a clunky title. It's a better kind of avalanche-breaker: a reminder to Icelanders of a village that always gets the sun. And of how art and place are sometimes the same thing.

And, in the meantime, Flateyri has been saved: the tourists have started to come, and with them new businesses are able to open, and the villagers can see a way to stay.

Rules for New Fathers

WHEN OUR FIRST SON, Finnur, was born, Olanda and I decided to move back to Australia. We left in 2007, three years after I had first taken the teaching job in Ísafjördur. Like Halldór, I have tried to keep my distant home close to me in other ways – in the sagas, and in writing about them.

Back in Brisbane, life was busy. I got a job lecturing at Queensland University of Technology, and a year after we returned, Olanda fell pregnant with our second son, Magnús.

It was a summer of storms. Some nights, the thunder was like a giant's whip, cracking against the side of house. The floors felt like kindling about to be lit by the sheer force of that noise.

We waited. Waiting, I discovered, was about waiting rooms, and instructional sessions at which nurses explained to you, very patiently, how to be more considerate as a man. The instructor looked at me. 'You're here because you're here *for her*.'

I said I couldn't agree more.

We took the hospital tour. 'This is where you'll come in, this is where you'll take the lift. This is where you'll see the nurse at reception. Call ahead so we know you're coming.'

And then a final rule that, for some reason, stuck more than any other. Our guide said, 'You mustn't ever park in the Emergency driveway. If you need to, drop your wife at the door and then park your car … in the car park. *Not* in Emergency.'

In my mind, being a good father and *not* parking near the Emergency ward became the same thing.

THE STORMS CONTINUED, and at around one-thirty one night, after the passing of a storm that was now just a distant white light – a fluorescent bulb running out – Olanda woke and said, 'It's time to go.'

Good. It was the middle of the night. We'd get a parking spot. But it was all happening fast, as it had with Finnur.

I rang ahead. 'Bring her in,' they said. 'Straight away.'

The back streets behind the hospital were rather lovely when empty. I went past the hospital car park, with its many free spaces, and into the Emergency driveway.

'I can drop you here,' I said. 'I'll just go and find a park.'

'No.'

'What do you mean, *no*?'

'You have to take me up. Now.'

Had she forgotten? Under no circumstances were we to park in front of Emergency. Wasn't that rule number one for delivering your wife to a hospital?

'Just get me to the ward!' she pleaded.

When the nurses saw Olanda they looked a little shocked and told her, 'It's happening.' Our midwife would be a West Indian lady called Carmen. She smiled warmly to Olanda, but reserved some other look for me. It seemed to say: Are you ready for this?

Yes, I thought. I'm ready. 'Um. But there *is* one thing. I'm actually parked in the Emergency section. I should probably go down and move the car.'

Carmen looked as if she couldn't believe what she was hearing. 'Forget about the car,' she said.

Then the storm was inside; the storm was us. I was calm, supportive. But I could see that Carmen wasn't convinced. Maybe she could tell that now and then I was still thinking about the car.

Later on, after Magnús was born and wrapped in his blanket, Olanda turned to me and said, 'Are *you* all right?'

She didn't need to ask. She'd done all the work. But there was one little thing. During the labour she'd clenched my hand, and my wedding ring had cut into the inside of my finger. I showed her that it was bleeding lightly.

For Carmen, this was too much. She turned on me and said, 'Just be glad it wasn't your testicles!'

AFTER DUE PAUSE and rest, and after Carmen had made sure that I wasn't stealing any of Olanda's toast, I was allowed back downstairs, and I moved the car.

I drove it to Mum's apartment and collected Finnur for a hospital visit to meet his new brother. They both got a present that day: a soft toy for Magnús, and a red toy car for Finnur.

'What do you want to do now?' I asked Finnur.

'Can we go for a milkshake?'

'Yes,' I said. I thought I'd have coffee, the Sun Coffee you have on the morning that your son is born.

A FEW WEEKS LATER, I went to the city registry office to put in the paperwork for Magnús's birth. There were forms, too – for vaccination schedules and a routine of check-ups.

But then another form arrived in the mail, this one with an Icelandic post mark. Accompanying it was a letter from the Íslendingabók database. They explained they were writing to ask about details missing from my entry in the database. I don't really know how, but they had my name and date of birth, and yet nothing else.

Would I kindly fill in my details and return the form?

I put the form on the top of a To Do pile in my study, alongside those for Magnús's registration. I thought I'd reply, but it didn't seem urgent. And then, over the months that followed, the letter worked its way down from the top to somewhere in the middle – between bills, applications for swimming classes, scraps of work brought home from the office.

Now and then, as I worked through the pile, it appeared, as though to ask for something. But I kept putting it back, underneath the busy world of parenting.

I let it sink, even though maybe one day I'd bring it to the surface again.

CHAPTER NINETEEN
(Richard)

The Disc of the World

The Ísafjördur café

Man Returns to Iceland

ÍSAFJÖRDUR HAS A SMALL café in a corrugated-iron house on the main street. Kári and I have come here this morning for coffee and pastries, before we take our leave of this town. After an hour, we're all done, and I go to pay at the counter. The young woman smiles as she gives me my change and politely wishes me a pleasant morning.

Outside, in the street, I recall something Kári said when I arrived in Iceland.

'Kári, when you picked me up at Keflavík, you told me that my very presence as a foreign media person would attract a lot of attention here. You said I'd be invited on all these talk shows and asked about my impressions of Iceland. Well, that hasn't happened, has it? We've been pretty much invisible since we got here.'

'You haven't noticed the attention you've been getting?'

'What are you talking about?'

'Everybody's being so nice to you! People are saying, "Hello! How are you today?"'

'That's because they're nice people, Kári.'

'No, no! They can tell straight away. "Richard Fidler! Oh, he's in town!" You thought that was normal behaviour?'

'Well, thank you very much, I feel much better now.'

'It's not that hard to be famous in Iceland, Richard. It's such a small country. Even *I* was famous in Iceland once, but only for a few days.'

I ask him when this happened.

'This was when I came to live here in Ísafjördur with Olanda. The local newspaper ran a huge front-page story. Colour photo and everything. They ran it under the headline: "Man Moves Back to Iceland and He Chose Ísafjördur".

'This was front page?'

'This was front page,' he nods. 'And in the article they called me "Lawyer and Doctor-Professor Kári Gíslason".'

'Wow.'

Kári nods. 'But it didn't stop there. Someone at the national paper, the *Morgunblaðið*, saw the local story and thought, "This is big news!" And so they ran their own story, with a picture of me sitting in a boat right here in the fjord.'

'What was the headline this time?'

'It was: "Iceland's Roots Run Deep".'

'That's amazing.'

'And that wasn't the last of it either, Richard. The next day I got a call from one of the TV channels, and they invited me to come down to Reykjavík to be interviewed on the whole "Man Returns to

Iceland" story. But at that point I thought the whole thing had got out of hand and I politely declined.'

'So if you were once such a celebrated individual here in Ísafjördur, how come no one's stopped you in the street and said, "My old friend Kári! What are you doing back in Ísafjördur?"'

'Well, I *have* noticed that now and again people have slowed down as they've passed us. They know it's me.'

Heimskringla

IN SNORRI'S TIME, ambitious Icelanders seeking fame and recognition would have to travel to Norway, to the court of the king. Despite their proud republican traditions, Icelanders have always been drawn to the glamour and mystique of the Norwegian kings, and Snorri Sturluson was no different.

Snorri sailed to Norway twice: first as a young man with his star on the ascendant; then, decades later, as an older man, shorn of much of his wealth and power, in flight from his enemies.

Sometime between these two Norwegian visits, he wrote the *Heimskringla*, his monumental history of the Norse world, told through the lives of its kings. The *Heimskringla* is history conceived as a series of biographies, and this is what makes it so much fun to read. In the mind of a great chieftain like Snorri, the world isn't shaped by vast impersonal forces, but by leaders like him, who impose their will on events, or succumb to the will of others.

The *Heimskringla* has a majestic sweep that befits the grandeur of its subjects: it begins with the legendary Swedish Yngling dynasty, follows the unification of Norway under Harald the Finehair and concludes in the year 1177, just a few years before Snorri's birth.

Heimskringla – which translates as *The Disc of the World* – is compiled from earlier histories and oral narratives. But it does give us some insight into Snorri's perception of the greater world beyond Iceland. The disc of the world, he notes, is surrounded by the outer ocean, whose waters run in at Gibraltar and flow all the way to the land of Jerusalem. The Black Sea is said to divide the Earth into three parts: Asia, Europe and the cold northern lands, which he calls Swithiod – lands of giants, dwarves and blue men.

Snorri never travelled beyond Scandinavia, and it seems he imagined the wider world as being much like Iceland, only grander and warmer in places. In the *Heimskringla*, he narrates the epic journey of the crusader king Sigurd Jerusalem-Farer to Constantinople in 1110. Sigurd, he writes, was welcomed into the Queen of Cities through the imperial Golden Gate, and was invited by the emperor to attend an afternoon of games at the Hippodrome.

Constantinople was then by far the biggest city in Europe, and the Hippodrome was the world's most stupendous stadium: a gigantic, marble-clad, colonnaded Roman edifice, crowned with classical statues. It could hold 100,000 spectators, more than twice the entire population of Iceland at the time. Nonetheless, Snorri describes the Hippodrome as:

> *A high wall surrounding a flat plain, which may be compared to a round bare Thing-place, with earthen banks all around at the stone wall, on which banks the spectators sit; but the games themselves are in the flat plain.*

In other words: just like Thingvellir, only bigger.

SNORRI'S ADMIRATION FOR the great Norwegian kings is made clear throughout the *Heimskringla*. It's a book that intends to please, as well as entertain. But in one passage, Snorri perfectly expresses the soul of Icelandic independence and republican virtue.

This story takes place in 1024, when an emissary of King Ólaf of Norway arrived at the Althing. The ambassador had brought a message of good will from Ólaf, and an invitation for Icelanders to become his subjects and enjoy his protection. The king would be pleased, he announced, if the Icelanders would agree to make a gift to him of the tiny island of Grímsey (which was yet to discover the pleasures of chess).

Ólaf was widely admired in Iceland as a good and just king, and the assembled chieftains at the Althing were inclined to accept his proposal. But then someone noted that a man at the assembly named Einar had yet to speak, and he was asked for his opinion.

Einar said:

'I am being quiet on this question, because no one has asked for my view. But if I am to have my turn, then I will say that it's wrong for us in this land to put ourselves under the taxation powers of King Ólaf, and all such powers as he has over men in Norway. That loss of freedom would not be for us to bear on our own. Our sons and all our kinfolk who live here would also carry the cost. Such a bind would never be undone, or escaped.

'Now, although the king is a good man, which I truly believe him to be, in the future there will be other kings, and they will be different – some will be good, some bad. If our countrymen want to protect the freedom they have had since this land was settled, it is not wise to give the king the smallest spot through which to fasten himself upon the country, and not to give him any kind of tax or service that could have the appearance of a duty.

'On the other hand, I think it very proper for the people to send the king such friendly presents of hawks or horses, tents or sails, or other items as can be sent to him. That would indeed be worthwhile, if friendship comes in return. But on the matter of Grímsey, although the island does not produce much food, provisions could be taken over to feed an army. If there were a foreign force on the island, and they began to sail their longships, I think there would be a throng at every poor farmer's door.'

Einar had spoken well and aroused the chieftains' sense of national dignity. His speech swayed them, and they resolved to politely decline the king's offer.

Illustration by Gerhard Munthe, from Heimskringla,
1899 edition

BUT SNORRI WAS WRITING the *Heimskringla* in another era, more than 200 years after Einar's speech at the Althing. The values Einar had expressed were dying, and Snorri, as much as anyone, was responsible for this.

Here I am to Do the Work

1237: ON HIS FIRST visit to Norway, Snorri had been at the height of his powers, the richest and most brilliant figure in Iceland.

Now in his fifty-ninth year, he returned to Norway more or less a fugitive. His nephew Sturla had seized his lands, including his estate at Reykholt; his two eldest children were dead, and his only remaining son had been mutilated and traumatised. Nonetheless, Snorri still had his connections, his fine way with words, and his cunning. In Norway he planned to reconnect with his old friend Skuli, to bide his time and salvage what he could of his name and his power.

Snorri was welcomed in Trondheim with open arms by Skuli who invited Snorri to spend the winter with him. Snorri discovered that Skuli was as disgruntled as he was with contemporary events. The same 'bitter-mooded' cloud he'd left in Iceland was hanging over Norway too: relations between Skuli and his nephew King Haakon had deteriorated as Haakon had grown to adulthood and shrugged off Skuli's influence. Haakon had elevated Skuli from an earl to a duke, as a sop to his ambitions, but Skuli knew he was being sidelined and the tensions between uncle and nephew festered into mutual hatred.

Snorri and Skuli sat up together late into the night, scheming how they might prevail over their respective younger rivals, Haakon and Sturla.

Then, in 1238, shocking news arrived from Iceland that forced Snorri to accelerate his plans: Sturla was dead.

STURLA HAD BROKEN too many oaths, betrayed too many alliances. Success had made him arrogant and cruel.

His father Sighvat, Snorri's older brother, foresaw the trouble his son would one day bring down on both their heads. Sighvat met up with an old friend on the road and asked him, 'How long will it last, this great pride that my son Sturla has? He has more pride than any of us.'

His friend was careful in his reply: 'I think it will last a long time, because your son is so respected and admired. But what do you think?'

'I'm no prophet,' Sighvat said, 'but few men get to enjoy such power for very long. Still, he should be fine if he doesn't stumble over his own feet. But if he does, then he will fall with a crash.'

STURLA ADMITTED THAT he feared only one man in Iceland now: Snorri's former son-in-law Gizur, who had become the pre-eminent chieftain in the south. Haakon, possibly hedging his bet on Sturla, had recognised Gizur's abilities and appointed him as a personal retainer, which set Sturla's teeth on edge. Sturla was heard to say 'he could control the whole country if he could manage to overcome Gizur'.

In 1238 Sturla sent a friendly invitation for Gizur to join him at Reykholt. But when Gizur arrived, Sturla put him under arrest, forced him to swear an oath of loyalty, and insisted he leave Iceland for Norway.

Sturla had overplayed his hand. Gizur escaped Sturla's custody and returned to his lands determined to destroy the man who had perpetrated this outrage. Gizur formed an alliance with Kolbein, another former son-in-law of Snorri, who was also sick of the insufferable Sturla.

Kolbein told his men they should not rest until either Sturla was in hell, or they were.

TOGETHER, GIZUR AND KOLBEIN raised an army of more than 1600 men, a stupendously large force by Icelandic standards. Sturla, warned of the looming battle, convened with his father and one of his brothers and set up a watch-post above a strip of land between two rivers, where he expected Gizur and Kolbein to approach his estates. But Gizur brought his men up from the south, across a barren highland road that threaded its way between glaciers. He joined forces with Kolbein's men, and in the pre-dawn light of 21 August 1238, they moved towards Orlygsstad, the farm where Sturla and his men were sleeping.

Sturla woke up at dawn with a jolt. He'd had a bad dream and his face was sweating. He calmed himself and wandered outside to the outhouse, then returned and lay on his bed a while. Then one of his men ran into the longhouse shouting: 'The southerners! They're here! There's an army of them!'

Sturla leapt up and ran to the longhouse door. His men woke, grabbing their weapons in haste, and went out into the field to meet the enemy in disorder and confusion. There was no time to round up the horses. Sturla was outnumbered nearly two to one, and his men were exposed in a poor defensive position. They had rushed into battle so quickly they hadn't even had time to prepare their weapons. Sturla was hastily given a chain-mail tunic and a red cloak.

As the two forces edged towards each other, Sturla's men nervously egged each other on to keep up their morale. Kolbein's forces rode right up to the edge of the meadow. Almost at the same time, with some relief Sturla saw his father Sighvat arriving with his kinsmen.

Meanwhile, at the other end of the field, Gizur's forces pressed forward. Sturla picked up a big rock and lobbed it at one of Gizur's men, smashing him in the helmet and knocking him down. Suddenly a shout went up: Kolbein's men had come up behind Sturla's forces, and had them penned in.

Sighvat now brought his men into the field. He was an old man of sixty-eight, and small in stature, but he charged into the mêlée in a rage, swinging his double-bladed axe by the shaft, until he fell down, exhausted.

One of his men, Björn, rushed to protect Sighvat by holding his shield over him. Kolbein, watching from a distance, shouted out to his men, 'Who's that, hunkering down over there?'

'It's Sighvat,' they cried.

'Well why don't you kill him?' Kolbein shouted.

'Because Björn is protecting him.'

'Then kill him first!'

That was enough for Björn, who fled, leaving Sighvat exposed. Kolbein now walked up to the old man and speared him between the shoulder and the neck.

The deathstroke now imminent, Sighvat asked Kolbein for quarter to be given: 'Let us talk with one another, for you now have the upper hand in our affair.'

But before Kolbein could reply, one of his men rushed forward and smashed Sighvat in the head with a rock. Another came forward to strike, and then many more, and Sighvat Sturluson – Snorri's older brother – was dead. Kolbein's men stripped his corpse, leaving him only with his undershirt.

Sturla, penned in and under attack from many sides, fought back fiercely. He fell back, protected by the shield of a loyal follower, who was then cut down. Sturla lashed out with his spear, a legendary weapon named *Grásíða* that had once belonged to Gísli the Outlaw. It was beautifully decorated but not very strong, and he had to stop and straighten the spear blade several times with his foot.

Amazingly, Sturla was still unwounded, until one of Gizur's men leapt forward and stabbed at Sturla's face with his spear, cutting him to the cheekbone. Outraged at being struck by such a lowly warrior, Sturla cried, 'Now the lesser devils are tormenting me!'

Then another man thrust his spear into Sturla's throat, driving it up into the bottom of his mouth. Still, Sturla struck out once more with *Grásíða* and killed another of his attackers.

Then he was stabbed again.

Exhausted and bleeding badly, he leant on the shoulder of a friend and staggered out of the field. He croaked out a request for something, but the wound to his mouth made his words unintelligible. Then he fell to the ground.

Gizur now walked across to Sturla, pulled off his bloodied helmet, and said coolly, 'Here I am to do the work.' Gizur took a broad-axe from one of his men and struck Sturla hard in the head – so hard he leapt into the air. As he did so, his men said they could see the sky between the earth and Gizur's feet.

Sturla was dead. He was thirty-nine years old.

Gizur took his purse, his ring and his weapon, *Grásíða*.

Kolbein took over all Sighvat's chieftaincies in the northern quarter, and became the most powerful man in the north of Iceland.

Three of Sturla's brothers were also killed on that day. A fourth brother fled to Norway. The Battle of Orlygsstad was a crushing defeat for the Sturlunga clan, and the largest and bloodiest battle ever fought on Icelandic soil.

SNORRI RECEIVED THE NEWS at Duke Skuli's estate with mixed feelings. The Sturlungs were his clan too, and the death of his older brother Sighvat must have shocked and saddened him. But the death of Sturla was surely very welcome, and it meant that there would be a brief power vacuum, an opportunity for Snorri to reclaim his property and his chieftaincies. He prepared to return to Iceland in the spring.

On the eve of Snorri's departure from Norway, Duke Skuli held a farewell feast. Afterwards there would be rumours that Skuli had secretly made Snorri an earl that night. Such an honour could only be conferred by a king, but Skuli was ready to make his move against Haakon.

The next morning, Snorri went down to the quay and boarded his ship. But as he was preparing to leave, a messenger from the king rode up and handed Snorri a royal decree: all Icelanders were forbidden to leave Norway that summer without King Haakon's consent. Snorri read the letter carefully, put it aside and said, 'Nevertheless, I will go home.'

To defy the king would be deemed an act of treason by Haakon, but Snorri did it anyway. With any luck, his friend Duke Skuli would prevail against Haakon, and Snorri could eventually return to Norway as the first earl of Iceland, and the trusted ally of the new king.

CHAPTER TWENTY

(Kári)

Slow Good Luck

But later in the evening, when I was on my way out for a stroll to pass the time, my grandmother spoke to me at the door and brought me back into the kitchen.

'Perhaps you'd like a sugar-stick, just like in the old days when you were smaller, Grímur dear?' she said.

'Listen, grandmother,' I said. 'Don't you think it's some other Grímur you're thinking about? As far as I can remember, you always told me when I was small that sugar was bad for the teeth.'

'No, it's all the same Grímur,' she said. 'But it's quite true that sugar is unhealthy for teeth, except just on special occasions. But fortunately there have not been very many special occasions in this house.'

'Did you say "fortunately", grandmother?' I asked.

'Slow good luck is best,' she said.

—Halldór Laxness, *The Fish Can Sing*

AFTER OUR MORNING COFFEE, we load our gear back into the car and begin the return journey to Reykjavík. For hours, we wind up and down the fjords until we reach the first heaths. We climb up onto their barren tops. When we come off them, we're back in the wider pastures of Gudrún's country.

We still have a couple of days before we get back to the capital – before there'll be another chance to visit Íslendingabók, to find out whether the staff have returned from their holidays and can help us in the search for Snorri. Richard's worried that we're cutting it a bit fine, but I have faith in the way things work here. People are normally happy to help, even if looks like nothing much is happening.

That evening, we stop for an early dinner at the village of Búdardalur. We choose a local restaurant called Leifsbúd, named in honour of Leif Eriksson. It sits close to the waterfront, at the end of a slope that runs off the main road into the village.

We sit down and order. Íslendingabók is still on Richard's mind. He reminds me that we'll only have a couple days in Reykjavík before our flights back to Australia. 'What if the staff are still on leave?' he asks.

'Yes,' I reply.

He smiles. 'What do you mean, *yes*?'

'Well, things normally get sorted out. You don't need to push too hard.'

Richard waits for a moment before he replies.

'Really,' I say, before he has a chance. 'We don't need to push. It'll work out when we get to town.'

Outside, the wind is up. I watch a family forced into an involuntary run to reach their car. Most likely, it was somewhere near this very spot that Kjartan made his return from his years away in Norway, and where his future wife Hrefna first came across the ornate headdress he'd brought with him. I can almost see her holding the treasure in her hand, something too good to be true.

'Don't you think it's strange,' I ask, 'that Kjartan gave away the headdress?'

'But Gudrún was married when he got back,' says Richard. 'Then he sees Hrefna. I mean, you get that moment, don't you? He's upset. He looks around, and Hrefna is right there, just at the right moment. And so he decides he wants her.'

'But it's so reckless.'

'It's understandable, too.'

'Maybe he should have kept the headdress, anyway,' I say. 'To give to Gudrún when he saw her again. Even if she was married to Bolli. It was meant for her.'

For a while, we eat in silence. The restaurant is quiet: just the occasional sound of steps on the wooden floorboards, the coffee machine warming up, two waitresses chatting softly at the far end of a counter.

Richard says, 'Anyway, stop changing the subject. What are we going to do about Íslendingabók?'

'Sorry. I'm just thinking that sometimes it's fine to leave things the way they are – you know, even after it's all broken up. Kjartan should have given Gudrún the headdress, because it was her gift. All he had to do was look after it and then hand it on.'

'Right.'

'And then Gudrún might have forgiven him for being late.'

'Do you think so?' asks Richard.

'Yes.'

'Íslendingabók.'

'Kjartan rushed. That's where it all went wrong.'

Richard smiles. 'No. It went wrong because he took too long.'

Waiting

I'M NOT SURE what to say next. I know I'm wavering. Some days, I want nothing more than to examine the gift that my father gave me that day, check whether it's true. But other times I find myself thinking that the real task here is to learn how to leave it be, or just hold on to it, wrapped up as an unopened treasure, to pass on to the boys without question.

It must be five or six years now since Íslendingabók sent me the form asking for my missing details. I haven't told Richard about it yet, but I've brought the form with me, just in case. In case. I'm not sure just in case *what*, but when I left Brisbane a few weeks ago it seemed best to bring it along. Maybe just in case it's time that I filled it out.

Or not. Over the years, I've come to trust in a certain kind of slow luck – a feeling that's as hard to define as a sense of inheritance, but that says there's nothing wrong with waiting.

MY TWO BOYS hear rather a lot about Iceland. I tell them about Icelandic history, the way things were in the deep past, when Iceland wasn't a destination in the way it is now, and when many more people left than came. I also talk about old friends, like Gunnar who used to take me fishing, and how the older people I knew had had contact with the last breaths of a very different Iceland – of farmers, fishermen and villagers struggling on the very edge of Europe.

Probably, I go on a bit too much. But I also know they like it. If I tell one story, they demand another, and another. They love the sagas, although our younger boy, Magnús, sometimes covers his ears during the fight scenes. Once, on a drive through the south of Iceland, I told them the saga of Hallgerd's first two husbands, and how she met Gunnar at the assembly. When we got to the part about the second husband, and his impending death at the hands of Hallgerd's foster-father, Magnús called out from the back, 'Oh no, not that axe again!'

Their favourite stories, though, are the little adventures of my own early life in Iceland. I've learnt that they like tales with final scenes in which the past, in some way disrupted by the events in the story, is put back together again. Then the tale can reconnect them to the present, and how things have turned out. Such stories allow them to enjoy the problems we face in life, because they know these problems will be righted. And digressions are fine, too – they are common in the sagas, and the boys have learnt to trust in the patchwork quality of such tales.

Their favourite topic is how naughty I was as a boy. So I often tell them the story about how I was once dared to snap my hair, which had frozen stiff after swimming lessons. How the hair was so hard that it simply broke off, like icicles hanging from a roof.

And then another dare: to stick my tongue to a frozen window pane, letting it freeze on. And having to wait for the glass to thaw from my breath before I could pull my tongue off again.

'Aren't you getting bored of these stories?' I ask. 'You've heard them so many times.'

'No!' shouts Finnur. 'Never!'

So I tell them another one. 'You know how I sometimes went out fishing with Gunnar …'

'The one who owned *The Swan*?'

'Yes. But this story isn't about him. This is about another friend. His name was Steini. He also took me fishing – fresh-water fishing rather than out to sea. Both of these men thought I should know how to fish. That you weren't really an Icelander if you couldn't.'

STEINI WAS AN aircraft engineer. He'd married an Englishwoman, Molly, who was a close friend of my mum's. Once he took me to the local airport to look at the planes he worked on. We went inside the hangars and met the other engineers. They assumed I was Steini's son, and asked if I'd ever been in a shed as big as these. I answered that it was like walking into a room built for giants.

Steini was very good to me; he had a gentle manner, a little distracted but kindly. He smoked a pipe, and kept a collection of them on a wooden board that sat on a low shelf next to his leather reading chair. He was old-fashioned: his hair was cropped very short, like in the fifties. And yet he liked to play the song 'San Francisco (Be Sure to Wear Flowers in Your Hair)' whenever I came over to his house. 'Hippies,' he'd say, and laugh to himself good-naturedly.

But Steini was also a little odd – even at a young age, I could tell that. He had an enormous stack of popular detective magazines, which featured salacious true-crime stories from America. I couldn't understand why such a mild-mannered person would want to surround himself with these paper towers of crime and depravity.

But, more puzzling still, Steini the aircraft engineer said he was afraid of flying, and refused to board any aircraft that was taking off. Why would anyone want to fly in his planes if he never did so himself? But then lots of people did, and nothing bad ever happened.

But one day I couldn't resist it any longer. I asked him why he was so scared of flying. I told him I thought it seemed almost unbelievable.

'Oh, I don't know,' he said. 'Why are we afraid of anything?'

'Then why won't you fly?'

He wouldn't answer. Instead, he started talking about his wife Molly. 'You know what, Kári?' he said. 'I'm the luckiest man in the world. Can you imagine? Someone like me getting a girl like Molly. *That*'s what's unbelievable. She's one of a kind.'

I thought about it. Steini seemed all right to me. He had an amazing job and he didn't mind having me around while he worked. Why *wouldn't* Molly want to marry him? But I left that question for later. I was still more interested in the intriguing matter of why he wouldn't fly.

'But Kári,' he said, 'Molly loves her trips. She *needs* to travel. Can you imagine what it's like to live so far from your home? I could only ever live in Iceland. Poor Molly has to live here too. Because of me, she'll never be able to settle down in England, ever again.'

'But why don't you go travelling with her?'

'Well, I like her trips as well.'

'You do?'

'I mean, I like that she does them. They're good for both of us.'

Finally I got it. Steini might not be afraid of flying at all. He simply needed an excuse to stay behind. For a reason that I didn't know, their love demanded both closeness and distance. 'I don't need to see all those countries anyway,' he said happily.

So while Molly was flying round the world using Steini's share of heavily discounted staff flights, Steini himself would drive to his summerhouse for some fishing, reading, and other acts of stillness.

STEINI'S SUMMERHOUSE wasn't much more than a habitable shed – a dark red cabin with a couple of rooms and a make-do kitchen. It was close to Borgarnes, not far from where Snorri's ancestor Egil Skallagrímsson had lived a thousand years before. The cabin sat on the shore of a trout-filled lake, and one summer Steini became my second fishing instructor.

I didn't have the same luck on fresh water as I'd had on the sea in Gunnar's boat. There was much more skill involved in catching trout. But Steini set me up with a fine rod and lent me his collection of silver spoon lures. I stood on the pebble beach of the lake for a whole day without a single catch, and with barely a bite.

The next day, Steini took me out in his small boat, and as we motored along he told me to let out a long line. At last the trout were biting properly. But each time I pulled up the rod, they shook themselves free, flicking their tails in the air until they fell off the hook and splashed back into the green water.

'C'mon!' yelled Steini. 'Quicker! As soon as you feel a bite, pull up as fast as you can.'

I tried and tried, but each time the same thing: just as I thought I'd caught a fish, it twisted itself off the line.

Steini was becoming more and more frustrated with me. But secretly I admired the way the fish freed themselves. For a few seconds, they were in flight, silver spirits.

'We're not in luck,' said Steini, eventually. 'I'm not sure you're going to be a fisherman. Let's go back in.'

We motored slowly back to shore. But I wasn't quite ready to give up on all those trout. I now knew they were right there in the lake. 'Can I stay out a bit longer?' I asked.

'Where?'

I pointed to a spit of uneven rocks further along the beach. Steini carried the gear and helped set me up on the outcrop.

'You'll be all right here?'

I nodded. In fact, here I had the same feeling as on Gunnar's boat: the most luxurious sense of purposeful waiting.

I spent the rest of the day casting and drawing in. The weather was still and mild. I wasn't having any luck with the fish, but that wasn't the point any more. The point was merely having the chance to try.

When evening came on, I decided to stop. But I thought I would cast the line one last time, and left it out in the lake as I walked back along the shore, dragging the spoon across the face of the beach.

The line stopped, and shook a little. A bite. No, a hook. I couldn't believe it! A fish, hooked at last.

I didn't dare draw the line, for fear that I'd jinx it. That I'd see the fish leap into the air and free itself. So instead I kept walking along the beach until I was in front of the cabin. Then backwards I stepped, without drawing on the reel at all, until my trout was finally pulled ashore.

I'd caught it, and an hour later Steini cooked it for dinner.

'Maybe you'll be a fisherman one day after all,' he said. 'No one can say you haven't got the patience for it.'

I'VE DISCOVERED THAT Icelandic genes do not in themselves make you a fisherman. But over the years I did become good at waiting. Even as a child, I think I always knew that one day I would meet my father and my siblings. From early on, I expected it to happen in something like the way I'd caught the trout at Steini's summerhouse: as a late-arriving change of luck.

I trust this as a method, as, I think, do most Icelanders. As in other places where harvests and fish yields can be good and also very bad, people sometimes rush to make the best of the good times. But you only survive in the long run if you're patient. And during the quieter years, there's so much to look at here. The landscape is a story, full of hostility and strange turns, but very habitable too.

Looking out of the window now, in the restaurant at Búðardalur, I can't think of anything more enjoyable than just staying in the countryside, and allowing the eyes to absorb that story a little longer.

'I know it's not ideal, leaving things to the last minute,' I say to Richard. 'But I think it'll be fine. There's a saying here. *Það rættist.*

It'll work out. We'll get to Reykjavík and the Íslendingabók people will be back at work.'

Richard gives it some thought. 'How about emailing them now so that they have some notice?'

'From here?'

'Yes, drop them a line.'

'I do have a form,' I say.

'What form?'

I explain its rather long history. 'I could fill it in, and email that ahead.'

'Perfect,' says Richard. 'Please do it tonight, won't you?'

I agree to send it. When we get back to the hotel, it only takes a couple of minutes to fill in the details, and photograph it on my phone, and email it to Íslendingabók.

'I've done it,' I call out to Richard in the room next to mine.

There's no answer. So I repeat it, quietly, to myself instead. 'I've done it.'

CHAPTER TWENTY-ONE
(Richard)

The Book of Icelanders

Church window, Borg

KÁRI AND I HAVE been travelling across Iceland for two weeks – across the grassy plains of the south coast, through the dales of the west country and around the rocky fjords of the northwest. And now, after days and days of open country roads, we're merging onto a six-lane motorway on the outskirts of Reykjavík. The windscreen wipers are sweeping away the late-afternoon drizzle as we pass a big box hardware franchise, a car rental outlet, a business park. It's as though we've been living in an epic place outside of time, and now we're sliding back into the slipstream of the everyday world.

'The thing cannot be put off any longer, now that we're back in Reykjavík.'

'I know, I know,' Kári says defensively.

'We're both leaving in two days. It would be ridiculous to go home without an answer from Íslendingabók.'

I've asked him to call ahead, but again, he says it'll be better to just show up at Íslendingabók.

If I'm feeling a little exasperated, it's because I hate pressuring Kári, and because I do understand where his reticence is coming from. In most situations I would be just the same, preferring to wait for circumstances to gently evolve, for a serendipitous moment to present itself. However, we have a deadline for departure, and a radio series to complete, and I don't think we can let the question of his ancestry slide for another decade. I'm caught between a professional obligation, and a reluctance to discomfit my friend, or to cause him anguish.

In the morning I ask Kári how heartbroken he'll be if it turns out his father was wrong, or misled him, and he snaps at me. 'I came to terms with all this years ago. I'm not a victim. And you shouldn't see me that way.'

I feel terrible, and apologise at once. He broods for a little while then comes back, gives me a hug, and says, 'Let's go and sort this fucking business out once and for all.'

IN THE CAR, Kári says, 'Now that we're close to it, I'm actually excited, and a little bit nervous. But I've had to think about why I'm doing this. What's the point of it? That's partly because of you, Richard, because you keep asking difficult questions. Sometimes I would rather you didn't ask them, but they do force me to question my own motivation in all this.'

We look at the road ahead in silence for a little while. A summer shower has broken out, spattering rain across the windscreen.

'You know, it would be so easy to assume that the reason why I'm so attached to Iceland is because I had an absent father, and so I went searching for Iceland instead. But really, I've been looking for both of them.'

HALF AN HOUR LATER, we're swishing through the glass doors of Decode once again. The receptionist doesn't remember us. Kári asks if the Islendingbok researchers are back from holiday and if we can see them.

'No', she says. 'They are not back from holidays.' She looks blankly at us.

Kári is looking at a spot on the floor. It's time for me to try to cut through this knot of Icelandic reticence. I smile at her and place my ABC business card on the counter, and ask to speak to their media officer. She studies the card and says, 'Oh!'

She writes down a phone number next to a name: 'Jón Gustafsson'.

'He's at home with his family today,' she says. 'Perhaps he won't mind if you call him.' That, I figure, is as good an invitation as we're likely to get.

We thank her and step back outside to the concrete multi-storey car park. I call Jón's number.

'*Já?*' he answers. The way he says it, it sounds like 'Yow'. I can hear kids in the background. I introduce myself in English and explain the situation. Then I pass the phone to Kári, who converses with him in Icelandic. Kári thanks him and ends the call.

'He says it's his day off, but he'll see what he can do for us. It's really very kind of him,' Kári says, handing the phone back to me.

We're unsure what to do next, so we cross the road to a park to wait.

As we sit down at a picnic bench, a text message comes swooshing into my phone. I pass it to Kári.

'Jón wants to know my father's dates of birth and death,' he says, tapping in the details, which he's apparently committed to memory.

Half an hour passes, so we go back to our apartment. Walking up the gravel driveway, we see Einar pulling out in his car, the same Einar who rented us our first apartment in another part of Reykjavík.

'Oh, Richard and Kári!' he says. 'Nice to see you. I'm just visiting a friend who lives upstairs here.'

Kári shrugs. 'Reykjavík's a small town.'

ANOTHER TEXT COMES IN just as we're trudging through the door. Now Jón is asking for the birth dates for Finnur and Magnús, Kári's sons. Kári taps them into my phone; he's smiling and laughing now.

Another half-hour passes.

Swoosh. A new message from Jón. It's in Icelandic so again I pass it to Kári.

'He's linked me to my father,' he says, looking dazed. 'I'm now listed in Íslendingabók as Gísli's son.'

We slump back in our chairs.

'And now that it's happened,' he says quietly, 'I think that means more to me than the search for Snorri.'

ONE LAST TEXT MESSAGE: a username and a password for Kári. Now he can use Íslendingabók's online database.

The moment of discovery is upon us. For some reason, I had expected this would take place in a darkened bunker deep inside Decode, on a huge monitor screen.

Kári has already brought up the Íslendingabók website on his laptop.

'The page is still updating ... so I'm having to keep logging back in ... Ah. Here we go.'

Kári types in Snorri's name next to his own. He studies the screen in silence for a good ten seconds. Then he whispers, 'Direct descent.'

He beckons me around to the screen. I see a ladder of twenty-four names, with 'Kári Gíslason' at the bottom, and 'Snorri Sturluson' at the top.

Kári reads each one of the names of his antecedents:

Snorri Sturluson, born 1179
Thórdís Snorradóttir, born 1205

I'm delighted to see his lineage passing through Thórdís, the most independent-minded of Snorri's children.

Einar Thorvaldsson, born 1227
Ónefnd Einarsdóttir, born 1250
Eiríkur Sveinbjarnarson, born 1277
Einar Eiríksson, born 1320
Björn Einarsson, born 1350
Kristín Björnsdóttir, born 1374
Björn Thorleifsson, born 1408
Thurídur Björnsdóttir, born 1430
Helga Narfadóttir, born 1465

Kári's eyes are shining, but his voice gets stronger with each name he recites:

Páll Grímsson, born 1500

Erlendur Pálsson, born 1535

Margrét Erlendsdóttir, born 1600

Erlendur Illugason, born 1635

Davíd Erlendsson, born 1688

Guðmundur Davídsson, born 1710

I picture Kári's Icelandic ancestors, pulling their oars in the water across the distant centuries, each one of them converging upon this moment in time.

Malmfrídur Gudmundsdóttir, born 1767

Pétur Ólafsson, born 1804

Pétur Pétursson, born 1852

Steinnun Pétursdóttir, born 1885

Fríða Kristín Gísladóttir Ólafs, born 1911

Gísli Ólafsson Ólafs, born 1936

And finally:

Kári Gíslason, born 1972

KÁRI LOOKS UP from the screen, stretches out his arms, and declares, 'And now I can proudly say ... it means nothing!'

Our laughter is tinged with relief and a faint sadness that's hard to identify. I'm a little ashamed of my doubts now. Gísli's gift was real and true.

'And look!' Kári says. 'They've put in Finnur and Magnús too.'

I'm greatly moved by this. After all these years of estrangement, my friend and his two young sons have been gathered up into the

Book of Icelanders. The island has claimed her lost children. It's suddenly obvious this is more meaningful and precious than the bloodline connection to Snorri.

KÁRI POPS THE CORK of a champagne bottle he bought weeks ago. The audio equipment is recording this moment. We fill our glasses, rise to our feet and toast each other like Vikings.

'To Snorri!' says Kári.

'To Snorri!' I repeat. Then I look nervously at the recording device.

'Can we do that again?' I ask. 'The clink of the glasses didn't quite sound right.'

THE NEXT DAY is our last in Iceland. Kári and I return to Decode to personally thank Jón Gustafsson for helping us so handsomely.

And there is one more awkward question I have to ask before we leave for the airport. As pleased as we are with the results, I can't help but wonder why Íslendingabók was so willing to accept Kári as Gísli's son, merely on his say-so, without a scrap of DNA evidence.

We meet Jón in the lobby. He seems a little embarrassed by our earnest tributes to his human decency. I had suggested to Kári we give him a bottle of wine, but he said that people don't really do that in Iceland. Instead we clasp the object of our gratitude by the shoulders and tell him what a fine upstanding fellow he is, but Icelanders don't seem to do that either.

Jón asks us politely about the progress of our saga project. I'm about to ask the awkward DNA question, but before I do, Jón says, 'There is one thing that perhaps I should have mentioned yesterday. I knew your father's family, Kári.'

'You did?'

'I grew up next door to their house. I used to play games with your brothers and sisters.'

We're a little stunned by this. Neither of us knows what to say.

'You know,' says Jón, 'you look a lot like him.'

Part

IV

(Winter)

Poltergeists

I N DECEMBER, REYKJAVÍK huddles into itself. A year and a half has passed since we were last here. The blue and green of summer have long gone, and everything is dark and golden. The sun rises feebly at 10.30 each day, briefly trails its coat across the sky and then dips below the horizon at 2.30, seemingly worn out by the effort. It's cold, of course, but not as cold as I'd expected. As I arrive the winter snow is yet to fall, and a thick cloud blanket lies across the city.

Despite the darkness, the streets are as lively as they were last summer. The shops and cafés on Laugavegur are full. People walk down the street, arm in arm, nestled in their winter coats. There are miniature Christmas dioramas on window sills, lit with little electric candles. Behind the lace curtains I glimpse living rooms, with their books, tapestries and paintings, illuminated with that soft honey-coloured light. I tell Kári I'm coming to love this place, but he seems to be going the other way.

This time I stopped over in Paris for a few days to break up the long flight from Australia. On the way back to the airport, the taxi driver asked me where I was going.

'Iceland,' I said in a French accent, which came out as 'EES-lund'.

'Tu cherches le froid!' he said incredulously, wondering why anyone would choose to go to such a place in winter.

Kári arrived in Reykjavík two weeks before me, so he could reimmerse himself in Iceland and get some writing done. Our plan is to write, research and make some winter journeys. Olanda and the boys will arrive just in time for Christmas.

He has rented an apartment in Klapparstígur, the street that runs from Laugarvegur down to the bay. Bobby Fischer lived out his last days in an apartment block a few doors down from us. I have the downstairs room; Kári has taken the loft. When I arrived, he told me how glad he was to see me after a fortnight of solitude, writing in the apartment. 'Maybe I won't come back to Iceland for a while after we finish here,' he told me. 'Maybe I've had my fill of Iceland for a while, Richard.'

I'm happy to see him too. We talk for hours that evening over a bottle of wine, exchanging news about our families and making plans. I've been reading more about the sagas and early Iceland since our last trip eighteen months ago. There are two more sacred sites we need to visit: Helgafell, or Holy Mountain, on the Snaefellsnes peninsula, and Reykholt, where Snorri Sturluson met his terrible end. I want to meet some of the ghosts of Iceland too.

ICELAND HAS MANY more names for ghosts than the English language can muster. A *draugur* is a restless phantom that leaves its tomb and wanders about anxiously; a *skotta* is a violent female spirit; a *haugbúi* is a ghost who lives in a cairn and can be driven into a fury if disturbed; a *fépuki* is a spirit that goes looking for the money it left behind; and an *útburður* is the ghost of an infant left outside in the cold to die.

Útburður

THERE WAS ONCE a young woman in Iceland who became pregnant. She was poor and the child was unwelcome, so after giving birth, she wrapped it some rags and left it outside, where the infant died in the snow.

Perhaps she forgot about it after a while. Perhaps she didn't.

The following year, the young woman was invited to a local dance, but she couldn't go because she had no fine clothes to wear.

On the night of the dance, she went into the sheep's fold to milk the ewes. As she sat on her little stool, she complained to the sheep that she really ought to be at the dance, and it was only for the want of a proper dress that she couldn't go.

Then a small, strained voice welled up from under the floor and sang:

> Mother mine, in the fold, fold,
> You needn't be so sad, sad,
> You can wear my rags,
> So you can dance,
> And dance.

Struck numb with terror, the woman was pushed past the point of sanity, and she never recovered.

THE EXPOSURE OF unwanted infants was a common practice in Iceland's early centuries. The nagging sense of shame and grief felt by those who had left a child to die manifested itself in the story of the *útburður*. They were said to hunch over like birds and crawl about on just one knee or an elbow, wearing the rags they were wrapped in when they died. An *útburður* would linger around the place of its death, sometimes emitting a piercing shriek. Sometimes they would hound the parent who abandoned them into insanity. In such Icelandic folk tales, ghosts often speak in verse, repeating the last word of each line like a funeral drumbeat:

> *Mother mine in the fold, fold,*
> *You needn't be so sad, sad ...*

THE NEXT EVENING, we're invited to the apartment of Kári's sister Bryndís and her partner Luca. Kári's eldest sister Fríða is also there. It's a warm, convivial night; Luca is from the north of Italy, and he generously opens a bottle of fine Italian red.

Iceland's stark beauty seems to have drawn Luca away from his temperate homeland. He was awarded a doctorate in criminal law some years ago, but lost interest in a legal or academic career. Instead he bought a Nissan Patrol and converted it into a 'super jeep' for Icelandic conditions. He now takes small groups of tourists into the highlands. Sometimes he takes them to Surt's Cave, where Oraekja is said to have been mutilated by Sturla.

Both Fríða and Bryndís left Iceland when they were younger to live in Europe, but eventually felt compelled to return to Iceland. I ask Fríða how Icelanders cope with the long winter dark. She says candlelight is very helpful in these months.

I tell them I've been reading stories of Icelandic ghosts, and I mention the tale of the *útburður*. To my astonishment, Bryndís softly sings the ghost-child's eerie refrain:

> *Móðir mín í kví, kví,*
> *Kvíddu ekki því, því,*

Ég skal ljá þér duluna mína,
Að dansa í,
Og dansa í.

I ask her how she knows that song.

'It's a lullaby' she says. 'This was sung to me when I was a child. It's well known here in Iceland.'

'Didn't it scare you as a kid?' I ask.

'Of course,' she says. 'All the good folk tales do that.'

The story of the *útburður* is like a cruel inversion of Cinderella: there is the young maiden who lacks the fine clothes to go to the ball, but no fairy godmother, just the ghost of her dead child, who offers its rags to her. I can't tell if the *útburður's* song is plaintive or menacing; like most Icelandic stories, it seems to offer you the option in the telling of it.

The Deacon of Dark River

IN THE MIDDLE of the nineteenth century, a man named Jón Árnason served as the National Librarian of Iceland in Reykjavík. Inspired by the Brothers Grimm, Jón compiled two volumes of Icelandic folk tales, including the story of the *útburður*. The best known of his stories is titled '*Djákninn á Myrká*' – 'The Deacon of Dark River':

THERE WAS ONCE a deacon who lived in the north of Iceland on a farm known as Myrká, which means 'Dark River'. The deacon was courting a young woman named Gudrún, who was the maid of a pastor who lived on the other side of the river.

One day, in early December, the deacon rode his horse Faxi to Gudrún's farm to make plans for Christmas. He promised to ride over on Christmas Eve and bring her back to Myrká, so they could enjoy the holiday together.

But as the deacon rode home that night, he was caught in a sudden, violent storm. In the blinding rain, he fell from his horse, head-first, into the icy river. His head struck a sharp stone and the poor man drowned.

The deacon's body was discovered the next day on the river bank by a farmer, and he was buried a week before Christmas. But the river was impassable, so this terrible news did not reach Gudrún, and she remained happily unaware of his death.

ON CHRISTMAS EVE, Gudrún was very glad to see the deacon waiting for her outside, astride his horse, just as he had promised. But she had barely enough time to pull on her coat as they set off, and she left one arm out of its sleeve.

They rode together through the night, the deacon's face hidden by a hat and a scarf. When they came to the river, his horse stumbled and the hat was knocked aside. At that moment, the moon came out from behind a cloud, and Gudrún could see the bloody wound on his head.

'The moon fades, death rides,' he said. 'Don't you see the white spot on the back of my head, Garun, Garun?'

(The ghost could not say her name, 'Gudrún', for it contains the Icelandic word for 'God' within it.)

'I see, as is,' replied Gudrún.

They did not speak another word until they arrived at the farm at Myrká.

The deacon said, 'Wait here, Garun, Garun, while I move Faxi, Faxi over the fence, fence.'

The deacon dismounted his horse, then slipped down into an open grave in the churchyard. As he did so, he grabbed the sleeve of Gudrún's coat to pull her in, but it was empty. Gudrún broke free and stood back.

The deacon groaned as he dragged the empty coat down with him. Gudrún watched as he disappeared into the dark pit. Then the grave filled up with dirt and all was quiet.

Three lunar halos: illustration from Olaus Magnus,
History of the Northern Peoples, *1555.*

Draugur

REYKJAVÍK'S MOST haunted residence is Höfdi House, a modest two-storey wooden mansion that stands on a treeless patch of land overlooking the North Atlantic.

Höfdi House was built in Norway and exported to Iceland in 1909 to serve as a residence for the French Consul. It was then purchased by Einar Benediktsson, a well-known lawyer and poet.

One day, in the course of his work, Einar was sent to the north of Iceland to investigate the case of a half-brother and half-sister who were alleged to have conceived a child between them, then murdered it. Einar questioned the woman, Sólborg Jónsdóttir, but she had poisoned herself earlier that morning, and in the course of the interrogation she fell into convulsions and died in his presence.

Later, back at Höfdi House, Einar's nerves were set on edge by sudden crashing noises, falling paintings, and the ghastly apparition of a woman in white, who wandered the house day and night. He was convinced it was Sólborg Jónsdóttir. Einar tried sleeping with the lights on, but she was not to be driven away. Eventually, tormented beyond endurance, he sold the house and walked away.

There were other short-term tenants who came then fled in horror. Both Marlene Dietrich and Winston Churchill had overnight stays during World War II.

Then in 1952, Höfdi House was taken up by the British Ambassador, John Greenway, who loved its distinctive Scandinavian design and made plans to renovate. But he too was kept awake by awful noises and by the spectral presence of the woman in white. The creaking could be explained by the presence of a thermal spring under the house, which might have been causing the structure to expand and contact, but there was no explaining the white lady.

Exasperated by sleeplessness and terror, Greenway telegraphed the British Foreign Office recommending the mansion be sold, and he took up a new residence in the centre of Reykjavík.

Höfdi House, Reykjavík

HÖFDI HOUSE REMAINED quiet and dark for decades, until October 1986, when it was announced that the two most powerful men in the world, US President Ronald Reagan and Soviet leader Mikhail Gorbachev, were coming to Reykjavík for a summit meeting. The Icelandic Government offered them Höfdi House as a venue.

It would be no ordinary meeting: the hastily put together two-day summit would later be described as one of the strangest episodes in the annals of nuclear diplomacy.

On the eve of the summit, President Reagan was seventy-five years old and approaching the end of his second term in office. Unlike his predecessors Richard Nixon and Jimmy Carter, Reagan rarely chose to involve himself in the intricacies of policy, preferring to set the ideological direction of his administration from the White House and let his staff get on with the details. Despite his reputation as a right-wing hardliner, Reagan was amenable to compromise, so long as his aides could persuade him the policy they were presenting for his approval was consistent with his conservative principles. In practice, this gave them plenty of leeway to exploit the boss.* One biographer of Reagan has likened the president to a child monarch, a naïve and manipulable ruler, humoured and protected by his courtiers.

But in Reykjavík, the ageing child monarch finally broke through the constraints of his minders. He and Gorbachev came stunningly close to concluding the biggest arms-control deal in history. Afterwards, the US media and America's allies wondered what on Earth had happened at Höfdi House.

---

* In 2014 I interviewed former Australian prime minister Bob Hawke, who recalled a meeting with Reagan at the White House. While being quick to praise Reagan's genial personality, he spoke of his amazement when, in the course of their diplomatic conversation, the president limited his comments to the recitation of lines from a set of cue cards he cupped in the palm of his hand.

ONE OF REAGAN'S CORE BELIEFS, shared by many in his administration, was that the communist Soviet Union was not merely a cynical, opportunistic world power, but a morally wicked entity, an 'evil empire' that should not be accommodated, but should be confronted with superior military strength. Cold War tensions escalated dramatically during his first administration (1981 to 1985), and the world edged towards a thermonuclear catastrophe. Reagan's secretary of defense mused aloud about fighting a 'winnable' nuclear war. Reagan himself had wondered if the world was living through the end times, the Christian apocalypse foretold in the book of Revelation.

There was, however, another aspect of the president's personality that many of his aides and the press missed at the time: a utopian desire to rid the world of nuclear weapons. Reagan believed such weapons of mass destruction were sinful. In 1979, just a year before winning the presidency, he was taken on a tour of the North American Aerospace Defense Command (NORAD) headquarters in Cheyenne Mountain, Colorado, the nuclear bunker that acts as an early-warning centre for potential missile attacks on the United States. Reagan marvelled at its command centre, which looked like the war room in *Dr Strangelove*.

For the first time, he was introduced to the prevailing strategic doctrine known as MAD, or Mutually Assured Destruction, which held that mutual self-interest would constrain the US and the Soviet Union from inflicting a nuclear holocaust upon the world. On the flight back to California, Reagan expressed how shocked he was by the apparent absurdity of MAD. He likened it to 'two men pointing cocked and loaded pistols at each other's heads'.

The following year Reagan won the presidency in a landslide. And when a group of advisors walked into the Oval Office and proposed an elaborate and expensive new scheme of missile defence, Reagan was easily persuaded to give the research his blessing.

The scheme was a very long way from realisation, little more a package of research proposals that were bundled together and came to be known as the Strategic Defence Initiative, or SDI. The scheme proposed to develop new technologies that would allow the US to knock down an enemy strategic nuclear ballistic missile in mid-flight. A fully functioning SDI would, in theory, create a virtual protective shield over the United States, making it safe from nuclear attack. Hostile missiles would be shot down from sophisticated laser weapons systems based on the ground and in space, which led journalists to dub the proposal 'Star Wars'.

The president, a former Hollywood actor who sometimes confused fiction and reality, was attracted to the idea of x-ray lasers in space. It might have resonated in his mind with a movie he starred in from 1940 called *Murder in the Air*, in which he played secret agent Brass Bancroft, charged with protecting a superweapon, an 'inertia projector' that 'would make the United States invincible in war, and in so doing, become the greatest force for world peace ever discovered'. Reagan became so excited by the prospect of SDI that he came to believe it was his own idea.

In March 1983, in a televised address from the White House, the president announced that America would pursue SDI research. The Soviet leadership – all too aware how far their pre-computer military systems lagged behind those of the United States – was badly spooked. Was it really possible the Americans might be able to shoot down all the Soviets' strategic missiles from space?

The answer was a firm 'No'. The idea amounted to shooting down a bullet with another bullet. SDI research, despite the expenditure of billions of dollars, never came close to a reliable, working prototype. But the Soviets – and US taxpayers, for that matter – weren't to know that.

THEN IN 1985, the leadership of the Soviet Union underwent generational change. After a succession of ailing, geriatric leaders, the Communist Party hierarchy turned to a younger man to lead the USSR. The new general secretary, Mikhail Gorbachev, understood the urgent need for greater openness and economic modernisation. Gorbachev badly wanted an arms agreement with the United States that would allow him to redirect scarce resources away from the military and towards food, housing and consumer goods. He shared Reagan's moral revulsion towards the hair-trigger nuclear trap the two superpowers had built.

Gorbachev presented an appealing new face to the world, not at all like that of his stone-faced predecessors. He was affable, reasonable and intelligent, a leader more in tune with the spirit of the 1980s. Western governments were suspicious of the Soviet charm offensive; Gorbachev tried to push through their scepticism with large, ambitious proposals for arms reduction.

In 1986, the moment was ripe for an arms deal: most of the hardline anti-communists in the Reagan Administration had been driven out by scandal or internal rivalries. The two figures closest to the president were now his secretary of state, George Schultz, and his wife Nancy, who both urged him to come to an agreement with the new Soviet leader and build a legacy as a peacemaker.

The first Reagan–Gorbachev summit was held in Geneva in November 1985. A personal relationship of sorts was established between the two men, but little was accomplished beyond that. Over the following months, negotiations stalled, so Gorbachev wrote to Reagan, proposing they meet again, somewhere halfway between Washington and Moscow. Reagan immediately agreed. The leaders and their entourages frantically prepared to convene in the haunted house in Reykjavík.

IT WAS COLD AND BLUSTERY when the delegations arrived in Reykjavík on Saturday, 11 October 1986. The American entourage took one wing of Höfdi House, the Soviets the other. The two leaders were scheduled to meet twice that day and once more on Sunday morning before flying home.

Reagan meets Gorbachev on the steps of Höfdi House

A media blackout was enforced once negotiations were underway, but on the Sunday morning journalists received a briefing that the teams had been up all night, and that a second leadership session had now been scheduled for later that day. Hopes were raised among the media pack that a breakthrough might be on the way.

These hopes were dashed in the late afternoon, when the two leaders emerged into the Icelandic twilight grim-faced and tight-lipped. Within the hour they were flying back to their respective capitals. Progress on arms reduction had stumbled on the issue of SDI research. The summit was written off as a failure. *Time* magazine's headline read 'No Deal: Star Wars Sinks the Summit'.

ONLY LATER DID the full story of that weekend in Reykjavík emerge.

The feverish atmosphere and close confines of Höfdi House seem to have made the two leaders giddy as they glimpsed what they might accomplish. The staffs of both men were shocked by the pace of the negotiations.

Gorbachev had opened with a radical suggestion: for both sides to cut the number of long-range strategic missiles by half, and to eliminate intermediate-range missiles based in Europe.

Reagan went a step further. 'It would be fine by me,' he said, 'if we eliminated *all* nuclear weapons.'

'We can do that,' Gorbachev replied.

Suddenly a major breakthrough was in sight, and the Americans became increasingly excited. The two delegations went back and forth well into the night, busily drafting and re-drafting proposals. Office space was sparse, so the Americans created an extra desk by taking a door off its hinges and laying it across an old bathtub.

THEN, IN THE FINAL HOURS of Sunday, the two sides reached an impasse. Neither was prepared to move on the Strategic Defence Initiative. Gorbachev insisted that America agree to confine Star Wars research to the laboratory for a decade. Reagan retorted that he had promised the American people he would not give up the SDI and that he wouldn't go back on his pledge. Since it was defensive in nature, he said he would be happy to share the technology with the Soviets once it was perfected.

'I doubt it,' snapped a tired and disappointed Gorbachev. 'You won't even share milking machine technology with us.'

Reagan walked out of the meeting, angry and upset. He was convinced, quite mistakenly, that Gorbachev's dramatic proposals had merely been an elaborate ploy to kill off the SDI.

Before they parted, Reagan said, 'I still think we can make a deal.'

Gorbachev replied wearily, 'I don't think you want a deal. I don't know what else I could have done.'

AS AIR FORCE ONE flew back to Washington, Reagan's aides struggled to string together a narrative that would explain to the media contingent at the back of the plane what had just happened. The president had met with the cunning Soviet leader, who had tried to trap them into abandoning the SDI, but Reagan had been too shrewd to fall for it. Contrary to rumours, the president, they said, had not offered to eliminate *all* nuclear weapons, only ballistic missiles over a ten-year period.

But Reagan himself wouldn't stick to the story. In Washington he told an amazed US congressional leadership that he had indeed offered to eliminate all nuclear weapons, if the Russians were prepared to accept the SDI.

The congressional leaders shook their heads at the president's recklessness. The depressing reality, ignored at Höfdi House, was that neither side could have delivered on their bold proposals. Reagan had failed to consult Congress, the Joint Chiefs of Staff or America's allies, who were nearly all opposed to the idea. British Prime Minister Margaret Thatcher was horrified: she had no intention of giving up 'her' nuclear weapons. Gorbachev too would likely have encountered multiple points of veto within the Soviet Politburo and the military. Even if both sides had reached an agreement that weekend, there was little prospect such a treaty would have been ratified.

STILL, THOSE TWO intoxicating days in Höfdi House had shown both sides how far the other was prepared to go. The following year Reagan and Gorbachev met again in Washington and signed the

Intermediate-Range Nuclear Forces Treaty, a less ambitious but still very substantial agreement on nuclear arms reduction that committed both sides to destroying all their short- and medium-range missiles based in Europe.

I can recall sagging with relief in 1987 when the news of the Washington treaty came through. At the height of the Cold War tensions of the early 1980s, I was finishing high school, and I had concluded the situation was intractable. I'd thought it was unlikely I would reach the age of thirty.

Maybe we'd get through this nuclear stalemate after all.

The Washington treaty was followed by another in 1991 that cut the number of long-range weapons by half. More agreements were signed in 1993 and 2002 that cut them back even further.

In 1993, President Bill Clinton downsized the SDI and shifted its focus to ground-based systems. The dream of a 'Star Wars' missile defence system was abandoned.

Six years after the Höfdi House summit, Mikhail Gorbachev came to visit former secretary of state George Shultz at Stanford University. They were both out of power: Schultz had retired and Gorbachev had been pushed out of office with the collapse of the Soviet Union. Shultz was pleased to see his Russian guest. 'When you and I entered office,' he said, 'the Cold War could not have been any colder. When we left it was basically over. What do you think was the turning point?'

'Reykjavík,' was Gorbachev's instant reply.

TODAY, HÖFDI HOUSE is uninhabited and closed to tourists, although it is sometimes used by the Icelandic Government for formal occasions. The whitewashed house stands quiet and lonely on its wind-blasted patch of land, seemingly shunned by its neighbours. Traffic roars past on the adjacent waterside motorway. On the day Kári and I come to see it, I strain to see a figure at the window but there's nothing there.

That night, I call Khym in Australia. She loves poltergeist stories. Neither of us really 'believes' in ghosts, but we lived with one for a while, not long after we got married. We were living in an apartment building in Sydney that was once part of a colonial jail. Whatever was in the place, it wasn't a malevolent thing, but it performed all kinds of uncanny tricks on us. The strangeness went on for months. One night, while we were washing the dishes together, Khym looked up at the ceiling and said, 'You're welcome to stay, but please don't frighten us.' After that, the disturbances stopped.

Khym suspects poltergeists are some kind of weird manifestation of shame and repressed rage we don't yet fully understand. On the phone that night, I told her the sad tale of Sólborg Jónsdóttir, her incestuous affair and the baby-killing. Khym found the nub of it right away: 'She did something she thought was right, but everyone else thought was wrong.'

Night Searches

A Picture of Gísli

BRYNDÍS AND LUCA live almost next door to where Richard and I are staying, and during the fortnight before Richard arrives I become a fairly regular visitor to their place. Now, a few nights after Richard's arrival, I leave him to his writing, and run through the rain and wind outside to say hello to my sister and her family. I'm met at the door by her two daughters, Indy and Opale. They're both lovely young women, Indy twenty-two, her younger sister seventeen. I've had a chance to get to know them over the years, during my trips to Iceland. And abroad, too: I first met Bryndís and her daughters in 1999, while Bryndís was living in Paris.

She hadn't been at the family lunch when my father told me about the connection to Snorri. But I spoke to her on the phone, and arranged to visit Paris on my way back to Brisbane.

Bryndís lived in a small apartment around the corner from the Place de la Bastille. She met me off the Eurostar from London at Gare du Nord. Indy was clutching at the side of her coat, and she had Opale, then only a few months old, in a BabyBjörn. She rushed over to me and held me, Opale squeezed between us but still sound asleep.

'Kári,' she said. 'So you are my brother.'

At the time I wondered, with a sense of real joy, how Bryndís and my other siblings could be so happy about my arrival, and so welcoming. Our father had protected them from me for so long, and yet they saw me as a gift. Of course they worried about their mother, Ólöf, and how it was affecting her. I didn't intrude on that part of what they were going through, but over the years that followed I sensed it, a slight silence about her that suggested some grief for what she had discovered, and her more pronounced unease around me.

That they were able to accept me and properly care for their mother at the same time taught me a lot about Gísli, and how he'd raised them to be compassionate and kind. It also suggested, perhaps, that they'd had to balance their knowledge of him with care for their mother before. I don't know whether he had other affairs, but I do know that he was a demanding husband, equally old-fashioned in his possessiveness of his wife as he was in his flirtations with other women.

Of course, the relationship with my mother was of another order: an affair that had produced me, back then a young man who turned up at their door unannounced, now a father still in search of his own. But my siblings have stayed true to me.

This evening, though, Indy and Opale look a little shocked when I arrive.

'Is everything okay?' I ask.

Indy says, 'Oh, I feel like crying when I see you. Nothing bad! But it's incredible how much you look like him. When I see you, it feels like Granddad's walking into the room. You're like a picture of him.'

I'm not really sure how to respond, so I give Indy a hug and joke that I must be a ghost, then. 'A friendly one, I promise.'

Bryndís takes my coat and ushers me in. 'Come on, Kári,' she says. 'Let me get you a drink. Or Luca, maybe you can serve.'

Luca's at the kitchen bench, putting out cheese while he watches a pot of mushrooms. 'Hello, Kári, my friend,' he says with his strong Italian accent. Sometimes he speaks in Icelandic with me, other times English. But the same accent is wonderfully present in both.

He pours out glasses of wine, and I take mine over to the couch to talk to the girls. Indy is sitting on her knees, looking for music to run through her laptop, but Opale, the younger of the two, lies curled into the hem of an over-sized jumper. She stretches out her arms and rests a hand on her sister's hair.

The view from the apartment is across the water to Mount Esja. It's dark outside, but now and then the mountain appears in relief when low clouds bunch against it and collect the illumination of the streetlights.

I call out to Bryndís in the kitchen, asking what she's making. It's both Icelandic and rather French. Her years away in Paris seem to have come back in her cooking; we're having mushroom soup, lamb, in which Iceland is more present, and a chocolate tart.

Over dinner, she joins in with her daughters in telling me that I look more and more like Gísli every year. My mum has mentioned it more lately too.

'It's strange,' I reply, 'to get closer to him in appearance as I get older.'

'Sometimes I can't believe it,' says Bryndís. 'Your mannerisms. They're *exactly* like his.'

For a minute, I wonder to myself what such likeness might mean. Actually, I find it a little imponderable, rather like the connection to Snorri – almost nothing more than a coincidence, a chance thing. Gísli and I barely knew each other. And yet there is some second part to it too, an unconditional connection that is very powerful in how I understand myself.

Bryndís disappears to one of the bedrooms, and comes back with a box of old photos. She tells the girls the story of how we all met, now seventeen years ago – the letter she got from me while she was living in Paris, and a first phone call that came just days after Opale's birth.

She pulls me over to the couch. 'I must have some pictures,' she tells the girls. 'Kári came to see us in Paris I took lots of pictures,' she adds. Her photos aren't really organised; each picture she stops at comes from a different decade, a different place.

Then she stops flicking.

'My God, look at this one.'

She has found a black and white photo of my father as a young man. He's slim and has his shirt off; his shoulders are strong, but there's something of the teenager's litheness in them too. He doesn't face the camera: his gaze is caught by someone in the distance. Or some*thing.*

There's such a lightness and ease there – as though he's looking entirely towards the future.

I find it a little overwhelming, and for a long while look at him in silence. 'How old do you think he is?' I ask eventually.

'Eighteen or nineteen,' says Bryndís. 'I think he was on a camping trip. He's so beautiful in this photo. You should have it.'

Normally, I'd offer some protest: 'Are you sure?' But this invitation I accept without being asked twice.

Searching

WHEN I GET BACK to the apartment, I Skype Olanda and the boys to say hello. It's Saturday lunchtime there; the boys have already had their morning swimming lessons, and in a minute they have to drive to Magnús's gymnastics class. I tell them how bright it looks there. Even online, the sunshine is startling, as though there are no shadows at all.

'It's so hot,' says Olanda. In fact, the warmest summer on record. But the boys' school term is nearly finished, and then they'll be on a plane to Iceland; they'll be joining me in just over a week, just after Richard leaves.

I tell them about the photo, and they ask me to hold it up to the camera. When Magnús and Finnur see it, they think it's an old photo of me.

'No,' I say. 'It's my father when he was very young.'

'Before you were born?'

'A long time before then.'

'We have to go, Dad,' says Finnur. 'We don't want to be late for Magnús's class.'

'That's fine. Off you go!'

WE HANG UP, and the brightness of the Brisbane summer flickers and disappears. I think about going downstairs to talk to Richard, but I think he's turned in for the night. And in any case … there's something bothering me: that ghost of a likeness that stands at the window. Reflections are clearer when it's dark outside.

I look at the picture again. It's true that we look similar, but also not. I've never been as handsome as Gísli is there. In fact, I'm not sure *he* was ever that handsome.

But yes, it feels like our faces meet somewhere inside that photograph – in our expressions, ways of looking, as much as in our appearance. I think that is why I was so keen to take it, to accept Bryndís's gift. I recognise him there. And, beneath the openness, a search for something in his life that feels like it might just as well have been my own.

Even if we hardly knew each other, in such moments I feel that I do know and understand him. It's difficult to say why, exactly, and so I am suspicious of the feeling. But while we met only four times and exchanged a few hundred words, I think I can hear him, sense his presence.

I tap the space bar on my laptop, bring up the Íslendingabók website, and enter my username and password.

I visit the site quite often now. I'm curious about my family lines, and I love clicking through the generations, reading the short, list-form biographies in each of my ancestors' individual entries. I can explore the generations between me and Snorri, and indeed beyond him. This database is quite extraordinary.

Of course, for me it all runs through Gísli.

I click on his name.

He was born in 1936 in Seltjarnarnes, a long peninsula on the west side of Reykjavík. In the nineteenth century, my family had its land here, and a farm close to the sea called Mýrarhús, or Marsh House, named after the wet soil of the area.

Above my father's name, that of his father. Ólafur Björnsson was born at that farm on 28 April 1908. On 17 June 1933, at the age of twenty-five, he married a girl three years his junior. Her name was

Fríða Kristín, and her family lived in a house in Ránargata, one of the slim streets near the old Reykjavík harbour.

They had three children: first Gísli, my father, and then Björn and Pétur – all handsome and bright boys. The youngest, Pétur, was born in 1943. Less than two years later, on 3 January 1945, their father Ólafur died.

I go back to Gísli's page, and check the dates. He was only eight.

Fríða Kristín never remarried, and chose instead to live with the memory of her husband. Gísli, as the oldest, went to work young, and helped her to raise the other two boys. She died in 2002, fifty-seven years after her husband Ólafur's death.

I met my grandmother Fríða. It was in 1999, the same year as I first met the rest of my Icelandic family. She invited me to visit her in her apartment in Ránargata, in the very same house she'd been living in when she met my grandfather.

In an attic room where she liked to sit in the evenings, she took out a picture of Gísli and his brothers.

'They were beautiful boys,' she said. 'Like you.'

'They look like trouble,' I said.

'Yes, that too.'

EVEN BEFORE HIS own children were born, Gísli became a father to his brothers. I know they have never forgotten that debt, how Gísli had to forego a full education in order to work to help his mother. My sisters tell me that he had a curious mind. He was obsessed with geology, and would collect samples whenever he travelled around the country. I don't know how he came to care so much about rocks, but Iceland is a place that draws you closer to them. The island's rock formations are immensely varied and colourful, like its unusual stories.

Gísli knew his family history inside out, and couldn't bear to be away from Iceland for more than a short time. He was also a very protective father. Whenever a boy came to visit his daughters, he'd quiz them on their family and relations. In a small country, it makes sense to check such things. But there was more to it, too. He knew he was descended from Snorri Sturluson, the noblest line of poetry.

The first son born to Gísli and Ólöf was christened Ólafur, a family name that honoured Gísli's father, the man he'd lost at the age of eleven.

In 1991, Ólafur was killed in an accident. It's a loss that I don't think Gísli ever recovered from. When I met him in 1999, eight years after Ólafur's death, I felt Ólafur's presence the whole day – in the way my siblings spoke about him, but also in how Gísli spoke to me. How kind he was to me that day, and calm about the fact that the secret of his paternity was over.

'You are descended from Snorri Sturluson,' he'd said.

A moment that is, I suppose, just one picture of Gísli. But also a picture of *us*, like the one that Bryndís gave me tonight.

Lament for the Lost Son

THE NEXT DAY, nearly a week after Richard joined me in Iceland, we drive north across the face of Esja, retracing a journey we made last year when we visited Laugar, Gudrún's farm in the mid-west. But the landscape is very different now. The fields are pale brown, and the grey light deepens the shadows in the rocks. There are horses out in the fields, but they stand perfectly still, their backs to the wind. They seem to have already begun the long wait for spring.

We drive through the town of Borgarnes and on to Borg, a farm where Snorri once lived, and where he must have learnt about *his* most famous ancestor, Egil Skallagrímsson, the warrior-poet.

Snorri was a poet and a politician, and I'm sure he was proud to be descended from Egil, for there had never been a more ambitious and at the same time more artistic Viking.

When we arrive at his farm it's bitterly cold. The rocks, usually a dark brown, seem to have paled in the white–blue light. We clamber up a small hill to where a cairn has been raised in honour of the area's first settler, Egil's father. Up here, you get a view back along the road we've come up: it sits under vast pyramids of scree, mountains that collect the wind and cast it across the low rocks of the nearby foreshore.

Richard's face has all but disappeared inside the thick hood of his coat and the scarf wrapped over his nose. 'When do we get out of this wind?' I hear his muffled voice ask. 'It's actually hurting my face.'

There's so little of it showing, I wonder how. But I feel the bite of it too. When I take my gloves off for a moment, my fingers burn so badly that I give up on taking pictures, and get my thick gloves back on.

The small chapel beneath us will be open; they almost always are in the countryside. We scramble back down the hill. As I'd hoped, the chapel door is unlocked. We're out of the wind. Amid the stillness of modest wooden pews, a small altar, and a hymn board that lists the last songs sung by the small congregation of Borg.

THE NORWEGIAN CHIEFTAIN Skallagrím came to Iceland during the exodus from Norway. He was one of the chieftains who suffered at the hands of King Harald the Finehair. One of Skallagrím's sons, Thórólf, was fair, promising, handsome and mild-mannered. He was popular with everyone.

Another boy, Egil, took after his father. He was difficult, bad-tempered and aggressive. He was also the ugliest man ever to live in Iceland. But he had a way with words.

It didn't always help him. When he was only six, Egil was invited to a ball game near Borg. He got the worst of the game, because he was playing against an older boy. When he lost, he took a hatchet to his opponent's head. A battle ensued, and many men died as a result of it.

Naturally enough, Egil's father wasn't pleased about the way this had gone. He could see that his son was taking after him, and he chided him for it. But his mother said, 'It's all right. Egil shows all the signs of becoming a great Viking. One day we'll make sure he has a ship of his own.'

Eventually, these two brothers left Iceland. They were conscripted into the army of King Athelstan of England, and fought at the Battle of Vin Moor in 937. And there Thórólf perished after a valiant fight.

After the battle, Egil sat at the end of the king's table, looking rather solemn.

The king looked along the table and saw him. 'What troubles you?' he asked.

Egil brought up the matter of compensation for his dead brother. King Athelstan gave Egil two chests of English silver to take back to his father as compensation for Thórólf.

Egil returned to his father in Iceland, but overlooked the matter of the English silver, and somehow managed to keep it all for himself.

He set up his farm at Borg. He married, and had sons of his own, and years passed in which Egil took on the quieter habits of farm life.

ON ONE OCCASION, a ship with a cargo of timber sat out in the bay. Workmen were collecting it off the ship. They'd row out in a smaller boat, and bring it back to the farm.

One of Egil's sons, Bödvar, was watching them work. He was developing into a fine young man. He asked if he could join them on their trips out to the ship. Eventually they said, 'Yes, come on. You can help. Get in the boat.'

They went out to the ship, and a wind came up and wrecked the boat. Bödvar drowned, along with all others on board.

Egil rode down to the shore and collected his son's body, then took it to the family's burial mound. He placed his son beside his father's remains. Then he came back to the farm, went up to his chamber and locked himself in. He would starve to death rather than live with the grief.

The household sent a message to Egil's daughter, Thorgerd, who lived a little to the north. She came to the farm and knocked on the door of his chamber. She told her father that she'd rather die with him than live without her brother and her father.

Egil opened the door and said, 'That's well spoken, daughter. Come in, and we'll die together.'

She said, 'Before we die, I think you should compose a verse for Bödvar. You're a poet, and he deserves a poem before we go.'

Egil said, 'Yes, I'll do that for him.'

'You'll need something to drink if you're going to do this properly.' She ordered some provisions and some water.

Egil drank the water in one gulp. Then he threw the cup on the floor. 'We've been tricked. It's milk.'

'Never mind. You compose the poem and then we'll go on with our plan.'

Egil began. He found it difficult to speak; difficult to come up with the words to do justice to his son. But eventually the poem came to him. And through the rhythm of the words, and through that side of himself that the words were able to reach, he recovered something.

When he finished the poem, his daughter said to him, 'This is too good to die with us. You must share it with the rest of the people in the house.'

Egil agreed. He went downstairs, and delivered the poem again. It begins with this verse:

> *My mouth strains*
> *To move the tongue,*
> *To weigh and wing*
> *The choice word:*
> *Not easy to breathe*
> *Odin's inspiration*
> *In my heart's hinterland,*
> *Little hope there.*

EGIL HAD SURVIVED his greatest loss. He was able to go on, and he lived into old age. He became decrepit, and felt exposed by his lack of physical strength. He decided that he had to do something about those two chests of English silver.

First, he thought he'd take them to the Thingvellir assembly, throw the silver on the ground, and watch everyone scurrying for it. His family was appalled by this idea, and persuaded him not to do it.

Instead, he took the chests of silver and two slaves for a walk, and buried the silver. The slaves never came back either.

People are still looking for that silver.

Parting Gifts

Stone cairn at Borg, the settlement of the Skallagríms

K**ÁRI TELLS ME** Egil's story inside the small timber church at Borg. We are both fathers, and our sympathies are naturally drawn into Egil's leaden grief for his drowned son.

As Kári speaks the words of Egil's lament, I'm surprised to find myself blinking back tears, and feeling the sting of my temporary separation from my children, Joe and Emma, on the other side of the world. I hear the hard Icelandic landscape embedded in the lines of verse:

> *The cracked rock-face crumbles,*
> *How can I keep*
> *My misery masked?*
> *My mind is in my face.*

As Snorri put the words of his ancestor to the page, was he thinking of the loss of his own son Jón Little Trout?

BACK IN REYKJAVÍK, we meet with Bryndís for coffee.

'How is your saga-telling going?' she asks.

I tell her we've just returned from Borg, and she gives us her version of Egil's story: the death of the beloved son, the exile to the bed chamber and the poetry that allows Egil to sing his way out of the room and back into the world again. Bryndís is as good at this as Kári; does every Icelander possess the storytelling gene? But she tells it from the point of view of Egil's clever daughter, Thorgerd. Bryndís delights in Thorgerd's slyness, which saves her father's life and goads Egil into creating the poem. I marvel at how Snorri's saga can be read as the howl of a grieving father, or as a parable of a clever daughter, depending on who's doing the telling.

'Where are you going next?' she asks.

'Reykholt,' I reply. 'I want to see where Snorri spent his final days.'

You Will Not Strike

1239: AFTER TWO YEARS of exile in Norway, Snorri Sturluson had taken the dangerous step of defying King Haakon's decree by returning to Iceland, where he was happily reunited with his wife Hallveig. Now that Sturla was dead, Snorri was once again the undisputed *paterfamilias* of the Sturlung clan, and could safely return to Reykholt.

Snorri's life soon slipped back into its old rhythms. He was asked to arbitrate several lawsuits, and this time the settlements he reached were reasonable, even generous. His chastened son Oraekja was given back the estate at Stafholt. A marriage was arranged between his nephew Túmi and one of Hallveig's sisters, and he hosted the wedding feast at Reykholt. It must have been hard going, in the sixth decade of his life, to build up his networks all over again, but Snorri had made a start.

Then, in the winter of 1240, the news came from Norway that his friend Duke Skuli was dead.

Skuli had launched his revolt and allowed his followers to proclaim him king. His army won their first battle against Haakon, but then were badly beaten at Oslo. Haakon's soldiers found Skuli holed up in a monastery with the last of his loyalists. The soldiers set fire to the building, driving the rebels outside. Skuli, choking on smoke, came out covering his head with his shield, shouting, 'Don't hit me in the face! It is not our custom to do that to a duke!' Haakon's men pulled out their swords and hacked him down.

Snorri had lost his chief ally in Norway. He must have known a triumphant and vengeful King Haakon would soon reach across the water to strike him down too.

SKULI AND SNORRI'S time was passing. Their ambitions had helped bring about an 'age of quarrels', when men with sharp blades would prevail over those with sharp tongues. Snorri's former sons-in-law Gizur and Kolbein were now the leading chieftains of Iceland. Snorri proposed a power-sharing agreement with them, but neither man was particularly interested.

Snorri rode to the Althing that summer with 100 men. Feeling vulnerable, he held court in a heavily guarded church at Thingvellir. Kolbein, infuriated by Snorri's hauteur, refused to see him; instead, he rode with his men in frenzied circles on the plains of Thingvellir below. Gizur arrived, huddled with Kolbein for a while, then met with Snorri in the church. Their discussion was apparently cordial, but without Kolbein present they were unable to reach a settlement. Hallveig was unwell, and stayed in her bed the whole time.

In these final months, the parish records at Reykholt note that Snorri ordered six calfskins to be made into parchment: an indication he was writing again. It may be that he wrote *Egil's Saga* at this time. The saga has an autumnal, elegiac tone not present in his other work.*

AS THE YEAR 1241 ground on, Snorri Sturluson could only look on helplessly as Hallveig grew weaker, and then died. The loss of his companion of sixteen years depressed and distracted him. 'This seemed a very great loss for Snorri,' the saga records, 'and so it was for him.'

Hallveig's two sons, Klaeng and Orm, were from an earlier marriage. Snorri invited them to Reykholt to discuss their inheritance, but he fell back into his customary habit of stinginess. He agreed to give them half of the gold and valuables that he and Hallveig had acquired, but he couldn't quite bring himself to hand over half the property, which the sons had a customary right to claim.

Klaeng and Orm left Reykholt angry and frustrated. They arrived at Gizur's door and asked for his support. Gizur agreed that Snorri's breach of custom was outrageous, and said he would certainly support their claim against Snorri.

One night, while drinking beer with his nephews, Snorri received a letter from an anonymous friend, warning him of danger. But the message was written in code and no one in the room was able to properly decipher it.

KOLBEIN WAS CALLED to a secret meeting with Gizur on the bleak highland road between the glaciers, the same place where they'd plotted the death of Sturla two years earlier.

---

* *Egil's Saga* contains a fine moment in which the old warrior-poet moans about his growing age and infirmity: 'My bald head bobs and blunders / I bang it when I fall; / My prick's gone soft and clammy / And I can't hear it when they call.'

When Kolbein rode up, Gizur pulled out a letter from King Haakon, naming Snorri as a traitor. The letter ordered Gizur to capture Snorri and bring him to Norway to face the king's vengeance. Failing that, Gizur was empowered simply to kill the old man.

Gizur rode down from the highlands and summoned his men. He passed around Haakon's letter. He told his followers that Snorri would never consent to being dragged abroad, so they would have to do the other thing. Among the men gathered at this meeting were Klaeng and Orm, and Árni the Quarrelsome. It says something of the times, and of Snorri's woeful inability to inspire loyalty, that three former sons-in-law and two step-sons had joined a conspiracy to murder him.

ON THE NIGHT OF 23 SEPTEMBER, Gizur rode out with seventy men to Reykholt. Arriving at the estate, he led a detachment towards the house where Snorri was sleeping.

Snorri, jolted awake by the noise, leapt from his bed and ran outside, to a smaller house nearby where Arnbjörn the local priest was staying. Arnbjörn told him to hide in the cellar under the storehouse.

Soon enough, Gizur came to the small house and demanded Arnbjörn tell him where Snorri was hiding. 'I can hardly come to an agreement with Snorri,' he said, 'if I can't find him.'

The priest now began to fear for his own life and offered to give up Snorri if Gizur promised to leave him unharmed. Five of Gizur's men opened the storehouse and tramped down to the cellar, where they found their quarry, alone and defenceless, an old man of sixty-two in his nightshirt.

In the cramped space, Gizur's lieutenant Símon gave the order to kill. The seething men unsheathed their swords.

Snorri had one last defence to call upon: his chiefly authority.

'You will not strike,' he commanded.

'Kill him now!' Símon ordered.

'You will not strike!' insisted Snorri.

Two men edged forward and drew back their swords. One blade was thrust into Snorri, and then a second. The third swordsman delivered the final cut, and Snorri Sturluson, the cleverest man in Iceland, died of his wounds on the floor of his cellar.

Snorri statue at Reykholt

Reykholt

KÁRI PULLS UP the handbrake in that slow easy manner of his, and we brace ourselves for the hostile weather outside. Ours is the only vehicle in Reykholt's carpark on this bleak day. The original buildings from Snorri's time are long gone; today there is a fine cultural centre, a library and a church with a tall, pencil-like steeple.

As we walk across the gravel carpark, the icy drizzle pricks the skin on my face and hands like tiny needles. The weather is so ridiculously awful it's making us laugh. Hopping up and down to keep warm, we walk over to a lawn with a solemn metal statue at its centre. Looking up we see the figure of Snorri Sturluson standing upright, dressed in a modest gown and hat, a book tucked neatly under his arm. The granite pedestal below his feet simply records his name in bold chiselled letters. I tell Kári it's quite a prim portrait for a man with such enormous appetites.

'Yes,' he says. 'And faintly absurd too. They've dressed him as a Lutheran scholar. The Lutheran church didn't even exist in Snorri's time.'

Still, I can't help but love a nation that reveres an author as its national hero, that commemorates him with such modest dignity.

We walk around to the side of the estate, where Snorri's outdoor bath has been reconstructed in a circle of hewn stone. Clouds of steam are trailing up into the frigid winter air. Directly next to the bath is the tunnel that once led to Snorri's home.

Kári and I are so cold we can barely talk, and we take shelter for a moment on the benches inside the little hutch next to the bath. I'm thinking of Snorri's last moments, of the cowardly murder that happened here.

'You will not strike' is remembered as the old man's defiant last stand. 'But to me,' I say, 'it seems more likely he was just cowering in terror, covering his face, screaming, "Don't strike!"'

'Yes, the line could be read that way,' Kári says. 'Snorri was a defenceless old man. All his life he'd dreaded that kind of death.'

'You might not want to hear this, Kári, but there will be those who would say he had it coming. He'd been so greedy and reckless with the lives of other people.'

Kári thinks for a moment. 'I think the challenge for us is to forgive him,' he says. 'We want him to have a brave death, a Ragnarok, but we just have to accept the squalid reality, that he died afraid in a cellar. We have to let ourselves not mind that.'

INSIDE THE MUSEUM at Reykholt, there's a permanent exhibition dedicated to Snorri's life and work, with text in both Icelandic and English. I wander over to read the panel that recounts the moment of Snorri's death. A middle-aged Icelandic woman is standing next to me.

'You know,' she whispers, taking me into her confidence, 'I'm certain Snorri never said "You will not strike."'

'Really? What do you think he said?'

'Snorri was a good Christian. He would have said, "Thou shalt not kill." This is what my priest thinks and I agree with him.'

IN ONE CORNER of the museum is a toy-like model of Yggdrasil, the world-tree from the *Prose Edda*, with four cartoonish dwarves holding up the perspex dome of the sky. At the roots I can see a little dragon, and the squirrel Ratatosk, but there doesn't seem to be enough room for the Norns.

In the *Prose Edda*, the Norns are three giantesses who live at the base of Yggdrasil. Every day the Norns gather water from a well, mix it with mud, and smear the chalky white clay all over Yggdrasil's branches to protect the tree from rot. The names of the three Norns are Urd, Verdandi and Skuld – That Which Once Was, That Which Is Becoming and That Which Is Yet to Come – and they shape the lives of men. As mythological creatures, they resemble the Three Fates of Greek legends, or the weird sisters from Shakespeare's *Macbeth*.

Pedestal of the statue at Reykholt

There are also norns who come to each child at birth to present them with the life that has been appointed to them. A kind norn will spin a long, prosperous life. A life filled with misfortune is the fault of a bad norn.

I ask Kári what kind of a norn he thinks attended Snorri's birth.

'I think Snorri was being looked after by the Norn of That Which Is Yet to Come,' he says. 'He had the great good fortune of being remembered.'

SNORRI'S DEATH DID nothing to quell the violent rivalry between Iceland's clans. By 1262, the island had exhausted itself with fratricidal violence, and the Althing agreed to surrender its sovereignty and accept union with Norway. Each chieftain swore an oath of loyalty to King Haakon and agreed to pay him tribute. Gizur was made Earl of Iceland. It was a sad, shabby end to three centuries of greatness.

Snorri's scholarly nephew Sturla Thórdarson* was exiled to Norway, where he became a liegeman to the king. He returned to Iceland in 1271 and wrote the story of his clan in the pages of *Sturlunga Saga*. His portrayal of his famous uncle, and of his role in the destruction of Iceland's commonwealth, is clear-eyed and unsympathetic.

Possession of Iceland eventually passed from Norway to Denmark, which imposed harsh trade restrictions, and Iceland slid further into hard, stony poverty. In the fifteenth century the advent of the global cooling period known as the Little Ice Age

---

*   Not to be confused with Snorri's other nephew and rival, who was also, unhelpfully, named Sturla.

made Iceland's winters longer, and its growing season shorter. The Black Death coursed its way through the island twice in the fifteenth century, scything away close to half the population each time.

The nation that had composed the sagas, settled Greenland and explored North America slid into a dark age of humiliation and poverty.

CHAPTER TWENTY-FIVE
(Kári)

The Heart's Hinterland

A FEW DAYS BEFORE CHRISTMAS, Richard prepares to leave
Iceland, while Olanda and the boys begin a long flight from
Brisbane to join me in Reykjavík. Richard and I have managed some
more short trips into the countryside, but the weather has been
against us: strong winds have swept across the country. Whenever
we've stepped out of the car to look around, we've had to rush back
to get out of the bitter cold.

On the morning of Richard's flight, it's very wet and windy, too –
perhaps the perfect weather for leaving. I wake early to make him a
coffee and to say goodbye before he takes the bus out to the airport.
I'm sorry to see him go.

But it's not long before Olanda and the boys arrive. We move into
our own rented apartment just a few streets from the one I had with
Richard. Straight away, a different tempo takes hold, more like being
at home. Every day, while I'm working at one of the reading desks
in the National Library, Olanda takes the boys for a walk around
Tjörnin pond and down to the harbour. On the weekends, I join
them, and we follow Tjarnargata until we get to Tjörnin's southern

end. I show them the spot where one of the last turf houses in Reykjavík reputedly stood, until shortly after World War I.

It was only then, after that war finished, that Reykjavík fully emerged out of the ground. Out in the country, though, there were people living in turf houses for decades longer. My generation – those in middle age now – were the first to experience an entirely modern Iceland.

Sometimes I wonder if we should move back. Finnur loves it here, and wants to have a year or two of Icelandic schooling. I mention that it might not be as much fun living here as it is to visit. And the language would be difficult to learn.

'But that's the point, Dad,' he says. 'You get to learn something special. It's good to be challenged.'

I look at him, only ten years old but already the sentimental exile in formation. 'What about you, Magnús?'

'I like it in Australia,' he says, calm but very sure. Then he adds quickly, 'Don't get me wrong. It's great here. But I don't want to feel cold all the time.'

'Better to be too hot than too cold?'

'Yep.'

We sit down at one of the benches along the pond. 'Kids here want to travel to places like Australia.'

'That makes sense,' Finnur says. 'They'd want to see what our lives are like. Just like we want to see theirs.'

IT'S NOT ALWAYS EASY to explain to the boys what I do for a living. They know that I write, and teach at a university. But why the long days in the library? How can it possibly take that long to read what I need to research, or to write a book about something I know as well as Iceland?

So, one day I take them to the National Museum to help explain what I do, and what makes the Icelandic sagas so special. The exhibits include some relics from the Viking age – swords, rune carvings, drinking horns, brooches, even combs of walrus ivory.

'Did the Vikings brush their hair?' asks Magnús.

'Yes, they took special care of their hair. Wherever you find Viking artefacts, there are usually combs too. And toothbrushes!'

'They must have liked to look good.'

But what I really want them to show them is a medieval manuscript, a page of vellum to help them understand that the survival of the sagas was an extraordinarily precarious enterprise, a little like the survival of the old Iceland of croft houses and subsistence farmers. How the stories might have perished with the Vikings, had it not been for the work of those who loved sagas.

A manuscript exhibition housed in another museum building downtown features a legal manuscript called *Skarðsbók Jónsbókar*. It's one of the most ornately decorated of the Icelandic manuscripts. Scholars believe that it was probably written at a monastery at Helgafell, in central Iceland – the very site where Gudrún ended her days as Iceland's first nun.

'Can you read it?' Finnur asks.

'Yes. You can probably make out some words too. Look, there's *mikil*. You know that one: "much". And *lögbók*. What does *bók* mean?'

'Book.'

'There you go, and *lög* is law. Law-book. You can read some words from a fourteenth-century manuscript.'

Finnur beams, and Magnús pushes him out of the way. 'Let *me* have a go.'

Skarðsbók Jónsbókar

I tell Magnús the date of the manuscript, 1363. He does the maths. 'That's 650 years,' he says, shaking his head in disbelief. 'How did it survive that long?'

I can't help but answer that it very nearly didn't. 'A lot came down to one man, and the decisions he made. He devoted himself to the sagas. Believe it or not, he almost lost the lot.'

It's just the kind of tale the boys love. We join the world created in a story while it is on the edge of some great danger, but with the certain hope that it'll work out in the end. We're here, after all, looking at the manuscripts, and trying to read the words. The sagas *must* have survived.

ICELANDERS DIDN'T FORGET about the sagas. The stories of the first settlers were reproduced in manuscripts long after the loss of the commonwealth, and over the centuries came to form part of an array of story types and scholarly works, from fantastical works to royal biographies.

But there were few libraries, and for hundreds of years it fell to farmers and merchants to keep the manuscripts in their own private

397

collections. It wasn't until the sixteenth century, when the first schools were established, that priests and teachers began to look for the most precious of the documents. Even then, they did so with a view to sending them abroad, to Sweden and Denmark, as treasures for the royal households of the most powerful nations in the region.

The most famous manuscript in Iceland was *Flateyjarbók*. Its title referred to a tiny island, Flatey in Breidafjördur, where the manuscript came from. In the mid-1600s, Bishop Brynjólf of Skálhot took an interest in the document, and began to press the farmer on the island to give it to him. Rare for both its beauty and its size, it held the largest single collection of sagas and poems of any medieval manuscript. The farmer wasn't overly keen to let go of it.

The farmer's name was Jón Finsson. He knew that he had the most precious document in Iceland, and refused the bishop's emissaries the gift of the manuscript. He said it would stay in Flatey.

There was nothing for it but for the bishop to make the trip himself. He rowed across to the island and met with Jón. If the farmer wouldn't give the manuscript away, would he at least sell *Flateyjarbók* to the bishop? No, said Jón, the manuscripts wasn't for sale.

Bishop Brynjólf, displeased with his failed errand, walked back down to the shoreline and prepared to push off from the island. Just as he was about to leave, word came that Jón had had a change of heart.

The bishop walked back to the farm. When the two men met again, Jón said he would, after all, give the manuscript away. Perhaps he had just wanted to make the donation on his own terms.

The bishop took the book, turned back to his boat, and sailed away with the most important treasure in Iceland. A few years later, it was packed onto a ship, and sent to the Danish court as a gift from bishop to king.

JÓN FINSSON OF FLATEY had cared for his manuscript. Other farmers were not as protective. One vellum script was found punctured with holes; it was being used as a kitchen sieve. Another had been cut up to make shoe soles. A page from an early copy of *Sturlunga Saga* had, in the years since its composition, been put to use as a tailor's waistcoat pattern.

Even when manuscripts were rescued from such situations, their transference from farms to libraries abroad was a dangerous one. In 1682, the Icelander Hannes Thorleifsson collected a cargo of books to take to the Danish king. His ship sank, taking him and all the manuscripts to the bottom. A few years later, when other collectors asked what Hannes had had with him, they were given the answer 'a load of parchment book rubbish'.

It seemed that the nation of storytellers could sometimes be reckless with its heritage.

Friendship and Fire

IN 1682, the same year as Hannes and his collection of sagas sank to the sea floor, a young Icelander called Árni Magnússon began a career that would alter the history of these documents, and with it the history of Iceland.

Aged nineteen, Árni travelled with his father to Copenhagen. He was on his way to begin university, for there were still none in Iceland. Árni had always showed great promise. As a child, he'd been sent from home to be raised by his maternal grandparents at Hvamm, the farm where, 500 years earlier, Snorri Sturluson was born. There Árni had come under the guidance of his grandfather Ketill, who taught him Latin and Greek.

In Copenhagen, Árni met a gifted young scholar called Thomas Bartholin. Although only four years older than Árni, Bartholin already held the high position of Keeper of the Royal Antiquities. Bartholin already had a large stock of Icelandic materials, but his own Old Norse–Icelandic language skills were patchy. He needed an Icelander to help him read the medieval manuscripts that were being shipped from Iceland as gifts and royal treasures.

When Árni applied for the job, he was told that he would have to sit a test. He was to translate a section of unsighted Icelandic manuscript into Latin, and give grammatical explanations as he went. Bartholin presented Árni with a text. I don't think he could have chosen a better one. It was *Njál's Saga*, the story of Gunnar and Hallgerd, and of Njál and his doomed family.

Árni passed the test, and Bartholin set him to work on a book he was writing about the Vikings, one of the first scholarly compendiums drawn from materials in the Icelandic sagas. Árni, the Icelander at court, was delighted, for he now had complete access to the greatest of the manuscripts, including *Flateyarbók* and Snorri's *Prose Edda*.

ÁRNI HAD FOUND a powerful friend and fellow enthusiast in Thomas Bartholin. However, his career was too closely bound to that of his employer. When Bartholin fell ill and died, Árni was very much on his own, and just another Icelander in the colonial capital.

He was told by Bartholin's family to auction the collection of manuscripts in Bartholin's estate, those documents in Bartholin's own possession. But rather than accept that this was the end of his scholarly career, Árni took a gamble, one that must have come from a deep affection for the sagas. Instead of selling the precious documents, he bought as many as he could, spending what meagre funds he had on manuscripts. He was even able to acquire the *Möðruvallabók*, which housed the largest collection of specifically *family* sagas, such as *Njál's Saga* and the stories of Gudrún, Bolli and Kjartan found in *Laxdaela Saga*.

He was building a library, but his place in Denmark had little foundation to it. Increasingly, it looked like he'd have to return to Iceland – to teach or pursue the life of a local priest. But his Icelandic friends told him to seek out the help of one Matthias Moth. He was brother of Soffia Amalia Moth, the mistress of King Christian V of Denmark. And he was also a noted manuscript collector, with one of the best libraries in the country.

Árni was reluctant. He couldn't see why someone of Moth's standing would take an interest in him. But eventually he made a tentative approach. To his surprise, Moth welcomed the contact, and shortly afterwards appointed Árni as his librarian. Árni moved with his manuscripts to Moth's house, and lived with the household. Once again, he had been able to cling on as an itinerant scholar for hire.

Árni and Moth became friends, and with their friendship came a change in how Árni was viewed back in Iceland. He was suddenly able to exercise influence over Danish government appointments related to his homeland. For many, such power would be an end in itself. For Árni, it meant that he could exert pressure on his countrymen to donate manuscripts. To him, of course.

This was how that most ornately decorated of all Icelandic manuscripts, the 1363 *Skarðsbók* version of *Jónsbók*, came into Árni's possession – the very manuscript on show in Reykjavík. The Icelandic owner of the work had sought Árni's help in becoming Bishop of Skálhot. In the end, the ploy didn't quite work, and the gift only secured him the headmastership of the cathedral school. Meanwhile, the successful candidate, Jón Vídalín, sent Árni every vellum manuscript in Skálhot Diocese. It couldn't hurt to have Árni and his connections on your side.

THANKS LARGELY TO MOTH, Árni was awarded the academic status of a professor. Others in the university questioned the promotion, for Árni had not yet published any of his own books, and, according to some, had done little more than steal and reuse old materials from Iceland.

But the title made little difference to Árni's immediate financial status. He was still poor, and dependent on Moth. He worried constantly that he'd have to return to Iceland to live. It seems this was the last thing he wanted to do. He was now thirty-three, but felt like he was drifting, and in all likelihood drifting back to the modest, closed life of the Icelandic priesthood.

One evening, Moth sent a servant upstairs to Árni's room to ask him down to dinner. When the servant came in, he found Árni lying on top of his bed, reading. He asked Árni whether he was unwell. Árni answered that he had no appetite.

After hearing this, Moth left the house and was gone for some hours. When he returned, he placed a letter on a plate and told the servant to take it up to Árni, with the message that he would probably find this more to his liking than bread and butter.

Árni held up the letter. It was from King Christian V, granting him the position of Royal Archivist. Árni rushed downstairs to thank Moth. A few years later, in 1701, he was also appointed to the Chair of Danish Antiquities by Christian's son, Frederik IV. With all these successes combined, the Icelander obsessed with his country's sagas could make his own home, in the residences of Copenhagen University, and build his collection yet more.

ÁRNI HAD BECOME one of the most influential Icelanders in mainland Scandinavia since Snorri Sturluson. And in 1702 his influence grew further. Much to his surprise, Árni received a commission from the Danish king to travel home and write a comprehensive account of living conditions in his country. The king had heard that the situation there was deplorable. It was time to take a proper account.

Árni was given a partner, the lawyer and poet Páll Vídalín, and a deadline. The task, it was thought, would take about a year.

It soon became clear that this had been hopelessly optimistic. By 1704, two years on, Árni wrote that they'd be done by 1708, which after all was only five years behind schedule. Then, in 1707, the country was struck by a smallpox epidemic. It was devastating. By 1709, the population stood at only 32,000, a quarter down on the population only two years before.

Árni survived the epidemic, and sought yet another time extension for his Iceland survey. No doubt it was very hard work: the roads were terrible, and many Icelanders resented the survey and its intrusion into their lives. Others, meanwhile, sought to use it as a chance to settle old disputes. They wrote countless letters to Árni, frustrating him with private matters. One was from a headmaster who hadn't been paid for three years. Another was written by a farmer who'd lent some tools to his neighbour, only never to get them back.

But there might have been another reason why Árni took so long to complete his survey. His commission gave him one extraordinary authority that scholars today suspect came as a result of Árni's own request. He had the special power to examine all the documents that existed in Iceland. The manuscripts of the entire country were suddenly laid out before him.

They say Árni had a special ability to sniff them out. If there was a manuscript in a house, he'd find it, no matter how poor its condition or to what use it was now being put. He visited Dýrafjördur, the fjord by Haukadalur, once home of Gísli the Outlaw, and there recovered a medieval copy of *Physiologius*, the Greek work of natural science – this was the manuscript famously being used as a kitchen sieve. While visiting old school friends, he implored them to return bits of manuscript they had stolen during their school days; it was a custom to tear parts off as youthful souvenirs. With these stray bits of parchment, Árni was able to reconstruct an ancient legal text.

In the end, Árni didn't complete his research until 1712, a decade after he had begun, by which time the patience of the Danish authorities was completely worn out. He was told that no more financial support for the project would be forthcoming. And yet he didn't present a summary of his findings to the king until 1716, thirteen years behind schedule. The completed documents were handed over in the autumn of 1720, eighteen years after Árni had first been approached to complete the one-year task.

The survey papers were shipped by royal navy frigate to Copenhagen, and with them the largest single collection of Icelandic saga manuscripts ever assembled to that point. By now, Árni was married. The couple moved into a two-storeyed timber house in Store Kannikestraede. It was a lovely home, but in one of the most crowded parts of Copenhagen. Into his new home, Árni piled his own manuscripts, and settled down to what he hoped would be many quiet years devoted to their study.

EARLY ON THE EVENING of Wednesday, 20 October 1728, a seven-year-old boy in the old western part of Copenhagen knocked over a candle. The inside of the boy's apartment began to burn. The family sounded the alarm, but soon the whole house was on fire.

It had been a hot, dry summer. That evening, a warm, southerly wind wound through the slim streets. The fire brigade began to arrive, but straight away it struck trouble: many of the streets were too narrow to access, and, after the summer, water inside the city was in short supply. As the blaze intensified and spread, fire fighters decided to get more water from the canals outside the city gates. But, fearing the desertion of conscripts, military officers ordered the gates shut, blocking the one ready source of water.

Árni, meanwhile, thought the fire would soon be contained. He didn't think it could reach his house, even though he was only a few streets away, and in among the old, fire-prone part of town. Perhaps the thought of it was just too awful to bear. For whatever reason, that night he did nothing. He left the manuscripts in his house.

The next day, the fire was still burning fiercely, and spreading through the city at an alarming pace. This was now a national catastrophe. Finally, Árni realised that his own home was in danger, and with it the manuscripts he'd been saving for decades. The streets were chaotic with people trying to move their possessions. All Árni had was a cart. With the help of his household and two other Icelanders, Jón Ólafsson and Finnur Jónsson, he began to load it.

Eventually, Árni and his companions began wheeling the cart, and as many documents as they'd been able to load onto it, through the burning streets of Copenhagen. But Árni's house was lost.

Much of his library was destroyed that day – how much, we don't really know. Certainly, Árni lost many of his own copies of manuscripts: a lifetime's study and transcription. The university library nearby perished completely, along with its collection of Icelandic literature. But Árni and his companions had saved the most valuable of the manuscripts, whatever could be fitted onto the back of a broken cart. Between them, the friends had managed to protect Iceland's national inheritance.

ÁRNI, THOUGH, NEVER recovered from the events of that day. His health deteriorated, and he died just over a year after the fire, on 7 January 1730. It would fall to others to reassemble and protect Árni's collection. Eventually his manuscripts were housed in a new royal library.

A hundred and fifty years later, the Icelandic independence movement began its struggle for an end to Danish colonial rule. Icelandic scholars who had followed in Árni's shoes, educated in Denmark and now schooled in the new nationalism of Europe, pressed the Danes for Icelandic home rule, and eventually for full independence.

In the nineteenth century, the Icelandic independence movement was led by a student of the sagas named Jón Sigurdsson, a hero of Icelandic history whose statute stands in the main town square of Reykjavík. In 1944, Icelanders voted in a national referendum to sever their constitutional links with Denmark and establish a sovereign republic. Ninety-five per cent of Icelanders voted in favour. A joyous national celebration was held at Thingvellir on 17 June 1944. A new flag of the Republic of Iceland was raised. Church bells rang out through the gorge and across the fields and into the mountains.

Icelanders also sought the return of the manuscripts. Árni had moved them to Denmark with good reason. In the old days, they'd often been neglected. But now they could take their place as the central monuments of Icelandic cultural life and nationhood.

The Danes had been poor colonial rulers, and for centuries had treated their island colony with disdain. But much was forgiven when, in April 1971, a Danish navy frigate sailed into Reykjavík harbour carrying with it a copy of *Flateyjarbók*, the very manuscript that the Bishop of Skálholt had once sailed out to Flatey to retrieve.

A photograph from that day says a great deal about Icelanders as a people. The old Reykjavík wharfs are as crowded as a concert hall. At the back, nearest to the photographer, people clamber up onto ship's containers and fish crates for their share of the view. The sagas were coming home.

Skarðsbók Jónsbókar, the manuscript I looked at with Finnur and Magnús, was also returned, four years later, in 1975. And so too *Möðruvallabók*, the manuscript of family sagas that Árni bought after his friend Bartholin's death. Their permanent home is the Árni Magnússon Institute in Reykjavík, the library where saga scholars now spend their long days reading about things they already know very well. It is where Richard and I met with Guðrún Nordal. And the very place where I sat when I first came back to Iceland, and thought about contacting my father and siblings.

The return of Flateyjarbók, *April 1971*

Hot Pots

THE WEATHER HAS turned cold, and the roads are icy. Each evening there's a news story about a reckless foreign visitor, how they're driving too fast, or wandering in the snow without enough cold-weather gear.

But it's hard to resist the call of the countryside, especially now that there have been heavy snowfalls. An old friend, Rakel, gives us the keys to her family summerhouse, offering it to us for the weekend. It's about half an hour past Thingvellir, the old site of the national parliament, on a road that climbs further up into the highlands.

I pack much too much cold-weather gear, and drive very slowly. I'm determined not to make the evening news. When we arrive at the summerhouse, the dashboard thermometer reads '−16°C', and the snow outside has dried and hardened. We joke that there must be a better word to use than 'summerhouse'.

We run inside and light the fire. Rakel has told us to make ourselves at home, and to run the hot pot* if we want. It's outside on the deck. For some reason, the tap is underneath the deck, in a storage space.

I go down under the house and lie on my back to find it – there's no room to stand or even crawl. Next to me is a wheelbarrow filled with water runoff. The whole load has frozen solid. The small rocks that I'm lying on have a coating of dry ice. But I find the tap and turn it on, and our hot pot begins to fill.

By the time it's ready, it's seven at night, very dark, but also intensely still. There's a faint line of Northern Lights in the sky. Olanda places candles in the snow around the tub, then we get into our swimmers, skip across the deck and jump in as quickly as we can.

Warmth and cold, a waterline of comfort and the biting hostility of the air. It's a very Icelandic combination, and one that has surely often meant the difference between perishing and survival. The

---

*   The local term for a hot tub.

geothermal waters are always here, no matter how far into the highlands you've come.

'What do you think, boys?' I say. 'Ready for a challenge?'

'Yes!'

'Why don't we have a roll in the snow?'

'What, in our swimmers?'

'Why not?'

We're not exactly brave about it. I tell the boys we mustn't run; it's too slippery on the deck. But we do walk pretty quickly, and we're lying in the snow just long enough to make three very hasty snow angels.

We run–walk back. The boys looked shocked, and for a minute I think I might have pushed them too far. Magnús says his skin is stinging, and Finnur can barely speak. But a minute later they've thawed out.

'Can we do it again?' they ask.

SNORRI, WE KNOW, loved his hot pot, if not the walk to get to it. I think he missed the point there, though. Surely some cold air on the skin is just as important as stepping into the warmth.

While we're in the country, we track back to Reykholt, which I want to show to the boys. The snow around Snorri's hot pot is undisturbed. I tell the boys that this is where their ancestor liked to sit and talk, to hear the local gossip, to think about his next steps in the endless disputes of his age. A place of contemplation, and no doubt composition too. 'I wonder how many sagas Snorri wrote here,' I say.

'But you can't write in a hot pot, Dad,' says Magnús. 'The paper would get wet.'

'Well, not *write*-write. More, you know, think-write. Don't you ever do that? Think about what you're going to write before you sit down to do it?'

'What do you mean?'

'Do you plan?'

'Yeah, at school we do. What we're supposed to do is … it's hard to explain. I'll write it down on a piece of paper. It's kind of easier to explain it that way.'

Magnús and Finnur at Snorri's hot pot

When we get back to the car, Magnús draws out a sheet of paper from his journal. For a couple of minutes, he writes, and then shows me.

'This is how it works:

'*Hook: the when, where and who of the story.*
A problem: the what.
How/event: trying to fix the problem.
Problem fixed.'

'That's it?' I ask.

'That's how you write a story,' concludes Magnús.

After

HEADING BACK TO Reykjavík, I wonder what the 'Problem fixed' section of my own story might be. The roads are no longer icy; thick, slow snowflakes are falling now, 'dog-paw' snow, as it's called, because of the soft impressions it makes on the road. Maybe that's all I need: a sense of delight and ease as we drive back into a familiar place after a weekend in the country, and a day trip to our ancestor's farm.

But there's one more step in the story.

Just before we reach our apartment, I turn off the main road towards the cemetery. I haven't been back here since I first visited a few years ago; somehow, there hasn't been a reason to. But I want Olanda and the boys to see where my father is buried, and my brother Ólafur too.

As we park the car, the snowfall gets heavier. There's about a foot of new snow in the cemetery grounds. It makes it difficult to orient ourselves; it takes me a while to find the high corner where they're buried.

But eventually I find the area, and its rim of dark trees. I turn around to tell the boys, but their attention has been captured by two white rabbits sheltering in leafless hedges nearby.

Finnur and Magnús crouch a little, then step as gently as they can towards the rabbits. The rabbits are very still, watching the boys as they come near.

'Boys,' I say, 'come over here. I want to show you where Gísli is.'

'But, Dad ...'

'Come on.' I join them at the hedge, and crouch so as not to scare the rabbits. In fact, they're rather tame. They must be used to distracting children who are meant to be making a family visit.

Finnur holds my hand. 'We'll come over and see the grave in a minute,' he says. 'We promise.'

And in a minute they do. We cross the fresh snow with all kinds of reasons for doing so. To say goodbye to Gísli, for now, and to let him meet my boys. And to thank him for the gifts I have.

Helgafell

IN LONDON, the streets are full of Christmas shoppers, and the wilds of Iceland already seem very far away. I spend a busy couple of days zooming across the city, seeing friends and keeping appointments. Kári is still in Reykjavík, now happily joined by Olanda and the boys. After the weeks of northern darkness, I'm ready to return to my family too. The promises of the Australian summer, the big blue sky and the beach are all tugging at my coat.

I buy some gifts for home in Covent Garden, then walk to the British Museum in Bloomsbury for a cup of tea with Naomi Speakman, the museum's curator of late medieval artefacts. Naomi had come on my radio program when she was touring Australia with a collection of beautiful medieval objects from the museum. Her area of responsibility includes the Lewis Chessmen, which I discover are one of the most popular exhibits.

This time, as I go to the chessboard display, my eye is drawn to the Viking queen. Her eyes are popping, and she holds her right hand to her cheek. It's not clear whether her expression should be read as shock, despair, grief or just mental absorption. She leans forward, like a spectator to a bloody disaster. Of all the chess pieces, she seems to bear the weight of war most heavily.

At Charing Cross I catch the Bakerloo line to take me back to my room in Maida Vale. Jammed into the crowded carriage, I flick through the photos of Iceland on my phone and a calmness settles upon me. Kári and I appear in very few of these pictures. When we are present, grinning gamely at the camera, we look like we're intruding; like a couple of guys photo-bombing the dignity of a raw and ancient landscape. The final images on my phone are pleasingly free of any human presence. A beach covered in shiny black pebbles. A lava field carpeted with sage-green moss. And, from my very last day in Iceland, there is a mountain side, thatched with fine, straw-like grass and split by a narrow path leading up to a metallic sky.

The troubled queen from the Lewis Chessmen

ON THAT FINAL DAY, Kári and I had driven out to the Snaefellsnes peninsula, a two-hour drive from Reykjavík. The peninsula juts out from the west coast of Iceland like a knobbly limb. Its tip is dominated by Snaefellsjökull,* a volcano so massive it can be seen from Reykjavík on a clear day. As the volcano came into view, I saw an odd, vortex-shaped cloud hovering over it, which looked like it was about to disgorge a UFO.

Jules Verne, in his classic work of science fiction *Journey to the Centre of the Earth*, imagined Snaefellsjökull as the gateway to a subterranean world of monsters and dinosaurs. Verne's novel begins with the purchase of an old manuscript of Snorri's *Heimskringla* by a German professor. Inside the book he discovers a coded, runic message, written by an Icelandic alchemist. Translated and decoded, the message reads:

Descend, bold traveller, into the crater of the jökull of Snaefell, which the shadow of Scartaris touches before the Kalends of July, and you will attain the centre of the Earth. I did it.

But this was December, so Kári and I would have to descend into the shadow of Scartaris some other time. We were there to honour a much smaller mountain nearby, named Helgafell.

HELGAFELL MEANS 'Holy Mountain'. In the Viking age it was a sacred site, dedicated to Thor, and a temple was built there in his honour. As we approached Helgafell, it looked like a lonely hump – an anomaly in the landscape, surrounded by smooth, grassy plains and a lake. It would have been easy for the first settlers to conclude it was placed here for a reason.

After the island's conversion to Christianity, Helgafell became the site of a monastery. *Laxdaela Saga* records that Gudrún lived out her

---

* The name translates as 'Snowy Mountain Glacier' for the heavy icy crust on its cap.

last years here as a nun, and was buried at the foot of the mountain. It would have been impossible for Icelanders to leave Gudrún's bones uncommemorated, and so as we walked around, we found a modest headstone surrounded by a white picket fence. The stone is engraved with her name, followed by the place and year of her death:

GUDRÚN ÓSVÍFURSD.
HELGAFELL
1008

I wished someone had thought to include the enigmatic last words of her tale: 'I was worst to the one I loved the most.'

A narrow dirt track led us to the top of the mountain. At the summit we were given was a panoramic view of the bay and the farmlands around it. Did this land look so very different when the first Vikings came ashore here?

Thor's Ness

There was once a man named Hrólf who lived on an island off the coast of Norway. Hrólf was tall and strong and took care to honour the gods. He kept a temple on the island to Thor, son of Odin.

Hrólf would have been content to spend his life there had he not made an enemy of the Norwegian king, Harald the Finehair, and been ordered to go into exile. But where could he go?

He had heard rumours of an island named Iceland, which was said to lie four days' sail towards the setting sun. People spoke of Iceland's rich virgin farmlands, which were yet to be claimed. So Hrólf made a sacrifice in the temple and asked if he should stay and fight, or leave and make a new life elsewhere. The message from Thor was unmistakable: he should sail to

Iceland. So he changed his name to Thórólf in honour of the
thunder god, and prepared to leave.

Thórólf bought a strong ship, and stored it with grain, cattle
and sheep. He dismantled the temple and stowed its timber
beams among the cargo. When all was ready, Thórólf boarded
the ship with his family, friends and slaves, and they sailed
west. They found their way by following the stars at night
and the birds during the day, and by singing their songs of
navigation.

They reached landfall on the south coast of Iceland, and then
sailed around to the west. Like Ingólf before him, Thórólf threw
the timber pieces from the temple high seat into the water, and
declared they would settle wherever Thor saw fit to send the
timbers ashore.

They found the timbers washed up on a headland. This
meant that Thor himself had come ashore at this very place, so
they named it Thor's Ness – the Peninsula of Thor – and they
began a settlement there. Thórólf carried fire around the land to
purge it of its unclean spirits.

Thórólf was both chieftain and priest of the new settlement.
He constructed a new temple to Thor, and carved the god's
image into its timber pillars. Inside the temple he made an altar,
with a heavy silver ring for swearing oaths, and a blood-bowl
for animal sacrifice.

The settlers were satisfied that Thor had made his home in this
strange new place of roaring mountains, soft grass and cracking
ice. They felt his presence seeping into the stones and streams.

ON THE HEADLAND of Thor's Ness was a mountain so
majestic, so sacred, that Thórólf insisted that no one should

even glance at it without washing themselves first. He named it Helgafell – Holy Mountain. He said that Thor himself dwelt inside the mountain and they would all enter Helgafell when they died.

The headland where the timbers of the high seat had come ashore was set aside for the local assembly. This area was also declared to be a holy place, and Thórólf piously decreed that no one should defile the land by spilling blood or excrement upon it. Anyone who felt the need to shit was expected to travel out a safe distance to a rocky outcrop called Dritsker – Dirt Skerry.

In time, more people came to settle on Thor's Ness. Their farms grew prosperous, and relations between local families were cordial.

Thórólf lived well, then he grew old and died. His body was laid in the ground and a burial mound was raised over it. His farm at Thor's Ness was passed on to his son, whose name was Thorstein Cod-Biter, and soon the troubles began.

NEARBY LIVED ANOTHER CLAN, the Kjallakssons, who complained of having to leave the assembly at Thor's Ness to walk all the way to the Dirt Skerry to perform their ablutions. The Kjallakssons let it be known that next time, they would simply shit on the grass.

Thorstein Cod-Biter was affronted by their arrogance, and so he gathered a group of kinsmen and attacked the Kjallakssons while they were on their way to the assembly. The Kjallakssons fought back fiercely. There were many deaths, the land was soaked with blood and the ground was defiled anyway.

A chieftain from outside the district was sent to arbitrate a settlement between Thorstein's clan and the Kjallakssons. Both families agreed to share the costs and responsibility of maintaining the temple, and the tensions between them calmed. But the blood-defiled land was no longer sacred, and so the assembly place would have to be relocated to the other side of the headland.

THORSTEIN COD-BITER built a fine new farmhouse, and then another, with thirty free men working for him. In his twenty-fifth year, Thorstein and his wife Thóra had two sons: Börk the Stout, and Thorgrím, who became a chieftain.* The happy and peaceful tenor of life was resumed.

One evening in the autumn, a shepherd was tending sheep near Helgafell, when he saw the whole mountain side open up like a cabinet. The shepherd could see great fires burning inside, and he heard booming laughter and raucous conversation, and ale-horns being raised and drained. Then, over the ruckus, he heard a great thundering voice welcoming Thorstein Cod-Biter into the mountain, and offering him the high seat near his father.

The shepherd ran to the farmhouse to tell Thorstein's wife everything he'd seen and heard. Her mouth tightened.

'We will soon receive very bad news,' she predicted.

In the morning, some men arrived at the house to tell her that Thorstein had drowned on a fishing trip.

BY TWO O'CLOCK it was getting dark on Helgafell. It was so viciously, perversely cold, we could barely operate our frozen jaws to talk. Gusts of cold wind were smoothing down the tufts of long grass on the mountain, like a head of fine grey hair. I told Kári that

---

*   Both Börk and Thorgrim would appear in *Gísli's Saga*.

Helgafell felt like a good place for me to take my leave of Snorri, and of Iceland. For a while anyway.

'I like to think that Helgafell opened up again when Snorri died,' said Kári. 'And that he's enjoying an afterlife doing what he loved best: drinking, feasting, flirting, and exchanging lines of verse in good company.'

'He was too wicked for the Christian heaven,' I replied. 'He'd be happier here.'

IT'S NOW EARLY January and I'm back home, in the middle of a humid Australian summer. I check my email and there's a message from Kári, written in the departure lounge at Keflavík Airport, where he's waiting with his family to catch their flight. The message contains a small confession:

> On this trip, when you arrived and I picked you up at the airport, I wasn't sure about when I'd be back in Iceland. It was as though something had been completed, maybe I'd done enough for a while. But yesterday, as we were leaving, it suddenly felt very different. We got to the airport and unloaded all our bags onto the path outside the terminal building. The boys helped me stack the suitcases onto two trolleys, and then they and Olanda started going inside.
>
> It was incredibly windy and cold. But I wasn't quite ready to go in. So I let them go ahead, and turned around to take it in. Not a great view of Iceland from there: just tarmac, parked cars, the low brown fields around the airport. The sky was low and dark grey. But I started to cry. I couldn't quite believe it. It was as though the tears came from somewhere hidden.

I stood there a bit longer, took my last breaths, and ran inside
to join the others.

I reply to this email with the words of an Icelandic lullaby that has
always annoyed him:

> *Sleep, you black-eyed pig.*
> *Fall into a deep pit of ghosts.*

Acknowledgements

FIRSTLY, WE MUST thank Deborah Leavitt, Tony McGregor and Michael Mason from ABC Radio for commissioning the original four-part series of *Saga Land*, and to Steve Fieldhouse & Michelle Rayner for helping transform a billion terabytes of recorded material into a coherent stream of radio. Thanks also to Pam O'Brien and Michelle Ransom-Hughes for their impeccably sound advice.

Brigitta Doyle and Lachlan McLaine from ABC Books embraced the idea and the aesthetic of this book right from the start, and we are truly grateful for their wisdom, expertise, flair and enthusiasm. A great many thanks are owed also to our editor Emma Dowden, who patiently helped us knit this narrative together, and to the people at OetomoNew for their wonderful cover design. Matt Howard got the word out. Elizabeth Troyeur and Grace Heifetz gave us their insight, sage advice and encouragement.

Special thanks to the Creative Industries Faculty at Queensland University of Technology, and in particular Mandy Thomas, Paul Makeham, Gene Moyle, and Chris Carter for their ongoing support. *Saga Land* took on new life as a stage show thanks to Jane O'Hara and Justin Marshman at the Brisbane Powerhouse. Just before we left for Iceland, Nicholas Martin lent us his Holga 120SF camera, which captured the images in the first pages of this book.

In Iceland, we received kind and very timely help from Jón Gustafsson at deCODE Genetics. We're grateful to Guðrún Nordal and the Árni Magnússon Institute, Reykjavík, and Torfi Tulinius and Vésteinn Ólason for conversations about sagas and the Icelanders' affection for Snorri Sturluson. And to Rakel Bergsdóttir and Þórir Júlíusson for lending us their (winter) summerhouse, Kári Bergsson for joining us on a wet winter's afternoon in Reykjavík to take pictures, Kolbrún Bergsdóttir for her knitted woollen hoods, and Luca Pozzi for his fabulous taste in Italian wine and generosity in sharing it.

Kaffitár on Bankastræti offered us good coffee and a safe harbour to write in the darkness of many winter mornings. We were sustained on our travels by several bottles of Brennivín, a tub of *skyr* and several hundred Icelandic hotdogs; the perfect balanced diet for any saga enthusiast.

Eternal thanks to Rachel Tackley and Simon Harper for their kindness and for the sanctuary of their beautiful home in England with the concrete cow. Paul Ham, historian and *boulevardier,* who has somehow figured out how to make a living as a writer in Paris, is also to be warmly thanked.

Our families have weathered our Iceland project with great patience and love. We couldn't have written this book without Susan Reid, Fríða Gísladóttir, Bryndís Gísladóttir, Anna Gísladóttir, and Björn Gíslason. And most of all Khym and Olanda, and Finnur, Magnús, Emma and Joe.

Finally, a tip of the hat to the great Lee Dorsey, for goading us to make everything we do funky (from now on).

Endnotes

Epigraph

vii 'Hávamál' ('Advice from Odin'): from the thirteenth-century *Codex Regius* manuscript, translated by W.H. Auden and P.B. Taylor.

About This Book

xix Borges, *Conversations*, p. 74.

xxiv 'In the twelfth century, the Icelanders discovered the novel': Williams, Jonathan C., The Boreal Borges, Masters thesis, Brigham Young University, 2013.

xxiv 'I want to recall that kiss': Williamson, p. 219.

xxvi 'Iceland of the silent snow': Borges, *Islandia*.

1. To Iceland

3 Gerald of Wales, *The Topography of Ireland*: www.yorku.ca/inpar/topography_ ireland.pdf.

4 'Never not thinking about Iceland': www.independent.co.uk/travel/europe/a.sublime-search-for-the-ancient-sagas-in-iceland-7960165.html.

6 'Six days' sail north of Britain, near the frozen sea': Strabo, *Geography*, Bk I, Ch. 4.

6 'Crystal pillar': *The Voyage of Saint Brendan*, p. 53.

7 These monks, whom the Norse people called 'Papar': Lopez, p. 316.

8 They sent up an urgent prayer: Parker, p. 2.

9 'Thórólf Butter': *Landnámabók*, Ch. 5.

10 They were a hybrid group of pioneers: www.decode.com/the-majority-of.icelandic-female-settlers-came-from-the-british-isles/.

10 One account, written centuries later: *Íslendingabók*, Ch. 1.

11 They were not warlords or petty kings: Byock, p. 3.

3. Into the Landscape

5. A Parliament of Vikings

7. Fiery Play Around the Head

9. The Poets' Mead

10. Silver Birch Trees

11. Ultima Thule

169 'Truly, our life lasts a thousand years': Odo of Cluny, quoted in Holland, p. 41.

183 Gudríd the Far Travelled: Davis, p. 73.

183 Then a new threat emerged: Diamond.

184 One Inuit folk tale mentions a competition: Parker, Ch. 5.

13. The Sand Winter

202 Viking gravesites: Clover, 1993, p. 368.

206 'An outcast': *Grettir's Saga*, Ch. 72.

208 The outraged Gudmund appealed to the Archbishop of Trondheim: *The Life of Gudmund the Good*, Chs 81–82.

208 'He was led barefoot from one church to another': *Sturlunga Saga*, Ch. 92.

15. Darkness and Light

240 Thuríd the Sound-Filler: *Landnámabók*, Chs 145–146.

257 An outbreak of flu: Jón Magnússon, Introduction by Michael Fell who credits the Icelandic scholar Ólína .orvar.ardóttir for the theory, p. 66.

258 Thuríd Jónsdóttir grew old: *ibid.*, Introduction, p. xxviii.

17. Outlaws

281 Just as likely to have been fashioned in the south of Iceland: Brown, 2015.

282 Snorri Sturluson recounts a famous chess match: *Heimskringla*, Ch. 163.

282 An American scholar named Daniel Willard Fiske visited Iceland: Evans, p. 362.

286 'Didn't you know? He was your father': Nicolas.

286 'The Boy Robot': Cavett.

286 'Russian pigs': Brady, 2011, p. 41.

287 An admiration for Adolf Hitler: Jackson.

287 'I had to get rid of her': Cavett.

287 In the company of Brahms, Rembrandt and Shakespeare: Levy, p. 9

288 'Well, I still have my music': Brady, *Endgame*, p. 188.

288 'I object to being called a chess genius': Chun.

291 'We will not be forced to be generous': Darrach.

292 'In everything else you're a big jerk!': *ibid.*

292 His father was inside on his deathbed: *Bobby Fischer Against the World.*

292 'I don't believe in psychology': Edmonds & Eidinow, p. 185

293 'It won't happen again': *ibid.*, p. 189.

295 'I think we can agree he exists': *Bobby Fischer Against the World.*

297 'I thought I had destroyed a genius with my decision': Edmonds & Eidinow, p. 234.

298 A 'symphony of placid beauty': *Bobby Fischer Against the World.*

298 'That's a real sportsman': *ibid.*

300 A desire to 'sleep and sleep and sleep': Edmonds & Eidinow, p. 338.

300 He was simply frightened of losing: Chun.

301 'A satanical secret world government': *ibid.*

302 An interview on Philippines radio: www.youtube.com/ watch?v=GyT3p22RZf8.

302 'It goes back to the sagas': Tweedie.

303 'We got him to Iceland': *Bobby Fischer Against the World.*

304 Appearing at a press conference: www.youtube.com/watch?v=vkkxnpl8Siw.

304 'I'd had enough of him': *Bobby Fischer Against the World.*

304 'Soul is dead': Ólafsson, p. 129.

306 'Jesus he was a handsome man: Cavett.

19. The Disc of the World

325 The Hippodrome was the world's biggest stadium: Brown, 2012, p. 13.

325 'A high wall surrounding a flat plain': *Heimskringla*, Ch. XII, Pt 12.

329 'He could control the whole country if he could manage to overcome Gizur': *Sturlunga Saga*, Ch. 121.

22. Poltergeists

356 Names for ghosts: Swatos & Gissurarson, p. 49.

362 Höfdi House was taken up by the British Ambassador: Evans, pp. 172–173.

363 One of the strangest episodes in the annals of nuclear diplomacy: FitzGerald, p. 347.

363 A child monarch: Cannon, p. 374.

364 Reagan had wondered if the world was living through the end times: Schorr, D., Reagan Recants: His Path From Armageddon to Détente, *Los Angeles Times*, 3 January 1988.

364 'Two men pointing cocked and loaded pistols at each other's heads': FitzGerald, p. 28.

365 An 'inertia projector': *ibid.*, pp. 22–23.

365 SDI research never came close to a reliable, working prototype: www.mda.mil/ global/documents/pdf/testrecord.pdf.

367 'No Deal: Star Wars Sinks the Summit': *Time*, 20 October 1986.

368 'You won't even share miking machine technology with us': Ridgeway.

370 In 1993, President Bill Clinton downsized the SDI: '1987: Superpowers to Reverse Arms Race'.

370 'Reykjavík,' was Gorbachev's instant reply: www.youtube.com/ watch?v=zf99T8LYhPE.

24. Parting Gifts

387 'This seemed a very great loss for Snorri': *Sturlunga Saga*, Ch. 149.

393 The Black Death coursed its way through the island: J.R. Maddicott, 'Plague in Seventh-Century England', *Past & Present*, No. 156 (1997), p. 32 (www.jstor.org/ stable/651177).

26. Helgafell

416 Thórólf and the Holy Mountain: *Eyrbyggja Saga*, pp. 27–38.

Bibliography

Note: In the case of Icelandic names, it is conventional to list authors alphabetically in order of first name then patronymic.

The Sagas and Other Medieval Sources
(Listed by author name only where it is known)
Ari Thorgilsson, *The Book of the Icelanders (Íslendingabók)*, ed. & trans. Halldór Hermannsson, Cornell University Press, 1930
Ari Thorgilsson, *Íslendingabók*, en.wikisource.org
Brennu-Njáls Saga, ed. Einar Ól. Sveinsson, Íslenzk Fornrit 12, Íslenzka Fornritafélag, 1954
Egil's Saga, trans. Hermann Pálsson & Paul Edwards, Penguin Classics, 1976
Egils Saga Skalla-Grímssonar, ed. Sigurður Nordal, Íslenzk Fornrit 2, Íslenzka Fornritafélag, 1933
'Eirik's Saga', trans. Magnús Magnússon, *The Icelandic Sagas*, Folio, 1999
Eyrbyggja Saga, trans. Hermann Pálsson, Penguin, 1989
'Gísla Saga Súrssonar', *Vesfirðinga Sögur*, eds Björn K. Þórólfsson & Guðni Jónsson, Íslenzk Fornrit 6, Íslenzk Fornritafélag, 1943
'Gísli Sursson's Saga', trans. Martin S. Regal, *Gísli Sursson's Saga and The Saga of the People of Eyri*, Penguin Classics, 2003
Grettir's Saga, trans. G.H. Hight, London, 1914, omacl.org/Grettir/
'Groenlendinga Saga', trans. Magnús Magnússon, *The Icelandic Sagas*, Folio, 1999
'Hávamál (The Sayings of Hár)', trans. W.H. Auden & P.B. Taylor, web.archive.org/web/20050912100548/http://vta.gamall-steinn.org/havamal.htm

Heimskringla, ed. Bjarni Aðalbjarnarson, 2 vols, Íslenzk Fornrit 26, Íslenzka Fornritafélag, 1941

Landnámabók, northvegr.org/sagas%20annd%20epics/miscellaneous/landnamabok/003.html

Laxdæla Saga, ed. Einar Ól. Sveinsson, Íslenzk Fornrit 5, Íslenzka Fornritafélag, 1934

Laxdaela Saga, trans. Magnús Magnússon & Hermann Pálsson, Penguin Classics, 1969

The Life of Gudmund the Good, Bishop of Holar, trans. G. Turville-Petre & E.S. Olszewska, Viking Society for Northern Research, 1942, vsnrweb-publications.org.uk

Njál's Saga, trans. Robert Cook, Penguin Classics, 2001

Saxo Grammaticus, *Gesta Danorum*, Vol. I, trans. Peter Fisher, Oxford University Press, 2015

Snorri Sturluson, *Heimskringla: History of the Kings of Norway*, trans. Lee M. Hollander, University of Texas Press, 1991

Snorri Sturluson, *The Prose Edda*, trans. Jesse L. Byock, Penguin Classics, 2005

'The Story of the Conversion (Kristni Saga)', *Íslendingabók, Kristni Saga*, trans. Siân Grønlie, Viking Society for Northern Research Text Series Vol. XVIII, University College London, 2006, www.vsnrweb-publications.org.uk

Sturla Thórdarson, 'Íslendinga Saga', *Sturlunga Saga*, Vol. 2, ed. Guðni Jónsson, Íslendingasagnaútgáfan, 1981

Sturla Thórdarson, 'The Saga of Haakon Haakonsson', *Icelandic Sagas and Other Historical Documents Relating to the Settlements and Descents of the Northmen of the British Isles*, Vol. IV, trans. G.W. Dasent, Cambridge University Press, 2012

Sturla Thórdarson, *Sturlunga Saga*, trans. Julia H. McGrew, Library of Scandinavian Literature, Twayne Publishers, 1970

Viðar Hreinsson, gen. ed., *The Complete Sagas of the Icelanders*, Leifur Eiríksson, 1997

The Voyage of Saint Brendan, trans. Simon Webb, The Langley Press, 2014

Post-Medieval and Contemporary Sources

Andersson, Theodore M., *The Icelandic Family Saga: An Analytical Reading*, Harvard University Press, 1967

Anonymous, *Wonders of Creation: A Descriptive Account of Volcanoes and Their Phenomena*, T. Nelson & Sons, 1872

Auden, W.H., 'Journey to Iceland', *Selected Poems*, ed. Edward Mendelson, Faber & Faber, 1979

Auden, W.H., & MacNeice, Louis, *Letters from Iceland*, Faber & Faber, 2002

Auður G. Magnúsdóttir, 'Women and Sexual Politics', *The Viking World*, eds Stefan Brink & Neil Price, Routledge, 2008

Bagge, Sverre, *Society and Politics in Snorri Sturluson's Heimskringla*, University of California Press, 1991

Barone, Jeanine, 'Europe's Loveliest Cemeteries', *National Geographic*, 29 October 2014, intelligenttravel.nationalgeographic. com/2014/10/29/europes-loveliest-cemeteries/

Bobby Fischer Against the World, documentary feature film, HBO Documentary Films, LM Media Production & Moxie Firecracker Films, 2011

Brady, Frank, *Bobby Fischer: Profile of a Prodigy*, Courier Corporation, 1973

Brady, Frank, *Endgame: Bobby Fischer's Remarkable Rise and Fall – From America's Brightest Prodigy to the Edge of Madness*, Hachette, 2011

Bragg, Lois, 'Disfigurement, Disability, and Disintegration in *Sturlunga Saga*', *alvíssmál* 4 (1994): 15–32

Brown, Nancy Marie, *Song of the Vikings: Snorri and the Making of Norse Myths*, St Martin's Press, 2012

Brown, Nancy Marie, *Ivory Vikings: The Mystery of the Most Famous Chessmen in the World and the Woman Who Made Them*, Macmillan, 2015

Byock, Jesse L., *Feud in the Icelandic Saga*, University of California Press, 1982

Byock, Jesse L., 'The Icelandic Althing: Dawn of Parliamentary Democracy', *Heritage and Identity: Shaping the Nations of the North*, ed. J.M. Fladmark, Heyerdahl Institute & Robert Gordon University, 2002

Cannon, Lou, *President Reagan: The Role of a Lifetime*, Public Affairs, 2000

Cavett, Dick, 'Was it Only a Game?', *New York Times*, 8 February 2008, opinionator.blogs.nytimes.com/2008/02/08/was-it-only-a-game/

Chun, Rene, 'Bobby Fischer's Pathetic Endgame', *The Atlantic*, December 2002

Cleasby, Richard, Gudbrand Vigfússon & Craigie, William A., *Icelandic–English Dictionary*, Oxford University Press, 1957

Clover, Carol, *The Medieval Saga*, Cornell University Press, 1982

Clover, Carol, 'Regardless of Sex: Men, Women, and Power in Early Northern Europe', *Speculum*, Vol. 68, No. 2, 363–387, University of Chicago Press, 1993

Clover, Carol, & Lindow, John, *Old Norse–Icelandic Literature: A Critical Guide*, Cornell University Press, 1985

Clunies Ross, Margaret, *Prolonged Echoes: Old Norse Myths in Medieval Northern Society*, Odense University Press, 1998

Clunies Ross, Margaret, ed., *Old Icelandic Literature and Society*, Cambridge University Press, 2000

Darrach, Brad, 'The Day Bobby Blew It', *Playboy Magazine*, July 1973

Darrach, Brad, 'Bobby Fischer Was a Genius and a Jerk', *Daily Beast*, 19 December 2015, www.thedailybeast.com/articles/2015/12/19/bobby-fisher-was-a-genius-and-a-jerk.html

Davis, Graeme, *Vikings in America*, Birlinn, 2009

Diamond, Jared, 'Why Societies Collapse', *ABC Science*, www.abc.net.au/science/articles/2003/07/17/2858655.htm

Edmonds, David, & Eidinow, John, *Bobby Fischer Goes to War*, Faber & Faber, 2011

Einar Ól. Sveinsson, Formáli, *Laxdæla Saga*, Íslenzk Fornrit 5, Íslenzka
  Fornritafélag, 1934
Einar Ól. Sveinsson, *The Age of the Sturlungs: Icelandic Civilization in the
  Thirteenth Century*, trans. J.S. Hannesson, Cornell University Press,
  1953
Einar Ól. Sveinsson, Formáli, *Brennu-Njáls Saga*, Íslenzk Fornrit 12,
  Íslenzka Fornritafélag, 1954
Einar Ól. Sveinsson, *Njál's Saga: A Literary Masterpiece*, ed. & trans.
  Paul Schach, University of Nebraska Press, 1971
Ellison, R.C., 'The Kirkjubol Affair', *Witchcraft in Continental Europe*,
  ed. Brian P. Levack, Routledge, 2013
Evans, Andrew, *Iceland*, Brandt Travel Guides, 2014
Finlay, Alison, Introduction, *Snorri Sturluson Heimskringla, Volume I:
  The Beginnings to Óláfr Tryggvason*, trans. Alison Finlay & Anthony
  Faulkes, Viking Society for Northern Research, University College
  London, 2011
Finnur Jónsson, *Ævisaga Árna Magnússonar*, Íslenzka Fræðafélag, 1930
FitzGerald, Frances, *Way Out There in the Blue: Reagan, Star Wars and
  the End of the Cold War*, Simon & Schuster, 2001
Franco, Zenon, *Spassky: Move by Move*, Everyman Chess, 2016
Gísli Pálsson, ed., *From Sagas to Society: Comparative Approaches to
  Early Iceland*, Hisarlik, 1992
Greenfield, Jeanette, *The Return of Cultural Treasures*, Cambridge
  University Press, 2007
Gudbrand Vigfusson, Prolegomena, *Sturlunga Saga Including the
  Íslendinga Saga of Lawman Sturla Thordsson and Other Works*, Vol. 1,
  Clarendon Press, 1878
Guðni Thorlacius Jóhannesson, *The History of Iceland*, Greenwood,
  2013
Guðrún Ása Grímsdóttir & Jónas Kristjánsson, eds, *Sturlustefna:
  Ráðstefna Haldin á Sjö Ártíð Sturlu Þórðarsonar Sagnritara 1984*,
  Stofnun Árna Magnússonar, 1998

Guðrún Helga Sigurðardóttir, 'Harpa in Reykjavík: Iceland's Symbol of Recovery', *Nordic Labour Journal*, 30 January 2017

Guðrún Kvaran, 'Hvað Þýðir Nafnið Esja?', *Vísindavefurinn*, 7 March 2000, visindavefur.is/svar.php?id=190

Guðrún Nordal, *Ethics and Action in Thirteenth-Century Iceland*, Odense University Press, 1998

Guðrún Nordal, *Tools of Literacy: The Role of Skaldic Verse in Icelandic Textual Culture of the Twelfth and Thirteenth Centuries*, University of Toronto Press, 2001

Guðvarður Már Gunnlaugsson, 'Manuscripts and Palaeography', *A Companion to Old Norse–Icelandic Literature and Culture*, ed. Rory McTurk, Wiley-Blackwell, 2005

Hastrup, Kirsten, *A Place Apart: An Anthropological Study of the Icelandic World*, Clarendon Press, 1998

Helgi Ólafsson, *Bobby Fischer Comes Home: The Final Years in Iceland*, New in Chess, 2013

Holland, Tom, *Millennium: The End of the World and the Forging of Christendom*, Hachette, 2011

Hughes, Robert, *The Fatal Shore*, Random House, 2010

Jackson, Caroline N., 'Mentor Helped Young Bobby Fischer Make Right Moves', *The Villager*, Vol, 77, No. 37, 13–19, February 2008

Jochens, Jenny, *Women in Old Norse Society*, Cornell University Press, 1995

Jochens, Jenny, *Old Norse Images of Women*, University of Pennsylvania Press, 1996

Jón Jóhannesson, *A History of the Old Icelandic Commonwealth*, trans. Haraldur Bessason, University of Manitoba Icelandic Series Vol. 2, University of Manitoba Press, 1974

Jón Magnússon, *And Through This World with Devils Filled: A Story of Sufferings*, trans. Michael Fell, Peter Lang Publishing, 2007

Jónas Kristjánsson, *Eddas and Sagas: Iceland's Medieval Literature*, trans. Peter Foote, Íslenzka Bókmenntafélag, 1988

Jónas Kristjánsson, *Icelandic Manuscripts: Sagas, History and Art*, trans. Jeffrey Cosser, Icelandic Literary Society, 1996

Ker, W.P., *Epic and Romance: Essays on Medieval Literature*, Dover, 1957

Le Goff, Jacques, *Constructing the Past: Essays in Historical Methodology*, Cambridge University Press, 1985

Levy, David, *How Fischer Plays Chess*, Ishi Press, 2009

Lindow, John, Lönnroth, Lars, & Weber, Gerd Wolfgang, eds, *Structure and Meaning in Old Norse Literature: New Approaches to Textual Analysis and Literary Criticism*, Odense University Press, 1986

Lopez, Barry, *Arctic Dreams*, Harwill, 1986

Maddicott, J.R., 'Plague in Seventh-Century England', *Past & Present*, No. 156, 1997

Lönnroth, Lars, *Njál's Saga: A Critical Introduction*, University of California Press, 1976

Magnús Magnússon, *Iceland Saga*, Tempus, 2005

Malm, Mats, 'The Nordic Demand for Medieval Icelandic Manuscripts', *The Manuscripts of Iceland*, eds Gísli Sigurðsson & Vésteinn Ólason, Árni Magnússon Institute, 2004

Már Jónsson, *Árni Magnússon: Ævisaga*, Mál og Menning, 1998

Már Jónsson, 'AM 344 fol. Handrit sem Árni Magnússon Eignaðist Ungur', *Góssið hans Árna*, ed. Jóhanna Katrín Friðriksdóttir, Stofnun Árna Magnússonar, 2014

Maxwell, I.R., 'Pattern in *Njáls Saga*', *Saga-Book* XV (1957–1961), 17–47

Mercer, M., 'Menagerie', *Royal Armouries*, royalarmouries.org/power-house/institutions-of-the-tower/menagerie

Miller, William Ian, *Bloodtaking and Peacemaking: Feud, Law, and Society in Saga Iceland*, University of Chicago Press, 1997

Minnis, A.J., *Medieval Theory of Authorship: Scholastic Literary Attitudes in the Later Middle Ages*, Scolar, 1984

Mitchell, Stephen, *Heroic Sagas and Ballads*, Cornell University Press, 1991

Nicolas, Peter, 'Chasing the King of Chess', *Los Angeles Times*, 21 September 2009

Parker, Philip, *The Northmen's Fury: A History of the Viking World*, Random House, 2014

Petersen, Irene Berg, 'How Vikings Navigated the World', *ScienceNordic*, 9 October 2012, sciencenordic.com/how-vikings-navigated-world

Quinn, Judith, 'From Orality to Literacy', *Old Icelandic Literature and Society*, ed. Margaret Clunies Ross, Cambridge University Press, 2000

Ridgeway, Rozanne, '"The Cold War Was Truly Over" – The 1986 Reykjavík Summit', Moments in U.S. Diplomatic History, Association for Diplomatic Studies and Training

Schach, Paul, 'Character Creation and Transformation in the Icelandic Sagas', *Germanic Studies in Honor of Otto Springer*, ed. Stephen J. Kaplowitt, K & S Enterprises, 1978

Scholes, Robert, & Kellog, Robert, *The Nature of Narrative*, Oxford University Press, 1966

Sigurður Nordal, Formáli, *Egils Saga Skalla-Grímssonar*, ed. Sigurður Nordal, Íslenzk Fornrit 2, Íslenzka Fornritafélag, 1933

Sigurður Nordal, 'The Historical Element in the Icelandic Family Sagas: The Fifteenth W.P. Ker Memorial Lecture Delivered in the University of Glasgow, 19 May 1954', University of Glasgow, 1957

Sigurgeir Steingrímsson, 'Árni Magnússon', *The Manuscripts of Iceland*, eds Gísli Sigurðsson & Vésteinn Ólason, Árni Magnússon Institute, 2004

Sørensen, Preben Meulengracht, *Fortælling og Ære: Studier i Islandingesagaerne*, Aarhus Universitetsforlag, 1993

Stefán Karlsson, 'The Localisation and Dating of Medieval Icelandic Manuscripts', *Saga-Book*, Vol. XXV (1998–2001), 138–158

Sumarliði R. Ísleifsson with Daniel Chartier, eds, *Iceland and Images of the North*, Presses de l'Université du Québec, 2011

Swatos, William H., & Loftur Reimar Gissurarson, *Icelandic Spiritualism: Mediumship and Modernity in Iceland*, Transaction Publishers, 1997

Torfi H. Tulinius, *The Enigma of Egil: The Saga, the Viking Poet, and Snorri Sturluson*, trans. Victoria Cribb, Cornell University Library, 2014

Turner, Victor, 'An Anthropological Approach to the Icelandic Saga', *The Translation of Culture*, ed. T.O. Beidelman, Tavistock, 1971

Tweedie, Neil, 'Bobby Fischer's Final Bizarre Act', *Daily Telegraph* (UK)

Úlfar Bragason, 'The Art of Dying: Three Death Scenes in *Íslendinga Saga*', trans. Anna Yates, *Scandinavian Studies* 63 (1991), 453–463

Vésteinn Ólason, *Dialogues with the Viking Age: Narration and Representation in the Sagas of the Icelanders*, trans. Andrew Wawn, Mál og Menning, 1998

Wanner, Kevin, *Snorri Sturluson and the Edda: The Conversion of Cultural Capital in Medieval Scandinavia*, University of Toronto Press, 2008

Weber, Bruce, 'Bobby Fischer, Chess Master, Dies at 64', *New York Times*, 18 January 2008

White, Hayden, *The Content of the Form: Narrative Discourse and Historical Representation*, John Hopkins University Press, 1987

Williamson, Edwin, *The Cambridge Companion to Jorge Luis Borges*, Cambridge University Press, 2013

Willis, Gary, *Reagan's America: Innocents at Home*, Heinemann, 1988

Further Listening

'Saga Land 1: The Story of Gunnar', *Conversations*, ABC Radio National, Brisbane, 14 March 2016 www.abc.net.au/radionational/7224384

'Saga Land 2: The Story of Gudrún', *Conversations*, ABC Radio National, Brisbane, 15 March 2016 www.abc.net.au/radionational/7224428

'Saga Land 3: The Story of Gísli', *Conversations*, ABC Radio National, Brisbane, 16 March 2016 www.abc.net.au/radionational/7224464

'Saga Land 4: Egil the Viking', *Conversations*, ABC Radio National, Brisbane, 17 March 2016 www.abc.net.au/radionational/7224488

Plate Captions & Image Credits

First pages – Summer – by the authors

1. A valley in southern Iceland
2. A house in Ísafjördur
3. Seljavellir, southern Iceland
4. Dettifoss, northeast Iceland
5. The slopes of Hlídarendi
6. Borg
7. Inside the chapel at Borg
8. Reykjavík shoreline
9. Geirthjófsfjördur, Westfjords
10. Jökulsárlón, southern Iceland
11. Borgarnes
12. The rift at Thingvellir
13. Tjörnin pond, Reykjavík
14. Haukadalur, Westfjords
15. Geirthjófsfjördur, Westfjords
16. An abandoned manor, Westfjords

Final pages – Winter – by the authors

17. The beach at Fródá, Snaefellsnes
18. Skógafoss
19. Hallgrímskirkja
20. Leif Eriksson statue, Reykjavík
21. Seaweed at Snaefellsnes
22. The Berserks' Lava Field, Snaefellsnes
23. Helgafell
24. A stone and wood loom at Erik the Red's farm, Haukadalur
25. Moss at Skorradalur, mid-west Iceland
26. Thingvellir
27. Winter grass at Helgafell

28. Wandering sheep
29. Öxarárfoss, Thingvellir
30. Borgarnes
31. Höfdi House, Reykjavík
32. The authors, Skólavördustígur, Reykjavík

Maps by Clare O'Flynn, Little Moon Studio
1 Richard Fidler; **16** Kári Gíslason; **31** Christian Krogh/public domain/ Wikimedia Commons; **41** Kári Gíslason; **45** Kári Gíslason; **58** Kári Gíslason; **67** Richard Fidler; **72** Richard Fidler; **79** Kári Gíslason; **82** Richard Fidler; **85** Kári Gíslason; **87** public domain/Wikimedia Commons; **95** public domain/ Wikimedia Commons; **112** Kári Gíslason; **123** Kári Gíslason; **128** Richard Fidler; **126** Kári Gíslason; **132** public domain/Wikimedia Commons; **138** public domain/Wikimedia Commons; **152** public domain/Wikimedia Commons; **154** Richard Fidler; **171** Richard Fidler; **173** public domain/Wikimedia Commons; **184** Creative Commons/Number 57; **186** public domain/Wikimedia Commons; **193** Kári Gíslason; **199** Kári Gíslason; **212** Alamy; **214** Kári Gíslason; **225** Kári Gíslason; **239** Richard Fidler; **241** Richard Fidler; **259** public domain/Wikimedia Commons; **264** Kári Gíslason; **272** Kári Gíslason; **278** Langeid sword by Ellen C. Holthe, Museum of Cultural History, University of Oslo; **279** Richard Fidler; **281** Creative Commons/Rob Roy; Bobby Fischer Against the World, documentary feature film, **285** still from *Bobby Fischer Against the World*, HBO Documentary Films, LM Media Production & Moxie Firecracker Films, 2011; **305** David Attie/Getty Images; **313** Kári Gíslason; **316** Kári Gíslason; **322** Richard Fidler; **327** public domain/Wikimedia Commons; **344** Richard Fidler; **352** Richard Fidler; **361** public domain/Wikimedia Commons; **362** Kári Gíslason; **367** public domain/Ronald Reagan Presidential Library; **375** Kári Gíslason; **384** Kári Gíslason; **389** Richard Fidler; **391** Richard Fidler; **397** Árni Magnússon Institute, Reykjavík; **407** Árni Magnússon Institute, Reykjavík; **410** Kári Gíslason; **414** Creative Commons/Nachosan

Index

In the case of Icelandic names, it is conventional to index people by their first name. This index follows that convention – for example, look for 'Gizur Thorvaldsson' not 'Thorvaldsson, Gizur'.

Richard Fidler presents 'Conversations with Richard Fidler', an in-depth, up-close-and-personal interview program broadcast across Australia on ABC Radio. It is one of the most popular podcasts in Australia, with over three million downloaded programs every month. Richard is the author of the bestselling book *Ghost Empire*.

Kári Gíslason is a writer and academic who lectures in Creative Writing at QUT. Kári was awarded a doctorate in 2003 for his thesis on medieval Icelandic literature. He is the author of *The Promise of Iceland* and *The Ash Burner*. As well as memoir and fiction, he also publishes scholarly articles, travel writing and reviews.

PLATE 17

PLATE 18

PLATE 19

PLATE 20

PLATE 21

PLATE 22

PLATE 23

PLATE 24

PLATE 25

PLATE 26

PLATE 27

PLATE 28

PLATE 29

PLATE 30

PLATE 31

PLATE 32